Gregory of Nyssa
THE LIFE OF MOSES

THE CLASSICS OF WESTERN SPIRITUALITY
A Library of the Great Spiritual Masters

Gregory of Nyssa
THE LIFE OF MOSES

TRANSLATION, INTRODUCTION AND NOTES
BY
ABRAHAM J. MALHERBE
AND
EVERETT FERGUSON

PREFACE
BY
JOHN MEYENDORFF

PAULIST PRESS
NEW YORK • RAMSEY • TORONTO

Cover Art:
The artist WILLIAM RABINOVITCH is a painter and sculptor who since 1973 together with artist partner Arthur Guerra has directed the Rabinovitch and Guerra Gallery in New York City's SoHo. He has studied at the San Francisco Art Institute, Whitney Museum Program, Boston Museum School of Fine Arts and a number of European schools. He has exhibited at the Allan Stone Gallery in New York City and the Monterey Peninsula Museum of Art in Monterey, California; he has also had a one-man show at the Casa Americana in Madrid and other galleries. In 1977 he was Project Director of the highly successful Whitney Counterweight, an artist-initiated museum-scale event held in dialogue with the Whitney Biennial.
Of his cover painting he says: "The water color is meant to convey a stained glass effect in order to bring out the luminosity, fluidity, and intensity suggested by Saint Gregory's life. I have worked in an expressionistic style reminiscent of the highly expressive Greek icon and Mosaic art but reinterpreted in a twentieth century way so as to create a kind of aesthetic bridge with his time. The figure of Gregory conveys the degree of asceticism and necessary mystery he espoused as a correct way toward the path of enlightenment. His serious bearded countenance was further suggested by an eleventh century miniature. To me, the triangle form beyond the halo conveys his strong sense of the Trinity and the unity of man. Another aspect of the triangle suggests its allusion to Mount Sinai and the idea that the achieving of each summit creates new horizons emphasizing Gregory's idea that progress itself is perfection."

Note: *The Life of Moses* is published in cooperation with Cistercian Publications Inc., Kalamazoo, Michigan, and is Number 31 in their series, *Cistercian Studies*.

Design: Barbini Pesce & Noble, Inc.

Library of Congress
Catalog Card Number: 78-56352

ISBN: 08091-2112-3 (Paper)
ISBN: 08091-0239-0 (Cloth)

Published by Paulist Press
Editorial Office: 1865 Broadway, New York, N.Y. 10023
Business Office: 545 Island Road, Ramsey, N.J. 07446

Printed and bound in the
United States of America

vi

CONTENTS

The Editors of this Volume:

ABRAHAM J. MALHERBE is Professor of New Testament Studies at Yale Divinity School. After completing his Doctoral work at Harvard, he went on for further studies at the University of Utrecht before taking New Testament teaching positions at Abilene Christian College and Dartmouth College before coming to Yale in 1970. His books include *World of the New Testament, Social Aspects of Early Christianity* and *The Cynic Epistles: A Study Edition.* Some of the journals in which his articles have appeared include *Journal of Biblical Literature, Journal of Ecclesiastical History, Restoration Quarterly, Journal of Theological Studies,* and others. Professor Malherbe is on the Editorial Board of the *Journal of Biblical Literature.* Born in Pretoria, South Africa, he lives with his wife Phyllis and their three children in Hamden, Connecticut.

EVERETT FERGUSON is Professor of Church History and Director of Graduate Studies in Religion at Abilene Christian University. After completing his doctoral work, "With Distinction," at Harvard, where he was a John Harvard Fellow, in 1957, he became Dean of Northeastern Christian Junior College, in Villanova, Pennsylvania. His books include *Early Christians Speak* and his articles have appeared in *Harvard Theological Review, Greek Orthodox Theological Review, Journal of Theological Studies, Studia Patristica* and others. Dr. Ferguson was born in Montgomery, Texas. He lives in Abilene with his wife Nancy and their three children.

JOHN MEYENDORFF is Professor of History, Fordham University and Professor of Patristics and Church History, St. Vladimir's Seminary, Tuckahoe, New York. Father Meyendorff is an internationally esteemed authority on Orthodox Spirituality. His books include *St. Gregory Palamas and Orthodox Spirituality* (1959), *Gregory Palamas* (1959), *The Orthodox Church* (1963), *Orthodoxy and Catholicity* (1966), *Christ in Eastern Christian Thought* (1969), *Byzantine Theology* (1974), and *Byzantine Hesychasm* (1974). Dr. Meyendorff is presently on a research fellowship at the Dumbarton Oaks Center for Byzantine Studies, Washington, D.C.

Acknowledgments

I t is with pleasure that we acknowledge our indebtedness to those who have had a special interest in our preparation of this volume. We undertook the task in response to a suggestion by Professor Johannes Quasten that a translation of Gregory's *Vita Moysis* into English was long overdue. Professors George Williams and Milton Anastos have encouraged us in patristic studies. The libraries of Abilene Christian College and Harvard University always graciously acceded to our requests, trifling and audacious alike. Zelma Odle preserved us from the grossest inelegancies of language; only our obstinacy is responsible for those that remain. Finally, we hope that the publication of this book may in some small way repay our families for the neglect it caused them. The manuscript was awarded a prize by the Christian Research Foundation in 1967.

Preface

The Christian Church, by receiving freedom and favors from the Empire of Rome, was endowed with a new opportunity and new responsibilities. It was now in a position of addressing itself not only to the simple folk in a few major cities with its "Good News" of the coming Kingdom in the risen Lord Jesus, but the entire world of educated aristocrats and intellectuals, trained in the traditions of syncretic Hellenism, was now ready to listen.

One of the major problems faced by Christianity in these new circumstances was that its Scriptures were Jewish Scriptures, that it claimed that Jesus was the Messiah foretold by Jewish prophets and that, therefore, the message of Jesus was not understandable except against the Old Testament background. Now the Hellenistic mind could hardly be receptive to the religious history of the obscure "barbarian" nation of the Jews. The Greek philosophical tradition and, in particular, the mystagogical trends of Neo-Platonism were open to a syncretistic absorption of Oriental religions, but not to the absolute claims of the Mosaic or Christian faiths.

At the time when Gregory of Nyssa was writing his *Life of Moses*, others had already tried to build a bridge between Hellenism and the Jewish Scriptures and, among them, particularly the Jew Philo and the Christian Origen. Gregory is indebted to them both. But his approach, as also that of the other two "Cappadocian Fathers"—his elder brother Basil and his friend Gregory of Nazianzus—more than that of his predecessors, was a witness to the Church. Gregory and his friends were influential Christian bishops, concerned not only with intellectual pursuits or individual mysticism, but also with orthodox doctrine, with the Church as a sacramental body and as an institution, now closely connected with the Roman state. The major achievement of their lives was that they had succeeded in maintaining their commitments to the Church, to Scripture, and to the Hellenistic tradition, without compromise and with intellectual and spiritual integrity. The synthesis which they produced was not necessarily a perfect synthesis—which was impossible because of their rejection of syncretism and their obvious prior and ultimate commitment to the Christian faith—but their honesty and consistency won the respect of pagans and Christians alike.

Among the three "Cappadocian Fathers," Gregory of Nyssa was the youngest. He was also more inclined to daring speculation and to what is usually called "mysticism" than were his colleagues. One wonders, however, whether this term is adequate in the context of Eastern Christian spirituality. To the Western mind, mysticism is associated with forms of subjective, individual and necessarily esoteric knowledge, which, by definition, cannot be communicated to all. In early Christian and Byzantine Greek meanwhile, the term "mystical" is applied to forms of perception related to the Christian "mystery"; the text of the Eucharistic Prayer, for example, is frequently described as "mystical." Whereas saints possess this "mystical" perception in an eminent way because they have attuned themselves to the gift of grace, all Christians are equally the recipients of the grace itself and are therefore called, by imitating the saints, to acquire and develop the "mystical knowledge."

Gregory of Nyssa's spiritual writings have no other central theme than his notion of "spiritual senses," distinct from all other forms of created perception, and which make God accessible to man. In his *Life of Moses*, using the biblical account as a parabola of the Christian spiritual ascent, he describes how this meeting with God occurs "in the cloud," i.e., without the help of created vision, since God is totally invisible and incomprehensible to the created eye, and inaccessible to the created mind. He is, nevertheless, seen and perceived by man, when man, by baptismal and ascetic purification, by effort and virtues, is enabled to acquire "spiritual senses," which allow him to perceive, through communion in Christ and the Holy Spirit, the One who is beyond creation.

Clearly, Gregory reads the biblical text as an Alexandrian Greek. He does so deliberately, because one of his basic goals—the goal of the Church in his time—is precisely to make the Jewish Scripture relevant to educated Greeks. But the God who is perceived by Moses is still the God of Israel, the totally Other, the living and personal God, not a philosophical idea, the One of Plotinus. The best proof of it is the constantly recurring affirmation of God's infinity, and, therefore, of the impossibility of exhausting Him or comprehending Him, as the human mind comprehends a concept. Communion with God is a constant ascent "from glory to glory." Each step of this ascent includes the joy of further expectation, the knowledge that He always remains greater than anything we can know of Him, and also that He gives Himself to man without setting any limits, because of His own inexhaus-

PREFACE

tibility. Thus, in meeting God, there is never frustration, or satiety, but only the discovery of true Love.

It is on this point—more clearly than on any other—that Gregory, while being Greek, transcends the Greek mind itself and indicates to his contemporaries and to future generations, including our own, the path to the Living God.

John Meyendorff
Dumbarton Oaks
Center for Byzantine Studies
Washington, D.C.

Foreword

St. Gregory of Nyssa (c. 335-c. 395) belonged to the third generation of an illustrious Christian family of Cappadocia. He was himself the third son among ten children. His older sister Macrina and brother Basil (later bishop of Caesarea) were major influences on his religious development and education. Although appointed a reader in the church, Gregory decided to follow his father's career as a teacher of rhetoric and apparently married. Persuasion from family and friends led him to retire to his brother Basil's monastery.

Basil secured Gregory's appointment as bishop of the small town of Nyssa about 371/2 with the explanation that he did not want his brother to obtain distinction from his see but rather confer distinction upon it. Gregory took a prominent part in the second ecumenical council at Constantinople in 381, which signalled the triumph of trinitarian orthodoxy.

The emperor Theodosius defined correct doctrine not only in creedal terms but also in personal terms, and Gregory's name joined those of the bishops of Constantinople and Alexandria as standards of belief. Gregory was a speculative theologian of great originality. In addition to his clarifications of the doctrine of the Trinity, he made contributions to the doctrines of man, the soul and the resurrection, and the atonement.

In his later years Gregory turned to developing a philosophical theology of the spiritual life. Central to these later writings is the "Life of Moses," previously untranslated into English in its entirety. Gregory first summarizes the history of Moses and then draws moral and spiritual lessons from events in his life. The work develops the theme that the virtuous life is a perpetual progress based on the infinite goodness of God.

Renewed appreciation for Gregory's importance in patristic theology and in Christian spirituality is evidenced by the continuation of the new critical edition of his works begun by Werner Jaeger and the meeting of Gregory of Nyssa colloquia at Chevetogne (1969), Freckenhorst (1972), Leiden (1974), and Cambridge (1978).

Introduction

A lthough Gregory grew up in one of the strong Christian families of Cappadocia, his early life showed no great commitment to the Church.[1] This changed in 372 when, at the age of about forty, he reluctantly accepted appointment as bishop of Nyssa from his brother Basil, metropolitan bishop of Caesarea. After Basil's death at the beginning of 379, Gregory became one of the foremost champions of the orthodox faith against Arianism. The years following the Council of Constantinople in 381 witnessed Gregory's religious leadership in the church of the East, but during the decade before his death about 395 his influence began to decline. Turning from dogmatic controversies and administrative duties, Gregory gave attention to the spiritual life, and thus the influence of his saintly sister Macrina triumphed at last.

Circumstances of Writing

A precise dating of the *Life of Moses* is not possible. Several facts indicate that it was written in the early 390s.[2] The work

1

would seem to belong to Gregory's old age.[3] The treatment of the envy directed toward Moses reflects the envy of which he was the victim.[4] The emphasis on the incarnation and absence of argument about the deity of the Holy Spirit fits the time when attention was being turned from trinitarian controversy to Christology.[5] There is stated in the *Life of Moses* a mature doctrine of the spiritual life, anchored in biblical texts.[6]

The Jaeger edition of Gregory's works brings together as *Opera Ascetica* the *De instituto Christiano*, *On the Christian Profession*, *On Perfection*, *On Virginity*, and *The Life of Macrina*.[7] The *Life of Moses*, *On the Titles of the Psalms*, *Homilies on Ecclesiastes*, *On the Lord's Prayer*, *On the Beatitudes*, and *On the Canticle of Canticles* are then sometimes treated separately as dealing with the "mystical" aspects of the spiritual life.[8] The many interrelationships among these works make such a classification difficult to maintain.[9] The main difference is that the latter group takes the Scriptural text as the point of departure whereas the former group is more "topical."

"Perfection according to virtue" may be considered the theme not only of the *Life of Moses* but also of the *On Perfection* and *On the Christian Profession*.[10] Of the other exegetical works, the *Life of Moses* has the most in common with the Canticles commentary, some of the parallels with which the footnotes will document. These works would seem to belong to the same general period of Gregory's life. Daniélou placed the *Life of Moses* between *On the Canticle* and *On Perfection*, and Jaeger regards it as the immediate predecessor of the *De instituto Christiano*, which he considers the climax of Gregory's spiritual writings.[11]

The same complex of ideas recurs in all Gregory's writings. Hence, the genuineness of the *Life of Moses* has never been questioned. Several of Gregory's spiritual writings were written in response to requests for guidance in living the virtuous life.[12] Caesarius is named as the recipient of the *Life of Moses* in the conclusion of certain manuscripts of the treatise. Two others give his name in the title, one designating him a monk.[13] He is otherwise unknown. More important is the indication of the request that the work comes from a time when Gregory was acknowledged by the ascetics of Asia Minor as a master of the spiritual life, even as he had earlier been recognized by council and emperor as a master of Christian doctrine. The treatise thus takes its place as part of Gregory's program to provide an ideological undergirding for the monastic movement organized by Basil.

The *Life of Moses* has the form of a *logos*, that is a formal treatise, dealing (as its complete title indicates) with "Perfection in Virtue." It may have been designed for reading aloud in a household of ascetics.[14] There are four sections: (1) the Preface, or covering letter of introduction; (2) the History *(historia)*, or paraphrase of the Biblical story; (3) the Contemplation *(theoria)*, or spiritual meaning of the Scriptural narrative, which is his main concern; and (4) the Conclusion. The *historia* and *theoria* approach was common in catechetical instruction.[15]

The Philosophical Tradition

Philosophy had become religious in the Hellenistic age, and in late Roman times it had become contemplative and ascetic. The ascetic life in Christianity was a direct continuation of the contemplative life of Greek philosophy.[16] Gregory speaks in the *Life of Moses* about a solitary's withdrawal as a "greater philosophy" (I, 19).

By the 4th century the Greek philosophical traditions had merged into a modified Platonism known as Neoplatonism. Gregory has clear points of contact with the philosophical heritage of Hellenism. His relation to the preceding philosophical development has been a frequent object of study, for he, more than most of the fathers, was a philosophical theologian.[17]

3

Gregory reflects an honest ambivalence in regard to pagan learning. He has some harsh things to say about its inadequacies and dangers.[18] Very graphic is his figure of pagan education as "always in labor but never [giving] birth" (II, 11). The womb of barren wisdom is pregnant with wind and miscarries before coming to the knowledge of God. If it is necessary to associate with pagan wisdom, one must scatter the teachers of evil for their wicked use of instruction (II, 17). On the other hand, Gregory has some positive things to say about the usefulness of pagan learning. The ark in which the baby Moses was saved from the waters "was constructed out of . . . education in the different disciplines" (II, 7). "There are certain things derived from profane education which should not be rejected" in our striving for virtue (II, 37). Therefore the "learning of the Egyptians" is necessary; indeed, acquiring it is a divine command. The spiritual meaning of the "spoiling of the Egyptians" is that God "commands those participating through virtue in the free life also to equip themselves with the wealth of pagan learning" (II, 115). "Such things as moral and natural philosophy, geometry, astronomy, dialectic, . . . will be useful when in time the divine sanctuary of mystery must be beautified with the riches of reason."

Gregory's own lack of formal training in pagan education may have been a blessing.[19] He was introduced to the "classics" and acquired a basic knowledge from his brother Basil, but he was not spoiled by the "handbooks" and was freer to apply his own intellectual gifts in an original way.

Gregory makes specific reference to some of the good in pagan philosophy and its erroneous teachings:

> For example, pagan philosophy says that the soul is immortal. This is a pious offspring. But it also says that souls pass from bodies to bodies and are changed from a rational to an irrational nature. This is a fleshly and alien foreskin. And there are many other such examples. It says there is a god, but it thinks

4

of him as material. It acknowledges him as Creator, but says he needed matter for creation. It affirms that he is both good and powerful, but that in all things he submits to the necessity of fate. (II, 40)

In II, 287f. Gregory gives positive endorsement to Aristotle's ethical doctrine of virtue as the mean.[20] His greatest debt is clearly to Plato.[21] But all has undergone a profound transformation into a Christian synthesis.

The Exegetical Tradition

In the second part of the *Life of Moses*, the *historia*, Gregory summarizes the events of Moses' life from the biblical account in Exodus and Numbers. In the third part, the *theoria*, he refers back to these events as the bases for spiritual lessons. Thus the life of Moses becomes a symbol of the spiritual journey of the soul to God.

Gregory's treatise càn be securely connected to the earlier history of Scripture interpretation, especially the Alexandrian tradition, Jewish and Christian. In the literal treatment of Moses' life Daniélou has noted the presence of certain features from Jewish *haggada* — edifying amplification of the biblical text, accent on the miraculous with a denial of naturalist interpretations, and the suppression of shocking details or interpretation of them in a favorable sense.[22] Of more interest is the allegorical or nonliteral interpretation of the *theoria*. The allegorical method was well developed by Gregory's time.[23] Although Gregory uses his own originality in applying this tradition, we must take note of his predecessors.

The figure of Moses occupied a prominent place in the thinking of Jews and Christians.[24] Of special importance to Gregory is Philo,[25] who also wrote a two-part *Life of Moses*.[26] Philo's *Life*, in the manner of the Hellenistic biography of the

Peripatetic type, presents the "life" in order to give an example for a type of life.[27] Philo's first book goes through the life of Moses, presenting him as a king, in straightforward historical order with little attempt at allegory. The second part gives a topical treatment of the character of Moses, treating his work as a lawgiver, priest, and prophet.[28] Gregory similarly outlines the life and then takes Moses as a model of the spiritual life.[29]

Philo's *Life* is mainly a moral interpretation since it is primarily an apology addressed to the Greeks.[30] The *Questions on Exodus*[31] follows a different approach, giving a "literal" and then the "deeper"[32] meaning of each passage in turn. This work deals more with specific legal enactments than the *Life* and manifests more of a cosmological interest. Where Gregory perhaps differs the most from Philo is in the virtual absence of cosmological allegories.[33] Philo's *Allegorical Laws* reinterprets the historical narrative rather than the legal ordinances, as does the Jewish *haggada*.[34] Gregory largely ignores the legal sections of the Pentateuch. As a generalization, one may say that Gregory's *Life of Moses* draws its format from Philo's *Life of Moses* and its allegorical method from other Philonic works as this method had been transformed by Christian doctrinal interests.

Clement of Alexandria shows the first extensive Christian appropriation of Philo. He gives his own "life of Moses,"[35] which is an epitome of Philo and the Hellenistic Jewish tradition concerning Moses. The closest parallels in method and content to Gregory are to be found in Origen, whose *Commentary on Lamentations* follows the method of Philo's *Questions and Answers on Genesis* and *Exodus* in first discussing the literal meaning and then the inner meaning (διάνοια) in accordance with the "laws of ἀναγωγή."[36] The *Homilies on Exodus* offer many exact parallels of interpretation to those in Gregory.[37] The idea behind the *Life of Moses* may be the suggestions of *On First Principles* 4.3.12 (24)[38] in accord with the principles of interpretation stated in 2.5 (12). Gregory takes the "moral" allegories of Philo and extends them in the direction of "mysti-

INTRODUCTION

cism" by his application of them to the spiritual life. He goes beyond Origen, for whom the "spiritual" interpretation is an interiorization of the sacraments.[39]

That Gregory belongs to the Alexandrian school of interpretation may be seen from his exegetical terminology. Studies of Greek usage show *historia* and *theoria* often in juxtaposition.[40] For example, Origen can speak of something said not in its "literal interpretation" *(historia)* but in its "spiritual sense" *(theoria)*.[41] *Historia* was the regular term in use by all schools to designate the literal wording or actual event.[42] This simple account of the facts, or literal sense, was used by Gregory and others in the Alexandrian tradition for all types of literature and not just for "historical" narration.[43] *Theoria*, on the other hand, had a different meaning for the Alexandrian and Antiochian schools. For the Antiochian exegetes, the *theoria* was the prophetic vision;[44] in interpreting the Old Testament, they found passages in which the prophets by inspiration spoke of things having a typical significance beyond their own day. This future reference they called *theoria*. The Alexandrians, in contrast, used *theoria* in practically the same sense as *allegoria* and *dianoia*.[45] The latter (the "deeper meaning") had been the usual pagan word for a hidden sense in a writing. It came to be replaced by *allegoria*, which was used for all types of nonliteral exegesis.[46] Gregory shows a preference for *theoria*,[47] the "insight" into meanings beyond the range of the literal. The word could be used both for the sense contemplated in the text and for the method of reaching this "spiritual meaning."[48] This choice may be due to Gregory's preference for visual imagery, in accord with the Greek tradition generally, or to an accommodation to the Antiochian attack on *allegoria*. At any rate *theoria* became the predominant word for the allegorical sense in Cyril of Alexandria.[49]

In the *Life of Moses* Gregory indicates some of the criteria employed for finding a spiritual interpretation of the sacred text. These are the same considerations urged in the Alexan-

7

drian school.[50] The a priori consideration that "the Law does not instruct us how to eat" becomes the basis for an allegorical interpretation of the first Passover meal (II, 105). What he felt was unnecessary, superfluous, or out of place in a revealed law ("Nature . . . is a sufficient Lawgiver" with regard to eating, he affirms) pointed him to a hidden meaning.[51] Where something morally wrong is enjoined in the biblical text an allegorical meaning must be sought. The "spoiling of the Egyptians" was without moral justification and was an indication that "the loftier meaning is therefore more fitting than the obvious one" (II, 113-115; cf. the same consideration urged with reference to the Egyptians punished by the death of the first-born, II, 91f.). Furthermore, anything that in its literal sense would be unworthy of God points to an inner meaning. Thus, since the description of God as having a "back" and a "face" is incongruous with the divine nature, it must have a spiritual sense (II, 221-223). In this work in particular the impossibility of duplicating the exact circumstances of the ancient worthies becomes a justification for moving beyond the literal history (II, 49). Gregory asks the hermeneutical question in his Introduction (I, 14). The spiritual meaning is always happening (e.g., II, 119).

On the positive side, where Gregory is aware of various interpretations he does not reject any interpretation that leads to virtue (II, 191). What is edifying, or what provides a "useful lesson" (II, 205) or "advice profitable to men" (II, 301), therefore, governs his interpretation. But this is not a sufficient criterion for Gregory: The slaying of the idolators by the Levites is given a practical, moral interpretation and then a spiritual meaning as well (II, 205ff.). The reasonableness or fitness of things is urged as a basis for a deeper meaning. Since spots on garments are no hindrance to ascending to God, the command to wash clothes before approaching Sinai must mean removing stains from the outward pursuits of life (II, 155). Especially at points where he finds warrant in the New Testament for a nonliteral interpretation of the Old (II, 179) and where he finds Christ pointed to by the Old (II, 148, 151), Gregory turns to allegory.

For his nonliteral interpretations, Gregory looks not only to the Alexandrian tradition but also to certain common Christian interpretations of the Old Testament, particularly with reference to Christ, the Church, and Christian ordinances.[52] These were already found in the New Testament, the apostolic fathers, Justin, and Irenaeus, and should not be regarded as unique to any one school of thought. Moses was an important figure in Christian thought as the leader of the people of God, a man of God, and a precursor and type of Christ.[53] We find summaries of his career, particularly the episodes of the Exodus, frequently in Christian authors.[54] These often read much like the framework within which Gregory developed his treatise. The treatment of Moses in the Latin fathers is quite different from that of Gregory, however; they discuss different events than does he, and where they mention the same events, they are concerned with more practical, moral questions.[55]

Although Gregory does incorporate some items of traditional interpretation and does show the results of many influences, especially from the Alexandrian tradition, there is much in him that is new, and certainly the whole synthesis is original. The material and the method are old, but the product is new. And Gregory invites anyone who will to obtain a more profitable interpretation than that which he offers.[56]

Qualities of the Spiritual Life

Gregory's spiritual theology has come in for great attention in recent years.[57] The Life of Moses is a particularly important formulation of his Christian spirituality.[58]

Gregory calls attention to those features of Moses' life which may be considered a withdrawal from active involvement in the affairs of men: In Midian "he lived alone in the mountains away from the turmoil of the marketplace" (I, 19); and on Sinai, leaving the people behind, "he boldly approached the very darkness itself" (I, 46). Gregory encourages the solitary life or life among those of "like disposition and mind" (II, 18). But there is still the return to society for service. The Moses who had known the discipline of the desert gained the hearing of the people (II, 55), and he who had been instructed by God in the thick darkness "went down to his people to share with them the marvels" that he had seen (I, 56). Practical philosophy must be joined to contemplative philosophy (II, 200).

Asceticism is emphasized. The life of virtue demands "austerity and intensity" (II, 2). Asceticism is a "greater philosophy" than the learning of the Egyptians (I, 19). Gregory interprets the coverings of the tabernacle as the mortification of the sinful flesh and the ascetic way of life (II, 187), and he considers asceticism the adornment of the Church.

The control of the passions is a theme often repeated in the work. For example, Gregory affirms that it is impossible to flee the Egyptian life except by destroying utterly the first birth of evil (II, 90). "For when he slays the beginning, he destroys at the same time what follows after it" (II, 92f.). Again, to the washing of the garments and the keeping of animals away from the mountain in preparation for the Sinai theophany he gives the moral interpretation of keeping body and soul stainless and keeping sense perception under control (II, 154, 156). Envy, pride, and pleasure, as enemies of the spiritual life, come in for extensive treatment in the late parts of the treatise.

On the positive side, the two parts of religious virtue are the knowledge of God and right conduct (II, 166). The virtues of faith, hope, and a good conscience receive special stress. The rod of Moses is once "the word of faith" by which he prevailed (II, 36); the staff of each Israelite is "the message of hope" (II, 108). "The voice which is melodious and ascends to God's hearing is not the cry made with the organs of speech but the meditation sent up from a pure conscience" (II, 118). Indicative of this strong moral note throughout is the moral interpretation of the priests' garments (II, 189-201).

In spite of this general trend of the treatise, the tendency of recent studies has been to see in the *Life of Moses* the crowning work of Gregory's "mysticism."[59] In view of the lack of precision with which the word "mysticism" is frequently used and of Gregory's close ties with the philosophical development, we have preferred to speak of his "spirituality." There are passages, notably the treatment of Moses on Sinai, that have a "mystical" ring about them, but Gregory's prevailing concern is with moral virtues and the qualities of the soul that would attain to God. The close of the *theoria* expresses Gregory's concern:

> For he who has truly come to be in the image of God and who has in no way turned aside from the divine character bears in himself its distinguishing marks and shows in all things his conformity of the archetype; he beautifies his own soul with what is incorruptible, unchangeable, and shares in no evil at all. (II, 318)

The climax of Gregory's spirituality is "to follow God" (II, 250-252). The one who "waits upon the divine voice and prays that he might follow behind" is the true servant of God. It is notable that the treatise says little about specific disciplines—prayer, meditation, listening to Scripture—as the way to God. The concern is with moral—in the broad sense—qualities.

At several places in the treatise Gregory alludes to points that form part of the general theological framework of his spiritual doctrine.[60] Man was made in the image [the mirror] of God (II, 47, 318). By his fall into sin, this image was tarnished (II, 45). Christ took upon himself our nature in order to restore us to our original nature (II, 30, 175). Conversion restores man's capacity to reflect the divine nature (II, 47, 207, 214ff.).

INTRODUCTION

There is an incessant transformation into the likeness of God as man stretches out with the divine infinity (II, 225f., 238f.); there is an ever-greater participation in God (I, 7; II, 62). Thus we come to the most distinctive teaching of the *Life of Moses*, and the theme that holds the whole work together, the idea of eternal progress.[61] The ancients saw perfection in achievement, but Gregory (like the later Stoic moralists) denied the possibility of perfection in this sense. Developing hints in Philo and Origen, who had described the spiritual life as a succession of steps, Gregory went on to make progress itself perfection. Gregory Nazianzus expressed a similar idea of infinite progress in the never-completed journey to God.[62]

This theme of eternal progress is announced in the preface (I, 5-10). The same language used of the infinity of God (II, 236) is used here of virtue: "How then would one arrive at the sought-for boundary when he can find no boundary?" Because "the one limit of perfection is the fact that it has no limit," there is no stopping place in the racecourse of virtue (I, 5-6; cf. II, 242). Perfection is unlimited, and so unattainable; hence, perfection is redefined: "The perfection of human nature consists perhaps in its very growth in goodness" (I, 10). A long section (II, 219-248) develops the theme of eternal progress in relation to the divine infinity. "Thus, no limit would interrupt growth in the ascent to God, since no limit to the good can be found nor is the increasing of desire for the good brought to an end because it is satisfied" (II, 239). Moses' attainments throughout the work serve to emphasize the truth that from each summit attained new horizons continuously open out. "Activity directed toward virtue causes its capacity to grow through exertion" (II, 226), Gregory asserts. Moses "always found a step higher than the one he had attained" (II, 227). Participation in virtue dilates the capacity for more virtue. The flesh can know satiety, but the spirit cannot (II, 59ff., 230). This perpetual growth does not imply a lack of satisfaction. Although

12

one's desire is increased with each participation in God (II, 230, 238), this experience is unlike the recurrence of desires for physical things (II, 59ff.). This progress toward virtue is achieved by stability in the good (II, 243). It is unlike the exertions of those in error; their motion, like that of a man trying to climb a sand dune, results in no progress (II, 244). In both the preface (I, 5) and the body of the work (II, 225) Gregory quotes Philippians 3:13 to express man's continual reaching out for a greater participation in the good. As he nears the end Gregory once more reiterates that the only perfection available to men in this life is to be found in progress toward perfection (II, 305-314): "The continual development of life to what is better is the soul's way to perfection."

Although Gregory makes much of the sequence of events in Scripture,[63] this fact should not be pressed in an absolute sense. Moses' life is not made to fit a schematized progression of spiritual experience.[64] Some things do logically precede others in one's spiritual development, but the experiences of life may not be reduced to a formula. The stages of Moses' life are a pattern not so much in their order as in their constant going on to new things.

Although Gregory's debt to Origen is immense,[65] the Cappadocian has made significant modifications in Alexandrian spirituality. The goal is now different: In Gregory, "continued progress" replaces the "static unity" of the still Greek-based system of Origen. Brooks Otis has also discerned a significant difference in the whole mood of the two spiritualities. If we contrast Origen's *Homilies on the Song of Songs* or his twenty-seventh *Homily on Numbers* with the *Life of Moses*, it is clear that a gulf separates the two spiritualities: Origen's is governed "by the omnipresent possibility of temptation and sin" while Gregory's is "concerned almost exclusively with the sinless life of the saved or blessed."[66] This is perhaps overstated, but it may serve to point up the partial appropriation of the Christian view by each of these great thinkers. The one understood the idea of progress, and the other, the awareness of the power of sin.

Gregory's "perfectionism," or what may be called theologically "synergism," were part of the Greek tradition and have remained in Eastern theology. It would be fruitful for someone to trace the idea of "eternal progress" in the later spiritual thought of the Eastern churches. Werner Jaeger has demonstrated the general influence of Gregory on Macarius and the spiritual life of the Eastern Church.[67]

Doctrinal Emphases

Although the *Life of Moses* hardly reflects the whole of Gregory's doctrinal concerns, there are certain doctrines that come in for special attention and may be related to his whole system of thought.

God:[68] Gregory's spiritual teaching is firmly based on his theology, and the fundamental doctrine for his spirituality is the divine infinity. At the very beginning of the *Life of Moses* Gregory affirms that God is absolute Good and absolute virtue. As such he is unlimited and infinite, since goodness is defined by its opposite and the divine nature does not admit of an opposite (I, 7).

In three major sections, and these the most important passages in the book, Gregory develops this doctrine of God—the burning bush (II, 22-26), the revelation of the Law at Sinai (II, 162-166), and the request to see God (II, 221-222, 231-239, 249-255). God is true Being, for he is the only self-subsisting nature; on him all else depends for existence. God is all-sufficient; by participation in him other things have being (II, 23-25). The infinite God is invisible and incomprehensible (I, 46). Since he transcends all cognitive thought and representation, he is ultimately unknowable, being beyond all sense

14

knowledge and intellectual concepts (II, 162-165, 234f.). The divine nature has no boundary (II, 236-238). Man's partial experience of God comes in constantly following him; to see God is to know him as unknowable. "To follow God wherever he might lead is to behold God" (II, 252). "This truly is the vision of God: never to be satisfied in the desire to see him" (II, 239; cf. 234).

Christ:[69] The incarnation, virgin birth, and two natures of Christ occupy a prominent place in Gregory's interpretations. He finds six figures of the incarnation in the story of Moses: the burning bush (II, 20f.), Moses' rod changed into a serpent (II, 26-27, 31-34), Moses' hand becoming leprous (II, 26-30), the manna (II, 139), the tabernacle (II, 174), and the tablets of stone (II, 216). By these figures he is able to emphasize the perpetual virginity of Mary (II, 21), both the preexistence and createdness of Christ who had no human origin (II, 175f.), and Christ's becoming sin for us and transforming our nature (II, 30-34).

This emphasis on the incarnation does not mean the cross is neglected. Figures of the cross are found in the outstretched arms of Moses in prayer when he removed the plagues from Egypt (II, 78) and interceded for Israel against the army of Amalek (II, 150f.), in the wood that sweetened the waters of Marah (II, 132), in the bunch of grapes suspended on wood and brought back from Canaan by Joshua (II, 267f.), and in the brazen serpent (II, 273). Moreover, the skins dyed red and the hair used in the tabernacle are taken as referring to the blood and death of the passion (II, 183). But, surprisingly, Gregory does not make explicit reference to the passion in his treatment of the passover (II, 103, but cf. 98 and 102). It is perhaps characteristic that the figures of the cross mentioned by Gregory were already traditional, whereas the figures of the incarnation are original developments.

The Holy Spirit and Angels:[70] In view of Gregory's role in establishing the deity of the Holy Spirit in the doctrinal controversies of his time, it is striking that the Holy Spirit appears so seldom and then never in a strictly theological context. The Holy Spirit was the means of the incarnation (II, 216), and now "grace . . . flourishes through the Spirit" (II, 187). Gregory commends those before him who interpreted the cloud that led the Israelites as the Holy Spirit (II, 121), and he considers the lamps in the tabernacle to represent the rays of the Spirit (II, 181). Elsewhere it is angels who take the role of assisting God's people. Thus angels are said to aid the righteous in their fight against evil (II, 51, 45). Their nature, like that of man's intellectual soul, is incorporeal (II, 51). The tabernacle offers opportunity for explaining the functions of various ranks of angels (II, 179f.).

Man and the Soul:[71] Human nature at its beginning was unbroken and immortal (II, 215). But this human nature fell into sin (II, 45). At the time of man's disobedience to the divine will there was placed around his nature a "dead and earthly covering of skins" (II, 22), so that mankind is now characterized by mortality and passions. Bodies, once having received an initial thrust downward, continue in that direction, whereas the soul, incorporeal and airy, unless hindered rises upward toward God (II, 224f.).

There are three aspects of the enfleshed soul—the rational, the spirited, and the appetitive (II, 96, 123). The appetitive part of the soul is filled with earthly desire and is never satisfied (II, 60f.). Nevertheless, the lower parts of the soul are not wholly bad. They support and give drive to the rational part. For the proper functioning of the soul the rational part must be in control, holding the appetitive and spirited together and directing them. The moral exhortations of the treatise repeatedly stress the need for the rational to restrain and control the passions. "All the movements of our soul are shepherded . . . by the will of guiding reason" (II, 18).

Free Will and Divine Cooperation:[72] The place of the freedom of human choice in Gregory's thought is fundamental to the *Life of Moses*. The *theoria* begins with the teaching that we are

16

in some manner our own parents, "giving birth to ourselves by
our own free choice in accordance with whatever we wish" (II,
3). Since the fall, each individual is placed between an angel
appointed in God's providence to help him and a demon who
contrives to corrupt his nature (II, 45f.). Placed between these
contenders, man chooses which one he follows and makes the
one with whom he sides the victor (II, 14). Gregory is com-
pelled to give extensive treatment to a major obstacle to his
view—God's hardening of Pharaoh's heart (II, 73-88). He
insists that the initial movement away from God is man's. God
sends the same influences; they incline one man in one direction and another in another. "We men have in ourselves, in our
own nature and by our own choice, the causes of light or of
darkness, since we place ourselves in whichever sphere we
wish to be" (II, 80). "Since then in the same place evil comes to
one but not to the other, the difference of free choices distinguishing each from the other, it is evident that nothing evil can
come into existence apart from our free choice" (II, 88).

In keeping with this emphasis, divine activity is seen as a
cooperation, which comes to assist the soul that has made the
first moves toward virtue. The Holy Spirit guides toward the
good those who are worthy (II, 121). "For truly the assistance
which God gives to our nature is provided to those who correctly live the life of virtue" (II, 44).

Baptism:[73] Following general Christian tradition, Gregory
treats the crossing of the Red Sea as a type of baptism (II,
124-129). Consistent with his doctrine of redemption, Gregory
sees baptism primarily as a victory over the forces of evil.
Those who have been in slavery drown the tyrant in the water.
By the "saving baptism" the passions are put to death. The
"mystical water" brings death to the enemy and life to the
friend of God. But Gregory is well aware that no magical
transformation takes place in the water. A good part of his
discussion has to do with the inconsistency of allowing the
"Egyptian army" (passions) to follow one along in life after the

baptismal liberation. Elsewhere he warns that lusts remain in the faithful (II, 277). Gregory refers to those who perform baptism as "those who wash away the blemish of sins," "those who administer grace," and "those who share in the free gift" (II, 185).

Universal Salvation: [74] The *apokatastasis*, or the return of all things to God, is clearly taught in the treatise. Thus the return of light after the three days of darkness over Egypt is interpreted as the "final restoration which is expected to take place later in the kingdom of heaven of those who have suffered condemnation in Gehenna" (II, 82). The punishment of fire is real for those who imitate the Egyptians in their manner of life (II, 83), but it will not be eternal. Moses' outstretched hands represent "the healing of pain and the deliverance from punishment" (II, 84).

Scripture: It is characteristic of Gregory's later writings that he gives a Scriptural grounding to his spiritual doctrine. Not only is the whole *Life of Moses* based on the Scriptural narrative, but also the spiritual interpretations are given a Scriptural basis wherever possible. The frequent Scriptural citations will bear this out. In the Introduction he says: "It seems good to me to make use of Scripture as a counselor in this matter" (I, 11). The prophets and apostles are the instruments of the Spirit, trumpeting forth the divine message (II, 159). The treatise is replete with such affirmations of the divine nature of Scripture. The Spirit who has inspired Scripture must guide its interpretation (II, 173).

Church Life[75]

Indications of the Church life of the time are, by the nature of the treatise, sparse but revealing. Gregory writes at the time of the triumph over idolatry and reflects the numerous conversions in the 4th century (II, 203). He also knows that many of these converts did not remain faithful or develop the Christian character. "Many of those who have . . . identified themselves with the Gospel are today still threatened by the Adversary with onslaughts of temptations" (II, 56f.; cf. 127f.).

Gregory also reflects the heresies that challenged the Church's doctrine in the 4th century (II, 16, 161, 218). One motive for withdrawal, when those who reject the "rule of truth" are in power, is flight from controversies in the Church.

Gregory is conscious of his position of influence and views the episcopal office in paternal terms (I, 2). His predecessors are "fathers" (II, 13), and his own task is to provide nourishment with the "laws and customs" of the Church (II, 12). Where there is no explicit Scripture teaching, the "tradition of the fathers" provides a trustworthy guarantee of doctrine (II, 45).

Gregory also reflects the heresies that challenged the priestly offices of the Church. Not all the people should trust themselves forward to learn the mysteries, but should select some worthy person to hear the divine things and to teach them (II, 160). Moses' flight to Midian and return with the message of liberation is said to teach "that he who has not equipped himself by this kind of spiritual training to instruct the multitude must not presume to speak among the people" (II, 55). On many occasions, Gregory notes, one may however see selfish and ambitious men arrogating to themselves God's ministry (II, 279). They seek a life of luxury and do not show the discipline of the priesthood (II, 286). He has much to say against the presumptions of those he considers unworthy of the priesthood, and his remarks seem to reflect his personal experiences with such men (II, 283).

The treatment of the tabernacle (II, 184-188) offers Gregory an opportunity for consideration of the structure of the Church. The pillars of the Church are the apostles, teachers, and prophets who brought the light of the Gospel to men. In the Church the sacrifice of praise and incense of prayer are offered to God daily. The lavers of the tabernacle are those who administer baptism. The courts refer to the harmony, love, and peace of those who believe. The Church is especially beautified by the ascetic way of life, symbolized by the red-dyed skin and coverings made of hair for the tabernacle.

The Old Testament Worthies in Gregory[76]

Each Old Testament worthy became for Gregory the model of a virtue.[77] Thus he says: "Scripture teaches us that Noah was righteous, Abraham faithful, Moses meek, Daniel wise, Joseph chaste, Job blameless, and David great-souled."[78] In his panegyric on Meletius, Gregory declares that he possessed the gentleness of David, the understanding of Solomon, the goodness of Moses, the scrupulousness of Samuel, the chastity of Joseph, the wisdom of Daniel, and the zeal of Elijah.[79]

Abraham is described in *Against Eunomius* in terms very similar to those applied to Moses.[80] Abraham surpassed his countrymen in their own wisdom, the philosophy of the Chaldaeans. The migration of Abraham was no mere spatial journey: He stretched his human capacity in order to attain to God. Making each new discovery a stepping stone to another, he ever "strained ahead for what was still to come" (Phil. 3:13, the text verse of the *Life of Moses*). He left all sense perception behind and arrived by faith at the knowledge that God is greater and more sublime than any token by which he may be known. Abraham and Moses are brought together as spiritual examples in an encomium on Stephen.[81] It is characteristic that this passage says more about Moses than about Abraham.

Events of Moses' life are several times taken as a pattern of virtue in Gregory's writings.[82] There are several extensive summaries of Moses' life and spiritual triumphs.[83] In one passage Gregory brings together three stages of Moses' experience of God: "The manifestation of God to the great Moses began with light; afterwards God spoke to him in the cloud; next when Moses became more exalted and perfect he saw God in the darkness."[84] The most extensive passage on the life of Moses outside the *Life* itself deserves to be quoted in full, for it reads almost like an outline of our treatise and shows that its theme had already assumed some importance for Gregory.[85]

> *The much desired face of the Lord once passed Moses by, and thus the soul of the lawgiver kept on going outside its present condition as it followed the Word who led the way. Who does not know those ascents which Moses attained? He was always becoming greater and never stopped in his growth. He had attained growth even at the beginning when he considered the reproach of Christ more exalted than the kingdom of Egypt, and chose to be ill-treated in company with God's people rather than to enjoy for a time the pleasures of sin.* [86] *He grew again when, at the time the Egyptian was oppressing the Hebrew, he fought on behalf of the Israelite and killed the foreigner. Surely you perceive the spiritual meaning in this history. Once more he excelled himself when he devoted a long time to the philosophical life as a solitary in the wilderness. Next, he was enlightened by the fire upon the bush, and his hearing was illumined with the beams of life by means of the Word. There he stripped from his feet the dead coverings of skins. He destroyed the Egyptian snakes with his rod and removed his people from the tyranny of Pharaoh. He was led by the cloud, divided the sea, drowned the tyrant, sweetened the waters of Marah, struck the rock, was nourished with the food of angels. He heard the trumpets, braved the burning mountain, touched the peak, came under the cloud, entered the darkness where God was, received the covenant, and became an unapproachable sun to those who came near because light radiated from his face. Indeed, how could anyone relate all his ascents and various theophanies? Nevertheless, this man who had experienced such things, this very Moses who through such attainments had been elevated to divinity, still was not satisfied. He besought God to see him face to face, although Scripture had already testified that he was counted worthy of*

speaking with God face to face. But neither his speaking as friend with friend nor the intimate conversation with God stopped his desire for more. Rather, he says, If I have found favour in your sight, make yourself known to me.[87] *God granted the requested favor. He who said, I have known you above all men,*[88] *passed by him while he was shadowed by God's hand at that divine place in the rock so that after God passed by he could only see his back. Scripture teaches by this, I think, that he who desires to behold God sees the object of his longing in always following him. The contemplation of his face is the unending journey accomplished by following directly behind the Word.*

Translating the Life of Moses[89]

"The language and the thought of Gregory of Nyssa have often discouraged translators."[90] The *Life of Moses* has suffered from this discouragement, but new interest in Gregory's place in the development of Christian spirituality has directed attention to this treatise.

The Latin translation printed by Migne was made by George of Trebizond (1395-1484) at the end of the 15th century. It represents an inferior manuscript tradition and does nothing to improve George's bad reputation as a translator. Jean Daniélou published a French translation in the first volume of *Sources Chrétiennes* in 1942, before he completed his collation of the principal manuscripts of the *Life of Moses*. This translation is reprinted in the second edition (1955) along with a critical Greek text established by him. The translation is often loose in relation to the Greek text. It is accompanied by notes, our debt to which is evident in our own notes. Of the most help in our translating has been the German rendering by Manfred Blum in the *Sophia* series (Freiberg im Br., 1963). Some extensive excerpts from the *Life of Moses* have been translated into English by Herbert Musurillo in *From Glory to Glory: Texts from Gregory of Nyssa's Mystical Writings* (London, 1961), but no complete English translation has been published.

22

We have translated from an eclectic Greek text.[91] We have made our own collation of the text established by Musurillo for the Leiden edition (begun by Werner Jaeger and continued by Hermann Langerbeck) with that of Daniélou in *Sources Chrétiennes*. The variants are, for the most part, of little consequence for an English translation. Our effort has been to stay as close to the Greek text as English style permits. Inasmuch as the other translations tend to be loose, we sought to convey the flavor of Gregory's style and produce a translation that would help the student working with the original.

Scriptural citations are given according to the Jerusalem Bible, except when more accurate translation is required to make sense out of Gregory's argument. Notes mark such deviations. Where the Greek version of the Old Testament differs significantly from the Hebrew a note has been made. Gregory was working from the Greek text of the Old Testament and this fact accounts for many of his interpretations. Scripture references given in the notes at the beginning of a section cover the entire section. Unless new biblical material is introduced, the Scripture references given in the first part of the treatise are not repeated when the historical events are given a spiritual meaning in the second part. The section numbers are those of Daniélou's Sources Chrétiennes edition.

Gregory of Nyssa
THE LIFE OF MOSES

BOOK I

The Life of Moses
or
Concerning Perfection In Virtue

Prologue

1. At horse races the spectators intent on victory shout to their favorites in the contest, even though the horses are eager to run. From the stands they participate in the race with their eyes, thinking to incite the charioteer to keener effort, at the same time urging[1] the horses on while leaning forward and flailing the air with their outstretched hands instead of with a whip. They do this not because their actions themselves contribute anything to the victory; but in this way, by their good will, they eagerly show in voice and deed their concern for the contestants.[2] I seem to be doing the same thing myself, most valued friend and brother. While you are competing admirably in the divine race along the course of virtue, lightfootedly leaping and straining constantly for the *prize of the heavenly calling*,[3] I exhort, urge and encourage you vigorously to increase your speed. I do this, not moved to it by some unconsidered impulse, but to humor the delights of a beloved child.

2. Since the letter which you recently sent requested us to furnish you with some counsel concerning the perfect life, I thought it only proper to answer your request.[4] Although there may be nothing useful for you in my words, perhaps this example of ready obedience will not be wholly unprofitable to you. For if we who have been appointed to the position of fathers[5] over so many souls consider it proper here in our old age[6] to accept a commission from youth, how much more suitable is it, inasmuch as we have taught you, a young man, to obey voluntarily, that the right action of ready obedience be confirmed in you.

29

3. So much for that. We must take up the task that lies before us, taking God as our guide in our treatise.[7] You requested, dear friend, that we trace in outline for you what the perfect life is. Your intention clearly was to translate the grace disclosed by my word into your own life, if you should find in my treatise what you were seeking. I am at an equal loss about both things: It is beyond my power to encompass perfection in my treatise or to show in my life the insights[8] of the treatise. And perhaps I am not alone in this. Many great men, even those who excel in virtue, will admit that for them such an accomplishment as this is unattainable.

4. As I would not seem, in the words of the Psalmist, *there to tremble for fear, where no fear was*,[9] I shall set forth for you more clearly what I think.

5. The perfection of everything which can be measured by the senses is marked off by certain definite boundaries. Quantity, for example, admits of both continuity and limitation, for every quantitative measure is circumscribed by certain limits proper to itself.[10] The person who looks at a cubit or at the number ten knows that its perfection consists in the fact that it has both a beginning and an end. But in the case of virtue we have learned from the Apostle that its one limit of perfection is the fact that it has no limit. For that divine Apostle, great and lofty in understanding, ever running the course of virtue, never ceased *straining toward those* things *that are still to come*.[11] Coming to a stop in the race was not safe for him. Why? Because no Good has a limit in its own nature but is limited by the presence of its opposite,[12] as life is limited by death and light by darkness. And every good thing generally ends with all those things which are perceived to be contrary to the good.

6. Just as the end of life is the beginning of death, so also stopping in the race of virtue marks the beginning of the race of evil. Thus our statement that grasping perfection with reference to virtue is impossible was not false, for it has been pointed out that what is marked off by boundaries is not virtue.

I said that it is also impossible for those who pursue the life of virtue to attain perfection. The meaning of this statement will be explained.

7. The Divine One is himself the Good (in the primary and proper sense of the word),[13] whose very nature is goodness. This he is and he is so named, and is known by this nature. Since, then, it has not been demonstrated that there is any limit to virtue except evil, and since the Divine does not admit of an opposite, we hold the divine nature to be unlimited and infinite. Certainly whoever pursues true virtue participates in nothing other than God, because he is himself absolute virtue.[14] Since, then, those who know what is good by nature desire participation in it, and since this good has no limit, the participant's desire itself necessarily has no stopping place but stretches out with the limitless.[15]

8. It is therefore undoubtedly impossible to attain perfection, since, as I have said, perfection is not marked off by limits: The one limit of virtue is the absence of a limit. How then would one arrive at the sought-for boundary when he can find no boundary?[16]

9. Although on the whole my argument has shown that what is sought for is unattainable, one should not disregard the commandment of the Lord which says, *Therefore be perfect, just as your heavenly father is perfect*.[17] For in the case of those things which are good by nature, even if men of understanding were not able to attain to everything, by attaining even a part they could yet gain a great deal.

10. We should show great diligence not to fall away from the perfection which is attainable but to acquire as much as is possible: To that extent let us make progress within the realm of what we seek. For the perfection of human nature consists perhaps in its very growth in goodness.[18]

11. It seems good to me to make use of Scripture as a counselor in this matter. For the divine voice says somewhere in the prophecy of Isaiah, *Consider Abraham your father, and*

Sarah who gave you birth.[19] Scripture gives this admonition to those who wander outside virtue. Just as at sea those who are carried away from the direction of the harbor bring themselves back on course by a clear sign, upon seeing either a beacon light raised up high or some mountain peak coming into view, in the same way Scripture by the example of Abraham and Sarah may guide again to the harbor of the divine will those adrift on the sea of life[20] with a pilotless mind.

12. Human nature is divided into male and female, and the free choice of virtue or of evil is set before both equally. For this reason the corresponding example of virtue for each sex has been exemplified by the divine voice, so that each, by observing the one to which he is akin (the men to Abraham and the women to Sarah), may be directed in the life of virtue by the appropriate examples.[21]

13. Perhaps, then, the memory of anyone distinguished in life would be enough to fill our need for a beacon light and to show us how we can bring our soul to the sheltered harbor of virtue[22] where it no longer has to pass the winter amid the storms of life or be shipwrecked in the deep water of evil by the successive billows of passion. It may be for this very reason that the daily life of those sublime individuals is recorded in detail, that by imitating those earlier examples of right action those who follow them may conduct their lives to the good.[23]

14. What then? Some one will say, "How shall I imitate them, since I am not a Chaldaean as I remember Abraham was, nor was I nourished by the daughter of the Egyptian as Scripture teaches about Moses, and in general I do not have in these matters anything in my life corresponding to anyone of the ancients? How shall I place myself in the same rank with one of them, when I do not know how to imitate anyone so far removed from me by the circumstances of his life?" To him we reply that we do not consider being a Chaldaean a virtue or a vice, nor is anyone exiled from the life of virtue by living in Egypt or spending his life in Babylon, nor again has God been

known to the esteemed individuals in Judaea only,[24] nor is Zion, as people commonly think,[25] the divine habitation. We need some subtlety of understanding and keenness of vision to discern from the history how, by removing ourselves from such Chaldaeans and Egyptians and by escaping from such a Babylonian captivity, we shall embark on the blessed life.

15. Let us put forth Moses as our example for life in our treatise.[26] First we shall go through in outline his life as we have learned it from the divine Scriptures. Then we shall seek out the spiritual understanding which corresponds to the history[27] in order to obtain suggestions of virtue. Through such understanding we may come to know the perfect life for men.

History of Moses

16. Moses is said to have been born when the tyrant's law sought to prevent the birth of male offspring.[28] Yet in his outward grace he anticipated the whole contribution which he would make in time. Already appearing beautiful[29] in swaddling clothes, he caused his parents to draw back from having such a child destroyed by death.

17. Thus, when the threat of the tyrant prevailed, he was not simply thrown into the Nile but was placed in a basket *daubed* along its joints *with slime and pitch*,[30] and so was given to the current. (This was recounted by those who carefully gave a narrative concerning him.)[31] Guided by some divine power, the basket moved to a certain place along the sloping bank where it was washed up naturally by the lapping of the waves. As the king's daughter happened to come to that grassy bank where the basket washed up, she discovered him when he gave a childlike cry in the ark. When she saw the outward grace evident in him, the princess out of her good will immediately adopted him and took him as her son. But when he instinctively refused a stranger's nourishment, he was nursed at his mother's

breast[32] through the contrivance of his close relatives.

18. After he had left childhood, and had been educated in pagan learning[33] during his royal upbringing,[34] he did not choose the things considered glorious by the pagans nor did he any longer recognize as his mother that wise woman by whom he had been adopted, but he returned to his natural mother and attached himself to his own kinsmen.[35] During a fight between a Hebrew and an Egyptian he sided with his countryman and killed the foreigner.[36] Then when two Hebrews fought with each other, he tried to restrain them, counseling them that because they were brothers they should make nature and not passion the arbiter of their disputes.

19. Having been rebuffed by the one in the wrong, he made this rejection the occasion for a greater philosophy.[37] Separating himself from association with the people, he thereafter lived alone. He became the son-in-law of one of the foreigners, a man with insight into what is noble, and perceptive in judging the habits and lives of men. This man saw in one act—the attack on the shepherds[38]—the virtue of the young man, how he fought on behalf of the right without looking for personal gain. Considering the right valuable in itself, Moses punished the wrong done by the shepherds, although they had done nothing against him. Honoring the young man Moses for these acts and judging his virtue in his manifest poverty more valuable than great riches, the man gave him his daughter in marriage and, in keeping with his authority, he permitted Moses to live as he wished. Moses lived alone in the mountains away from all the turmoil of the marketplace; there in the wilderness he cared for his sheep.

20. After he had passed some time in this kind of life, the history says an awe-inspiring theophany occurred.[39] At high noon a light brighter than the sunlight dazzled his eyes.[40] Astonished at the strange sight, he looked up at the mountain and saw a bush from which this light was flaming up like a fire. When he saw the branches of the bush sprouting up in flame as

if they were in pure water,[41] he said to himself, "I will go and see this great sight." As soon as he said this, he no longer received the marvel of the light with his sight alone, but (which is most astounding of all) his hearing too was illuminated by the rays of light. The light's grace was distributed to both senses, illuminating the sight with flashing rays and lighting the way for the hearing with undefiled teachings. The voice from the light forbade Moses to approach the mountain burdened with lifeless sandals.[42] He removed the sandals from his feet, and so stood on that ground on which the divine light was shining.

21. I think that the discussion should not dwell extensively on the bare history of the man. We should give attention to the matters we have proposed. After he was empowered by the theophany which he had seen, he was commanded to release his countrymen from Egyptian bondage. In order that he might learn more fully the strength implanted in him by God he tested the divine command by the things in his hands.[43] This was the test. When the rod fell from his hand, it became alive, a living creature (in fact it was a serpent); when he took it up again in his hand, it became what it had been before becoming an animal. When he withdrew his hand from his bosom, it looked as white as snow, but when he put it back in his bosom, it returned to its natural color.

22. Moses went down to Egypt and he took with him his foreign wife and the children she had borne him.[44] Scripture says that an angel encountered him and threatened death. His wife appeased the angel by the blood of the child's circumcision. Then he met Aaron, who had himself been brought by God to this meeting.

23. Later, the people in Egypt were gathered by Moses and Aaron into a general assembly and their release from bondage was announced all around to those who were already distressed by the hardships of their labors.[45] Report of this came to the tyrant himself. When he heard it his anger at both

the overseers of the work and the Israelites themselves was greater than ever. The levy of bricks to be made was increased[46] and a harsher command was sent down, not only to those slaving with the clay but also to those laboriously gathering chaff and straw.

24. Pharaoh (for this was the Egyptian tyrant's name) attempted to counter the divine signs performed by Moses and Aaron with magical tricks performed by his sorcerers.[47] When Moses again turned his own rod into an animal before the eyes of the Egyptians, they thought that the sorcery of the magicians could equally work miracles with their rods. This deceit was exposed when the serpent produced from the staff of Moses ate the sticks of sorcery—the snakes no less! The rods of the sorcerers had no means of defense nor any power of life, only the appearance which cleverly devised sorcery showed to the eyes of those easily deceived.

25. When Moses saw that all the subjects agreed with their leader in his evil, he laid a blow upon the whole Egyptian nation, sparing no one from the calamities.[48] Like an army under orders, the very elements of the universe—earth, water, air, and fire which are seen to be in everything—cooperated with him in this attack on the Egyptians, and changed their natural operations to serve human purposes.[49] For by the same power and at the same time and place the disorderly were punished and those free of wrong did not suffer.

26. At the command of Moses all the water in Egypt turned into blood.[50] The fish were destroyed because the water thickened, but to the Hebrews alone the blood was water when they drew it. Found among the Hebrews this water provided an occasion for the magicians to use their art in making the water appear bloody.

27. Similarly frogs covered Egypt in large numbers.[51] Their breeding in these numbers was not natural, but Moses' command changed the normal density of frogs. All the land

was in a sorry state, for the Egyptians' houses were being overrun with these creatures, while the Hebrews were free of this hateful plague.

28. Likewise, there was no distinction between night and day to the Egyptians, who lived in unchanging gloom.[52] To the Hebrews, however, nothing was out of the ordinary. It was the same with all the other things—the hail, the fire, the boils, the gadflies,[53] the flies, the cloud of locusts: Each had its natural effect on the Egyptians.[54] The Hebrews learned of the misfortune of their neighbors by report, since they experienced no similar attack themselves.

Then the death of the firstborn made the distinction between Egyptians and Hebrews still sharper.[55] The Egyptians were dismayed, lamenting the loss of their dearest children, while the Hebrews continued to live in total serenity and safety. Salvation was assured to them by *the shedding of the blood*.[56] At every entrance both the doorposts and the lintel joining them were marked with blood.

29. While the Egyptians were downcast at the fate of their firstborn and each individual was lamenting his sufferings and those of everyone else, Moses led the exodus of the Israelites.[57] He had previously prepared them to take away with themselves the wealth of the Egyptians on the pretext that it was a loan.[58] The history goes on to say that when they were three days out of Egypt, the Egyptian was angry that Israel did not remain in slavery, and after mobilizing all his subjects for war, he pursued the people with his cavalry.[59]

When they saw the deployment of the cavalry and infantry, they were panic-stricken since they were inexperienced in war and untrained in such sights, and they rose up against Moses. Then the history tells the most marvellous thing about Moses. He did two distinctly separate things at once: By spoken word he encouraged the Israelites and exhorted them not to abandon high hopes, but inwardly, in his thoughts, he pleaded with God on behalf of those who cowered in fear and he was directed by counsel from above how to escape the danger. God himself, the history says, gave ear to his voiceless cry.[60]

30. By divine power a cloud led the people.[61] This was no ordinary cloud, for it was not composed of the vapors or exhalations as normal clouds are. The winds did not press the vapors of the air into a misty composition; it was something beyond human comprehension.[62] Scripture testifies that there was something amazing about that cloud. When the rays of the noonday sun shone with great heat, the cloud was a shelter for the people, shadowing those below it and moistening with a light dew the fiery heat of the atmosphere. During the night it became a fire, leading the Israelites as in a procession with its own light from sunset to sunrise.[63]

31. Moses himself watched the cloud, and he taught the people to keep it in sight.[64] When the cloud had guided them along their course, they came to the Red Sea, where the Egyptians coming from behind with their whole army surrounded the people. No way of escape from their terrors was open to the Israelites in any direction, because they were trapped between their enemies and the water. It was then that Moses, urged on by divine power, performed the most incredible deed of all. He approached the bank and struck the sea with his rod. The sea split at the blow, just as a crack in glass runs straight across to the edge when a break occurs at any point. The whole sea was split like that from the top by the rod, and the break in the waters reached to the opposite bank. At the place where the sea parted, Moses went down into the deep with all the people and they were in the deep without getting wet and their bodies were still in the sunlight. As they crossed the depths by foot on dry bottom, they were not alarmed at the water piled up so close to them on both sides, for the sea had been fixed like a wall on each side of them.[65]

32. When Pharaoh and the Egyptians ran after them headlong into the sea along that newly cut path, the walls of

water came together again and the sea rushed in upon itself to assume its previous form, becoming to the eye a single body of water.[66] By that time the Israelites were already resting on the opposite bank from the long and strenuous march through the sea. Then they sang a victory song to God for raising a monument[67] unstained with blood on their behalf since he destroyed in the water the whole army of the Egyptians—their horses, infantry, and chariots.

33. After that, Moses pushed on, but when he had traveled three days without water he was at a loss how to relieve the thirst of the army.[68] They pitched camp near a pool of salty water, more bitter than the sea itself. While they were resting close to the water and were parched with thirst, Moses, acting on the counsel of God, found a piece of wood near that place and threw it into the water. Immediately it became drinkable, for the wood by its own power changed the nature of the water from bitter to sweet.

34. As the cloud moved forward, the Israelites followed their guide closely. They always rested from their march wherever the cloud indicated by stopping, and they departed again whenever the cloud led the way on.[69] By following this guide, they arrived at a place irrigated with drinkable water.[70] It was watered all around by twelve bountiful springs and shaded by a grove of date palms. There were seventy date palms which, even though few in number, made a great impression on those who saw them, because of their exceptional beauty and height.

35. Again their guide, the cloud, rose up and led them forth to another place.[71] But this was a desert with arid, scorching sand and not a drop of water to moisten the country. Here once more thirst exhausted the people. But when Moses struck a prominent rock with his rod, it gave forth water which was sweet and drinkable in greater abundance than was needed by even so large a host.

36. It was also there that the provisions which they had

laid in for the journey out of Egypt failed, and the people were famished.[72] Then the most incredible marvel of all occurred: Food did not grow out of the earth in the customary manner but fell like dew from heaven. For the dew was poured out upon them at daybreak and became food for those who gathered it. What was poured out was not drops of water as in the case of dew but crystal-like drops in the shape of coriander seed, tasting as sweet as honey.

37. With this marvel was seen also another: Those who went out to gather the food were all, as one might expect, of different ages and capacities, yet despite their differences one did not gather more or less than another. Instead, the amount gathered was measured by the need of each, so that the stronger did not have a surplus nor was the weaker deprived of his fair share. In addition, the history tells another marvel. Each one, when making provision for the day, laid up nothing for the morrow, but when some stingy person did store up some of the daily food for the next day, it became inedible, being changed into worms.

38. The history offers yet another astounding feature of this food, for one of the seven days of the week was observed by rest in keeping with a mystical ordinance. On the day before the day of rest, the same amount of food flowed down as on other days and the effort of those gathering it was the same, yet what was gathered was found to be double the usual amount, so that their need for food was no excuse for breaking the law of rest. Divine power was shown even more in that, whereas on other days the excess became worthless, on the day of Preparation for the Sabbath (which is the name of this day of rest) alone did what was stored up remain imperishable so that it in no way appeared to be less fresh than the new.

39. Then they waged war against a foreign nation.[73] The text calls those combining against them Amalekites. For the first time the Israelites were drawn up fully armed in battle array. The full army was not moved into battle; only picked

troops chosen for their merit undertook the war. Here Moses showed a new piece of strategy. While Joshua (who was to succeed Moses in leading the people) led the army out against the Amalekites, Moses, standing on a hilltop away from the furor of battle, was looking up toward heaven with a friend stationed on either side of him.

40. Then we hear from the history the following marvel: When Moses raised his hands to heaven, those under his command prevailed against their enemies, but when he let them down, the army began to give in to the foreigners' assault. When those who stood with him recognized this they stationed themselves on either side of him and supported his hands, which for some unknown reason had become heavy and hard to move. When his helpers became too weak to hold him in an upright position, they provided him a stone to sit on, thus helping Moses to raise his hands to heaven. From then on the foreign army was mightily defeated by the Israelites.

41. When the cloud which led the people in their journey continued to remain at the same place, the people could not move on, since there was no one to lead them to depart. All the necessities of life were provided for them without toil. The air from above rained bread already prepared for them, and the rock from below provided drink. The cloud in turn tempered the unpleasantness of being out in the open, forming a shelter from the heat by day and at night dispelling the darkness by shining with a torch-like radiance. So they experienced no discomfort in that desert at the foot of the mountain where they had pitched camp.

42. Here Moses guided them in a most secret initiation.[74] The divine power itself by marvels beyond description initiated all the people and their leader himself in the following manner. The people were ordered beforehand to keep themselves from defilements[75] of all kinds which pertain to both soul and body and to purify themselves by certain lustrations. They were to keep themselves pure from intercourse for a stated

number of days so that, pure of passion, they might approach the mountain to be initiated, cleansed of every emotion and bodily concern. (The name of the mountain was Sinai.) Persons alone were allowed at that time to approach the mountain, and of them men alone, and of them, in turn, those purified from every pollution. Every safeguard and precaution was taken against the approach of any animals to the mountain.[76] If somehow it did happen that any animal at all showed itself at the mountain, it was stoned by the people.

43. Then the clear light of the atmosphere was darkened so that the mountain became invisible, wrapped in a dark cloud.[77] A fire shining out of the darkness presented a fearful sight to those who saw it. It hovered all around the sides of the mountain so that everything which one could see smouldered with the smoke from the surrounding fire. Moses led the people to the slope, not without fear himself at the sight. His whole being so trembled with fright that his faintness of soul was not concealed from the Israelites, but he was terrified, as they were, at what he saw and his body shook violently.

44. The manifestation was of such a nature that it not only caused consternation in their souls through what they saw but it also struck fear in them through what they heard. A terrible sound ripped down from above upon everything below. Its first impact was harsh and intolerable to every ear. Its sound was like the blaring of trumpets, but the intensity and terribleness of the sound surpassed any such comparison. As it drew nearer, its blaring steadily increased to a more terrifying volume. This sound was sharp and clear, the air articulating the word by divine power without using organs of speech.[78] The word was not articulated without purpose but was laying down divine ordinances. As the sound drew nearer, it became louder, and the trumpet surpassed itself, the successive sounds exceeding in volume the preceding ones.

45. The people as a whole were incapable of enduring what was seen and heard. Therefore, a general request from all

42

was brought before Moses that the Law be mediated through him,[79] on the ground that the people would not doubt that whatever he commanded in keeping with the teaching from above was a divine command. So when all went down to the foot of the mountain, Moses alone remained and showed the opposite of what was to be expected of him. Whereas all other men feel confidence in the face of fearful things when in the company of their associates, Moses was more courageous after he had been left by himself. From this it became clear that the fear which had encompassed him at the beginning was an emotion not in keeping with his character but was experienced out of sympathy for those who were terrified.

46. Since he was alone, by having been stripped as it were of the people's fear, he boldly approached the very darkness itself and entered the invisible things where he was no longer seen by those watching. After he entered the inner sanctuary of the divine mystical doctrine,[80] there, while not being seen, he was in company with the Invisible. He teaches, I think, by the things he did that the one who is going to associate intimately with God must go beyond all that is visible and (lifting up his own mind, as to a mountaintop, to the invisible and incomprehensible) believe that the divine is *there* where the understanding does not reach.[81]

47. While there he received the divine ordinances.[82] These were the teachings concerning virtue, the chief of which is reverence and having the proper notions[83] about the divine nature, inasmuch as it transcends all cognitive thought and representation and cannot be likened to anything which is known. He was commanded to heed none of those things comprehended by the notions with regard to the divine nor to liken the transcendent nature to any of the things known by comprehension. Rather, he should believe that the Divine exists, and he should not examine it with respect to quality, quantity, origin, and mode of being, since it is unattainable.[84]

48. The word also adds what are right moral actions,

presenting its teaching in both general and specific laws. General is the law which is destructive of all injustice, namely that one must love his neighbor.[85] If this law were observed, it would certainly follow in consequence that no one would do any evil to his neighbor.[86] Among the specific laws was established honor for parents, and there was listed a catalogue of prohibited deeds.[87]

49. With his mind purified by these laws, as it were, he was led to the higher initiation, where a tabernacle was all at once shown to him by divine power.[88] The tabernacle was a sanctuary with beauty of indescribable variety—entrances, pillars, and curtains, table, candlestick, and altar of incense, the altar of holocaust and the propitiatory, and the inaccessible and unapproachable holy of holies.[89] So that their beauty and arrangement might not be forgotten and might be shown to those below, he was counseled not to represent these things in mere writing but to imitate in material construction that immaterial creation, employing the most splendid and radiant materials found on earth. Among these the most abundant was gold, with which the pillars were overlaid. With the gold, silver also made its contribution by beautifying the capitals and bases of the pillars so that by the changes of color at each end, I think, the gold might shine forth more brightly. There were also places where brass was considered useful, namely at the head and base of the silver pillars.

50. The draperies and the curtains and the outer wall of the sanctuary and the coverings stretched out in succession over the columns—each was finished out of an appropriate material by the weaver's art. The dye of these woven fabrics was violet, purple, and fiery scarlet, and some material had its natural brightness. For some things linen was used and for other things hair, in keeping with the purposes of the fabrics. There were also places where skins dyed red were suitable to the beauty of the structure.

51. After his descent from the mountain Moses, employ-

ing workmen, constructed these things according to the pattern shown to him.[90] While he was in that sanctuary not made with hands,[91] he was commanded how the priest should be adorned when he entered the sanctuary.[92] The law prescribed the details of the under and outer garments.

52. The first in order of the garments was not the hidden but the visible. There was an ephod embroidered of different colors with gold thread predominating. (The veil was also made of these colors.)[93] Clasps held the ephod together on both sides and provided a setting of gold for emeralds.[94] The beauty of these stones was due partly to their natural radiance—from them a green brightness was given forth—and partly to the marvellous skill of the engraving. (This was not the skill which carves out images of idols, but the adornment was the names of the patriarchs engraved six on each stone.)

53. From the clasps down the front the little shield-like ornaments hung loosely.[95] There were also intertwined cords plaited through one another in a netlike pattern hanging from the clasps on each side. They dropped down below the shield-like ornaments so that the beauty of the plaiting might, I think, be more conspicuous being enhanced by the background.

54. The ornament[96] made out of gold which hung down from the chest had on it stones of different kinds equal in number to the patriarchs.[97] These were arranged in four rows set three to a row, with the names of the tribes written on them. The tunic beneath the ephod extended from the neck to the toes and was suitably adorned with fringes. The hem was decked out beautifully, not only by the variety of skilled weaving but also by the hanging of gold ornaments. These were golden bells and pomegranates distributed alternately along the hem.

55. The fillet for the head was solid violet, and the metal-leaf frontpiece was of pure gold engraved with the ineffable letters.[98] There was also a girdle which held together the loose folds of the garment, as well as an adornment for the hidden parts of the body, and the other articles of clothing which

symbolically instruct concerning priestly virtue under the
form of clothing.

56. After he was instructed in these and other such things
by the ineffable teaching of God while he was surrounded by
that invisible darkness, and having surpassed himself by the aid
of the mystical doctrines, he emerged again out of the darkness.
He then went down to his people to share with them the
marvels which had been shown to him in the theophany, to
deliver the laws, and to institute for them the sanctuary and
priesthood according to the pattern shown to him on the
mountain.

57. He carried in his hands the holy tablets, which were a
divine invention and gift that needed no human cooperation to
be brought into existence.[99] Both the material and the writing
on them were equally the work of God. The writing was the
Law. But the people prevented grace: Before giving heed to the
lawgiver they rebelled in idolatry.[100]

58. Some considerable time had elapsed while Moses devoted himself to conversation with God in that divine initiation. He participated in that eternal life under the darkness for
forty days and nights, and lived in a state beyond nature,[101] for
his body had no need of food during that time. It was then that
the people, like a little child who escapes the attention of his
pedagogue, were carried along into disorderliness by uncontrolled impulses, and, banding together against Aaron, forced
the priest to lead them in idolatry.

59. When the idol had been made out of gold (it was a
calf), they exulted in their impiety; but Moses came to them
and broke the tablets which he had received from God so that
they might suffer a punishment worthy of their transgression
by having no share in the God-given grace.

60. He then purified his people's guilt with their own
blood when the Levites slew them,[102] and appeased the divine
by his own anger against the transgressors. Thereupon he
utterly destroyed the idol. Once more applying himself to the

matter for forty days, he received the tablets. The writing on them was done by divine power, but the material was fashioned by the hand of Moses.[103] He received them while for the same number of days he again lived beyond nature in a manner different from that to which we are accustomed and admitted to his body none of those sustenances which our nature requires.

61. Moses accordingly erected for them the tabernacle, delivered to them the laws, and established the priesthood in keeping with the teaching given to him by God. The workmanship on all the material objects was done according to the divine directions—the tabernacle, the entrances, and everything inside—the altar of incense, the altar of holocaust, the candlestick, the curtains, the propitiatory within the holy of holies; the adornment of the priesthood, the myrrh, the different sacrifices—the purifications, the thank-offerings, the offerings to avert evil, the propitiations for trespasses.[104] As he arranged everything in the required manner, among his family he aroused against himself envy, that congenital malady in the nature of man.

62. Even Aaron, who was endowed with the honors of the priesthood, and his sister Miriam, driven by a most female-like jealousy against the honor given to Moses by God, so railed against him that deity was provoked to punish their trespass.[105] Here Moses showed patience most worthy of admiration, because, when God punished the irrational envy of the woman, he made his nature prevail over anger and appeased God on behalf of his sister.

63. The multitude again fell into disorderliness.[106] What led to their transgression was a lack of moderation in regard to the pleasures of the table, for they were not satisfied to live healthfully and painlessly on the food which flowed down from above, but the craving for meat made them prefer slavery in Egypt to their present good circumstances. Moses took counsel with God concerning the passion which had overcome them,

and God instructed that they should not have such desires because he would give what they longed for. He sent flocks of birds like a cloud to fly close to the ground near the camp. The ease with which they could catch the birds led them in their craving for meat to stuff themselves.

64. Their immoderation at once became destructive to their bodies, and their satiety ended in sickness and death. This example became to them and to those watching them a sufficient cause for moderation.

65. Next, Moses sent spies into that region which they hoped to inhabit according to the divine promise.[107] When not all of them reported the truth, but some gave false and discouraging information, the people again rose in anger against Moses. God decreed that those who had no confidence in divine help should not see the promised land.

66. As they were crossing the desert, water again failed them—as did their memory of the divine power,[108] for the earlier miracle[109] of the rock did not give them confidence that their present necessities would be provided for. Abandoning their hopes for better things, they reviled Moses and God himself, so that the disbelief of the people seemed to intimidate even Moses. Nevertheless he performed for them again the miracle of changing that jutting rock[110] into water.

67. Again the pleasures of the table enslaved them, and their desires led them to gluttony. Although they lacked none of the necessities of life, disorderly youths were dreaming of the Egyptian plenty. They were disciplined by very severe scourges: Serpents within the encampment as they bit them injected deadly poison in them.[111]

68. When deaths caused by the serpents followed in rapid succession, the lawgiver, at the urging of divine counsel, cast a bronze likeness of a serpent and placed it on a height to be seen by the whole camp. In this way he stayed the harm done among the people by the serpents and delivered them from destruction. For he who looked on the bronze image of the serpent did

not fear the bite of the real serpent, since looking at it counteracted the poison by some mysterious antidote.

69. Some of the people again rose up against Moses' leadership and put pressure on him to transfer the priesthood to themselves.[112] Although he made supplication to God on behalf of the rebels, the righteous judgment of God was stronger than the compassion of Moses for his people. For the earth, opening up like a chasm at the divine will and closing up again, swallowed all those who set themselves, together with all their kinsmen, against the authority of Moses. When two hundred and fifty of those who raved about the priesthood were consumed by fire, the people were brought to their senses.

70. In order to persuade men that the grace of the priesthood comes from God to those who are worthy, Moses received rods from the most eminent man in each tribe, each man bringing a rod marked with his own name.[113] Aaron's rod was among them. Moses placed the rods before the sanctuary, and by them he made God's choice concerning the priesthood clear to the people. Aaron's rod alone budded and produced ripe fruit from the wood—and the fruit was the almond.

71. It seemed a very great marvel to the unbelievers that what was dried, polished, and rootless all at once produced the growth natural to things which are planted. Instead of earth, bark, moisture, roots, and time, it was the divine power at work in the wood.

72. Thereupon, when he led the army through foreign nations who blocked their passage, he swore an oath that the people would not pass through the fields and vineyards but would keep to the royal road, turning aside neither to the right nor to the left.[114] When the adversaries would not make peace on these terms, he prevailed in battle against the enemy and became master of the route.

73. Next, a certain Balak who ruled a greater nation known as the Midianites, panic-stricken at the experience of those who were destroyed and expecting to undergo nothing

less calamitous at the hands of the Israelites, brought in support not arms and men but magical arts in the person of a certain Balaam.[115] He was commonly reputed to be skilled in these things and was believed by those who employed him to be powerful in such matters. His augury came from watching the flight of birds,[116] yet he was a hard man to deal with, for with the cooperation of demons[117] he could bring utter ruin on men through this magical power.

74. As he followed those who were leading him to the king of that nation, he learned by the voice of his ass that the way was not propitious for him. Having learned in a vision what was to be done, he found that any harm to be inflicted by working magic was impotent against those who have God as their ally. Moved by divine inspiration instead of by demonic power, he uttered such words as were a clear prophecy of better things which would later come to pass. What prevented his making use of his skill for evil also brought him an awareness of divine power. Leaving divination aside, he acted as an interpreter of the divine will.[118]

75. Then the foreign nation was destroyed. The Israelites had the upper hand in the battle, but they in turn were overcome by licentious passion for their female captives.[119] When Phineas then with one blow ran those through who were entangled in dishonor, the wrath of God against those raving for unlawful unions abated. Then the lawgiver, ascending a high mountain, surveyed from afar the land which was prepared for Israel by the divine promise made to the fathers.[120] He departed from this human life, leaving behind no sign on the earth nor any grave as a memorial of his departure.[121]

76. Time had not harmed his beauty, neither dimmed his brightness of eye nor diminished the graciousness of his appearance.[122] Always remaining the same, he preserved in the changeableness of nature an unchangeable beauty.[123]

77. Those things which we have learned from the literal history of the man we have retraced in summary for you,

although we have of necessity so amplified the account as to bring out its intention. Now we must adapt the life which we have called to mind to the aim we have proposed for our study so that we might gain some benefit for the virtuous life from the things mentioned. Let us now begin the account of this life.

BOOK II

Contemplation on the Life of Moses

Birth and Childhood

1. Moses was born at the time Pharaoh issued the decree for male offspring to be destroyed.[1] How shall we as a matter of choice imitate this fortuitous birth of Moses? Someone will rightly raise the objection that it does not lie within our power to imitate in our own birth that famous birth. But it is not hard to begin the imitation with this seeming difficulty.

2. Everyone knows that anything placed in a world of change never remains the same but is always passing from one state to another, the alteration always bringing about something better or worse.[2] The narrative is to be understood according to its real intention. For the material and passionate disposition to which human nature is carried when it falls is the female form of life, whose birth is favored by the tyrant. The austerity and intensity of virtue is the male birth, which is hostile to the tyrant and suspected of insurrection against his rule.[3]

3. Now, it is certainly required that what is subject to change be in a sense always coming to birth.[4] In mutable nature nothing can be observed which is always the same. Being born, in the sense of constantly experiencing change, does not come about as the result of external initiative, as is the case with the birth of the body, which takes place by chance. Such a birth occurs by choice.[5] We are in some manner our own parents,

giving birth to ourselves by our own free choice in accordance with whatever we wish to be, whether male or female, moulding ourselves to the teaching of virtue or vice.[6]

4. We can most certainly enter upon a better birth[7] into the realm of light, however much the unwilling tyrant is distressed, and we can be seen with pleasure and be given life by the parents of this goodly offspring, even though it is contrary to the design of the tyrant. (The rational faculties[8] are what become the "parents of . . . virtue.")

5. When we lay bare the hidden meaning[9] of the history, Scripture is seen to teach that the birth which distresses the tyrant is the beginning of the virtuous life. I am speaking of that kind of birth in which free will serves as the midwife, delivering the child amid great pain. For no one causes grief to his antagonist unless he exhibits in himself those marks which give proof of his victory over the other.

6. It is the function of the free will both to beget this virtuous male offspring and to nourish it with proper food and to take forethought how to save it unharmed from the water. For there are those who present their children to the tyrant, delivering them naked and without forethought to the stream. I am speaking of life as a stream made turbulent by the successive waves of passion, which plunge what is in the stream under the water and drown it.[10]

7. Whenever life demands that the sober and provident rational thoughts which are the parents of the male child launch their good child on the billows of this life, they make him safe in an ark so that when he is given to the stream he will not be drowned.[11] The ark, constructed out of various boards, would be education in the different disciplines, which holds what it carries above the waves of life.

8. Although he is borne along by the rushing of the waves, the child is not carried far by the tossing of the waters where there is education. Instead he is washed to the side and the motion of the waters naturally thrusts him on the firm

bank, that is to say, outside the turmoil of life.

9. Experience teaches us that the restless and heaving motion of life thrusts from itself those who do not totally submerge themselves in the deceits of human affairs and it reckons as a useless burden those whose virtue is annoying. He who escapes from these things must imitate Moses and not spare his tears, even though he should be safe in the ark, for tears are the unfailing guardian of those saved by virtue.

10. Since the daughter of the king, being childless and barren (I think she is rightly perceived as profane philosophy), arranged to be called his mother by adopting the youngster,[12] Scripture concedes that his relationship with her who was falsely called his mother[13] should not be rejected until he had recognized his own immaturity. But he who has already attained maturity, as we have learned about Moses, will be ashamed to be called the son of one who is barren by nature.

11. For truly barren is profane education, which is always in labor but never gives birth.[14] For what fruit worthy of such pangs does philosophy show for being so long in labor? Do not all who are full of wind and never come to term miscarry before they come to the light of the knowledge of God,[15] although they could as well become men if they were not altogether hidden in the womb of barren wisdom?

12. Now after living with the princess of the Egyptians for such a long time that he seemed to share in their honors, he must return to his natural mother.[16] Indeed he was not separated from her while he was being brought up by the princess but was nursed by his mother's milk, as the history states.[17] This teaches, it seems to me, that if we should be involved with profane teachings during our education, we should not separate ourselves from the nourishment of the Church's milk,[18] which would be her laws and customs. By these the soul is nourished and matured, thus being given the means of ascending the height.

13. It is true that he who looks to both the profane doc-

trines and to the doctrines of the fathers will find himself between two antagonists.[19] For the foreigner in worship is opposed to the Hebrew teaching, and contentiously strives to appear stronger than the Israelite. And so he seems to be to many of the more superficial who abandon the faith of their fathers and fight on the side of the enemy, becoming transgressors of the fathers' teaching. On the other hand, he who is great and noble in soul like Moses slays with his own hand the one who rises in opposition to true religion.[20]

14. One may, moreover, find this same conflict in us, for man is set before competitors as the prize of their contest. He makes the one with whom he sides the victor over the other.[21] The fight of the Egyptian against the Hebrew is like the fight of idolatry against true religion, of licentiousness against self-control, of injustice against righteousness, of arrogance against humility, and of everything against what is perceived by its opposite.[22]

15. Moses teaches us by his own example to take our stand with virtue as with a kinsman and to kill virtue's adversary. The victory of true religion is the death and destruction of idolatry. So also injustice is killed by righteousness and arrogance is slain by humility.

16. The dispute of the two Israelites with each other occurs also in us. There would be no occasion for wicked, heretical opinions to arise unless erroneous reasonings withstood the truth. If, therefore, we by ourselves are too weak to give the victory to what is righteous, since the bad is stronger in its attacks and rejects the rule of truth, we must flee as quickly as possible (in accordance with the historical example) from the conflict to the greater and higher teaching of the mysteries.

17. And if we must again live with a foreigner, that is to say, if need requires us to associate with profane wisdom, let us with determination scatter the wicked shepherds from their unjust use of the wells—which means let us reprove the teach-

ers of evil for their wicked use of instruction.

18. In the same way we shall live a solitary life,[23] no longer entangled with adversaries or mediating between them, but we shall live among those of like disposition and mind who are fed by us while all the movements of our soul are shepherded, like sheep,[24] by the will of guiding reason.[25]

The Burning Bush

19. It is upon us who continue in this quiet and peaceful course of life that the truth will shine, illuminating the eyes of our soul with its own rays. This truth, which was then manifested by the ineffable and mysterious illumination which came to Moses, is God.

20. And if the flame by which the soul of the prophet was illuminated was kindled from a thorny bush, even this fact will not be useless for our inquiry.[26] For if truth is God and truth is light—the Gospel testifies by these sublime and divine names to the God who made himself visible to us in the flesh[27]—such guidance of virtue leads us to know that light which has reached down even to human nature. Lest one think that the radiance did not come from a material substance, this light did not shine from some luminary among the stars but came from an earthly bush and surpassed the heavenly luminaries in brilliance.

21. From this we learn also the mystery of the Virgin: The light of divinity which through birth shone from her into human life did not consume the burning bush, even as the flower of her virginity was not withered by giving birth.[28]

22. That light teaches us what we must do to stand within the rays of the true light: Sandaled feet cannot ascend that height where the light of truth is seen, but the dead and earthly covering of skins, which was placed around our nature at the beginning when we were found naked because of disobedience to the divine will, must be removed from the feet of the soul.[29]

When we do this, the knowledge of the truth[30] will result and manifest itself.[31] The full knowledge of being comes about by purifying our opinion concerning nonbeing.

23. In my view the definition of truth is this: not to have a mistaken apprehension of Being. Falsehood is a kind of impression which arises in the understanding about nonbeing: as though what does not exist does, in fact, exist. But truth is the sure apprehension of real Being.[32] So, whoever applies himself in quietness to higher philosophical matters over a long period of time will barely apprehend what true Being is, that is, what possesses existence in its own nature,[33] and what nonbeing is, that is, what is existence only in appearance, with no self-subsisting nature.[34]

24. It seems to me that at the time the great Moses was instructed in the theophany he came to know that none of those things which are apprehended by sense perception and contemplated by the understanding really subsists, but that the transcendent essence and cause of the universe, on which everything depends, alone subsists.[35]

25. For even if the understanding looks upon any other existing things, reason observes in absolutely none of them the self-sufficiency by which they could exist without participating in true Being.[36] On the other hand, that which is always the same, neither increasing nor diminishing, immutable to all change whether to better or to worse (for it is far removed from the inferior and it has no superior), standing in need of nothing else, alone desirable, participated in by all but not lessened by their participation—this is truly real Being. And the apprehension of it is the knowledge of truth.[37]

26. In the same way that Moses on that occasion attained to this knowledge, so now does everyone who, like him, divests himself of the earthly covering and looks to the light shining from the bramble bush,[38] that is, to the Radiance which shines upon us through this thorny flesh and which is (as the Gospel says) the true light and the truth itself.[39] A person like this

becomes able to help others to salvation, to destroy the tyranny which holds power wickedly, and to deliver to freedom everyone held in evil servitude.[40]

The transformation of the right hand and the rod's changing into a snake became the first of the miracles.

27. These seem to me to signify in a figure the mystery of the Lord's incarnation, a manifestation of deity to men which effects the death of the tyrant and sets free those under his power.[41]

28. What leads me to this understanding is the testimony of the Prophets and the Gospel. The Prophet declares: *This is the change of the right hand of the most High,*[42] indicating that, although the divine nature is contemplated in its immutability, by condescension to the weakness of human nature it was changed to our shape and form.

29. When the hand of the lawgiver was extended from his bosom it was changed to an unnatural complexion, and when placed again in his bosom, it returned to its own natural beauty. Again, *the only begotten God who is in the bosom of the Father*[43] is he who is the right hand of the most High.[44]

30. When he was manifested to us from the bosom of the Father, he was changed to be like us. After he wiped away our infirmities, he again returned to his own bosom the hand which had been among us and had received our complexion. (The Father is the bosom of the right hand.) What is impassible by nature did not change into what is passible, but what is mutable and subject to passions was transformed into impassibility through its participation in the immutable.[45]

31. The change from a rod into a snake should not trouble the lovers of Christ—as if we were adapting the doctrine of the incarnation to an unsuitable animal.[46] For the Truth himself through the voice of the Gospel does not refuse a comparison like this in saying: *And the Son of Man must be lifted up as Moses lifted up the serpent in the desert.*[47]

32. The teaching is clear. For if the father of sin is called a

serpent by Holy Scripture and what is born of the serpent is certainly a serpent,[48] it follows that sin is synonymous with the one who begot it. But the apostolic word testifies that the Lord was *made into sin for our sake*[49] by being invested with our sinful nature.

33. This figure therefore is rightly applied to the Lord. For if sin is a serpent and the Lord became sin, the logical conclusion should be evident to all: By becoming sin he became also a serpent, which is nothing other than sin. For our sake he became a serpent that he might devour and consume the Egyptian serpents produced by the sorcerers.

34. This done, the serpent was changed back into a rod by which sinners are brought to their senses, and those slackening on the upward and toilsome course of virtue are given rest, the rod of faith supporting them through their high hopes. *Only faith can guarantee the blessings that we hope for.*[50]

35. He who has some insight[51] into these things right away becomes a god[52] to those who resist the truth, who have been distracted to a material and unsubstantial delusion. They disdain the discussion of Being as so much idle talk,[53] as Pharaoh says: *Who is Yahweh, that I should listen to him? I do not know Yahweh.*[54] He considered valuable only the material and fleshly things which characterize lives governed by the most irrational sense.

36. If, on the other hand, he had been strengthened by the illumination of the light and had received such strength and power against his enemies, then, as one who has developed as an athlete by strenuous practice under his trainer, he would boldly and confidently strip for the contest with his opponents.[55] With that rod, the word of faith, in his hand, he would prevail against the Egyptian serpents.

37. The foreign wife will follow him, for there are certain things derived from profane education which should not be rejected when we propose to give birth to virtue.[56] Indeed moral and natural philosophy may become at certain times a

comrade, friend, and companion of life to the higher way, provided that the offspring of this union introduce nothing of a foreign defilement.[57]

38. Since his son had not been circumcised so as to cut off completely everything hurtful and impure, the angel who met them brought the fear of death.[58] His wife appeased the angel when she presented her offspring as pure by completely removing that mark by which the foreigner was known.

39. I think that if someone who has been initiated under the guidance of the history follows closely the order of the historical figures, the sequence[59] of the development in virtue marked out in our account will be clear. There is something fleshly and uncircumcised in what is taught by philosophy's generative faculty;[60] when that has been completely removed, there remains the pure Israelite race.

40. For example, pagan philosophy says that the soul is immortal.[61] This is a pious offspring.[62] But it also says that souls pass from bodies to bodies and are changed from a rational to an irrational nature.[63] This is a fleshly and alien foreskin. And there are many other such examples. It says there is a God, but it thinks of him as material.[64] It acknowledges him as Creator, but says he needed matter for creation.[65] It affirms that he is both good and powerful, but that in all things he submits to the necessity of fate.[66]

41. And one could describe in some detail how good doctrines are contaminated by profane philosophy's absurd additions.[67] When these are completely removed, the angel of God comes to us in mercy, as if rejoicing in the true offspring of these doctrines.

The Meeting with Aaron

42. We must return to the sequence in Scripture so that brotherly assistance might come out to meet us as we draw near

the conflict with the Egyptians. For we remember the incidents of fighting and quarreling which involved Moses at the beginning of the life of virtue, the Egyptian oppressing the Hebrew and on another occasion a Hebrew disputing with his countryman.[68]

43. For the one who has been lifted to the greatest virtue of soul by long training and supernatural illumination on the mountain, it is a friendly and peaceful encounter that takes place when his brother is brought by God to meet him. If this historical incident is taken in a more figurative spiritual sense, it will be found useful for our purpose.

44. For truly the assistance which God gives to our nature is provided to those who correctly live the life of virtue.[69] This assistance was already there at our birth, but it is manifested and made known whenever we apply ourselves to diligent training in the higher life and strip ourselves for the more vigorous contests.

45. So as not to interpret the figures by our own figure, I shall set forth my understanding about this more plainly. There is a doctrine (which derives its trustworthiness from the tradition of the fathers)[70] which says that after our nature fell into sin God did not disregard our fall and withhold his providence. No, on the one hand, he appointed an angel with an incorporeal nature to help in the life of each person and, on the other hand, he also appointed the corruptor who, by an evil and maleficent demon, afflicts the life of man and contrives against our nature.[71]

46. Because man finds himself between these two who have contrary purposes for him, it is in his power to make the one prevail over the other. While the good angel by rational demonstration shows the benefits of virtue which are seen in hope by those who live aright, his opponent shows the material pleasures in which there is no hope of future benefits, but which are present, visible, can be partaken of, and enslave the senses of those who do not exercise their intellect.

47. If, then, one should withdraw from those who seduce him to evil and by the use of his reason turn to the better, putting evil behind him, it is as if he places his own soul, like a mirror, face to face with the hope of good things, with the result that the images and impressions of virtue, as it is shown to him by God, are imprinted on the purity of his soul.[72] Then his brother brings him assistance and joins him, for the angel, who in a way is a brother to the rational and intellectual part of man's soul, appears, as I have said, and stands by us whenever we approach the Pharaoh.

48. If, while trying to parallel completely the historical account to the sequence of such intellectual contemplation,[73] someone should somehow discover something in the account which does not coincide with our understanding, he should not reject the whole enterprise. He should always keep in mind our discussion's goal, to which we are looking while we relate these details.[74] We have already said in our prologue that the lives of honored men would be set forth as a pattern of virtue for those who come after them.

49. Those who emulate their lives, however, cannot experience the identical literal events. For how could one again find the people multiplying during their sojourn in Egypt? And how again find the tyrant who enslaves the people and bears hostility to male offspring and allows the feminine and weaker to grow in numbers? And how again find all the other things which Scripture includes? Because therefore it has been shown to be impossible to imitate the marvels of these blessed men in these exact events, one might substitute a moral teaching for the literal sequence in those things which admit of such an approach. In this way those who have been striving toward virtue may find aid in living the virtuous life.

50. If the events require dropping from the literal account anything written which is foreign to the sequence of elevated understanding, we pass over this on the grounds that it is useless and unprofitable to our purpose, so as not to interrupt

the guidance to virtue at such points.

51. I say these things concerning the interpretation of Aaron in order to anticipate the objection which will arise from what follows in the narrative.[75] For someone will say that there is no doubt that the angel does share kinship with the soul in its intellectual and incorporeal aspects, that it already existed before our creation,[76] and that it is allied with those engaged in the fight against the Adversary, but that it is not right to see Aaron, who led the Israelites in the worship of idols, as a type of the angel.

52. To him we shall reply, passing over the sequence, with the point already made, that what falls outside our purpose is not to overthrow the agreement which exists elsewhere. Moreover, both words, "brother" and "angel," are alike applicable in the meaning they might have to opposite things.

53. For "angel" signifies not only an angel of God but also *an angel of Satan*.[77] And we call "brother" not only a good brother but also a bad brother. So the Scripture speaks of the good, *Brothers are proved in distress*,[78] and of the opposite, *Every brother will utterly supplant*.[79]

Deliverance Announced

54. Laying aside these matters for a later point[80] in our discussion where we shall give a fuller interpretation of them in their proper place, let us now turn to what is at hand. Moses, who had been strengthened by the shining light and had acquired such a brother as an ally and supporter, boldly delivered to the people the words of freedom, brought to their remembrance the nobility of their fathers, and gave his judgment how they could escape from their wretched labor of brick making.[81]

55. What then does the history teach us by this? That he who has not equipped himself by this kind of spiritual training to instruct the multitude must not presume to speak among the

LIFE OF MOSES

people. For you see how, while he was still young and had not
yet matured to so lofty a degree of virtue, two men who were
quarreling did not consider his peaceful advice worth accepting, yet now he addresses tens of thousands in the same way.
The history all but cries out to you not to be presumptuous in
giving advice to your hearers in your teaching unless the ability
for this has been perfected in you by a long and exacting
training such as Moses had.

56. When Moses had spoken these excellent words and
had offered his hearers freedom and had strengthened their
desire for it, the enemy was provoked and increased the suffer-
ing of those who hearkened to his speech. This is not unlike
what happens now. For many of those who have accepted the
word as a liberator from tyranny and have identified themselves with the Gospel are today still threatened by the Adversary with onslaughts of temptations.

57. Many of them do become more firmly established in
their faith as they are hardened by these grievous assaults, but
some of the weaker ones are beaten to their knees by these
misfortunes and say outright that it would have been more
useful for them not to have heard the message of freedom than
to endure these things for freedom's sake.

58. The same thing happened when the Israelites through
meanness of spirit blamed those who proclaimed to them deliverance from servitude.[82] But the Word will not cease at all
from leading on toward the Good, even if he who is yet young
and immature in understanding should, childlike, be fearful of
the strangeness of temptations.

59. For this demon who does men harm and corrupts
them is intensely concerned that his subjects not look to heaven
but that they stoop to earth and make bricks within themselves
out of the clay.[83] It is clear to everyone that whatever belongs to
material pleasure consists assuredly of earth or water, whether
one is concerned with the pleasures of the stomach and the
table or with the pleasures of wealth.

60. The mixture of these elements becomes clay and is so called. Those who yearn after the pleasures of clay and keep on filling themselves with them never keep the space which receives them full; for although it is always being filled, it becomes empty again before the next pouring. In the same way the brick maker keeps on throwing yet more clay into the mould while it is constantly being emptied. I think that anyone can easily perceive the meaning of this figure by looking at the appetitive part of the soul.[84]

61. For if he who fills his desire in one of the things which he pursues should then incline his desire to something else, he finds himself empty again in that regard. And if he should fill himself on this, he becomes empty and a vacant container once more for something else. And we never stop doing this until we depart from this material life.[85]

62. The straw and its chaff which those subject to the tyrant's orders were required to mix in the brick are interpreted by both the divine Gospel and the sublime voice of the Apostle as material for the fire.[86]

The Plagues on Egypt

63. Whenever someone who excels in virtue wishes to draw those who have been enslaved by trickery to a life philosophical and free, the one who schemes against our souls with many different deceits (as the Apostle says)[87] knows how to introduce the devices of trickery against the divine law. I am speaking here of the Egyptian serpents in the text, that is, of the many different evil tricks which the rod of Moses destroyed. We have probably already sufficiently interpreted the rod.[88]

64. Now he who possesses that invincible rod of virtue which consumes the rods of magic progresses along his course to greater marvels. Marvels are not performed for the purpose of terrifying those who happen to be present, but they look to

the benefit of those being saved. By these very marvels of virtue the enemy is defeated and his own people are strengthened.

65. If we first learn the general spiritual intent of miracles, we would then be able to apply this insight to individual miracles. True doctrine conforms to the dispositions of those receiving the word, for although the word presents to all equally what is good and bad, the one who is favorably disposed to what is presented has his understanding enlightened, but the darkness of ignorance remains with the one who is obstinately disposed and does not permit his soul to behold the ray of truth.[89] If our general understanding of these things is not false, the specific items would certainly not be different since the individual part is demonstrated with the whole.

66. So then, it is not marvelous at all that the Hebrew, although living in the midst of foreigners, remains unaffected by the evils of the Egyptians. One can also see the same thing happening now in populous cities where people are holding contradictory opinions. To some, the stream of faith from which they draw by means of the divine teaching is fresh and clear, but to others, who live as the Egyptians do and draw by means of their own evil presuppositions, the water becomes corrupted blood.[90]

67. And many times the master of deceit endeavors to turn the drink of the Hebrews also into blood by polluting it with falsehood, that is, by presenting our doctrine to us as different from what it really is. But he cannot make the water wholly unusable, even if he should easily turn it red by his trickery. For since he pays no attention to the optical illusion, the Hebrew drinks the true water, even though he is successfully misled by his adversaries.

68. The same applies to the frogs—ugly and noisy amphibians, leaping about, not only unpleasant to the sight, but also having a foul-smelling skin—they entered the houses, beds, and storerooms of the Egyptians, but they did not affect the life of the Hebrews.

GREGORY OF NYSSA

69. The breed of frogs is obviously the destructive offspring of the evil which is brought to life from the sordid heart
of men as though from some slimy mire.[91] These frogs overrun
the houses of those who choose to live the Egyptian life,
appearing on the tables, not even sparing the beds, and entering the very storerooms.

70. One sees in the sordid and licentious life that which is
indeed born out of clay and mire and that which, through
imitation of the irrational, remains in a form of life neither
altogether human nor frog. Being a man by nature and becoming a beast by passion, this kind of person exhibits an amphibi-
ous form of life ambiguous in nature. In addition, one will also
find the evidences of such an illness, not only on the bed, but
also on the table and in the storeroom and throughout the
house.

71. For such a man shows his profligacy in everything so
that everyone readily recognizes the life of the profligate and
the life of the pure man by what is valued in each one's
household. In the house of the one there are frescoes on the wall
which by their artful pictures inflame the sensual passions.[92]
These things bring out the nature of the illness, and through
the eye passion pours in upon the soul from the dishonorable
things which are seen. But in the house of the prudent man
there is every precaution and foresight to keep the eye pure
from sensual spectacles.

72. The table of the prudent man is similarly found to be
pure, but that of the man wallowing in the mire is frog-like and
fleshy. And if you search the storeroom, that is to say the secret
and unmentionable things of his life, you will discern there in
his licentiousness a much greater pile of frogs.

The Hardening of Pharaoh's Heart and Free Will

73. Let us not be astonished if the history says that the rod
of virtue did these things to the Egyptians, for it also says that

70

the tyrant was hardened by God.[93] Now, how could he be condemned if he were disposed by divine constraint to be stubborn and obstinate? Somewhere the divine Apostle also expresses the same thought: *Since they refused to see it was rational to acknowledge God, he abandoned them to shameful passions,*[94] speaking about those who commit sodomy and those who disgrace themselves by dishonorable and unmentionable profligacy.

74. But even if what has been said before is so stated by Scripture, and God does in this way entirely give up to dishonorable passions the one who gives himself up to them, still Pharaoh is not hardened by the divine will nor is the frog-like life fashioned by virtue. For if this were to be willed by the divine nature, then certainly any human choice would fall into line in every case, so that no distinction between virtue and vice in life could be observed.[95] People live differently—some live uprightly in virtue while others slide into vice. One would not reasonably attribute these differences in their lives to some divine constraint which lies outside themselves. It lies within each person's power to make this choice.

75. Who it is who is delivered up to shameful affections can be clearly learned from the Apostle: It is he who does not like to have God in his knowledge. God delivers up to passion him whom he does not protect because he is not acknowledged by him. But his failure to acknowledge God becomes the reason why he is being pulled down into the passionate and dishonorable life. (as Ammonites?)

76. It is as if someone who has not seen the sun blames it for causing him to fall into the ditch. Yet we do not hold that the luminary in anger pushes into the ditch someone who does not choose to look at it. Rather, we would interpret this statement in a more reasonable manner: It is the failure to participate in the light that causes the person who does not see to fall into the ditch.[96] In the same way, the thought of the Apostle should be clear, that it is those who do not acknowledge God who are delivered up to shameful affections, and that the Egyptian tyrant is hardened by God not because the divine

will places the resistance in the soul of Pharaoh but because the free will through its inclination to evil does not receive the word which softens resistance.

77. In the same way also, when the rod of virtue appeared among the Egyptians, it made the Hebrews pure from the frog-like life but showed the Egyptians to be full of this illness.

78. When Moses stretched forth his hands on the Egyptians' behalf, the frogs were instantly destroyed.[97] This can also be seen happening now. For those who perceive the outstretched hands of the lawgiver—you understand, surely, what the figure says to you, and perceive in the lawgiver the true Lawgiver and in his outstretched hands him who stretched forth his hands upon the cross[98]—those then who for a short time have lived with these sordid and frog-like thoughts, if they look to him who stretched forth his hands on our behalf, are set free from their evil life as their passion is put to death and left stinking.[99]

79. Truly, after the death of the frog-like emotions, the former manner of life of those who have been delivered from such an illness becomes to them a foul and odorous memory which disgusts the soul in shame. It is as the Apostle says to those changed from evil to virtue: *What did you get from this? Nothing but experiences that now make you blush.*[100]

80. In keeping with this insight of mine, consider the air which is darkened to the Egyptians' eyes by the rod while to the Hebrews' it is illuminated by the sun.[101] By this incident the meaning which we have given is confirmed. It was not some constraining power from above that caused the one to be found in darkness and the other in light, but we men have in ourselves, in our own nature and by our own choice, the causes of light or of darkness, since we place ourselves in whichever sphere we wish to be.

81. According to the history, the eyes of the Egyptians were not in darkness because some wall or mountain darkened

their view and shadowed the rays, but the sun cast its rays upon all equally. Whereas the Hebrews delighted in its light, the Egyptians were insensitive to its gift. In a similar manner the enlightened life is proposed to all equally according to their ability. Some continue on in darkness, driven by their evil pursuits to the darkness of wickedness, while others are made radiant by the light of virtue.

82. Perhaps someone, taking his departure from the fact that after three days of distress in darkness the Egyptians did share in the light, might be led to perceive the final restoration[102] which is expected to take place later in the kingdom of heaven of those who have suffered condemnation in Gehenna. For that *darkness that could be felt*,[103] as the history says, has a great affinity both in its name and in its actual meaning to the *exterior darkness*.[104] Both are dispelled when Moses, as we have perceived before, stretched forth his hands on behalf of those in darkness.

83. In the same way we would perceive the true meaning of the *furnace ashes*[105] which, according to the text, produced painful boils on the Egyptians. In the figure of what is called the "furnace" we perceive the threatened punishment of fire in Gehenna which touches only those who imitate the Egyptians in their manner of life.[106]

84. If anyone is truly an Israelite, a son of Abraham, and looks to him in life in such a way as to show by his own free will his kinship in race to the elect people, he is kept unharmed from that painful fire. The interpretation of Moses' outstretched hands which we have already given may become for those others also the healing of pain and the deliverance from punishment.

85. If one follows the sequence of our earlier investigations, he will have no trouble attaching to each plague the corresponding perception: those light gadflies which tormented the Egyptians with their unseen bites, the flies which

clung painfully with their bites to their bodies, the tillage which was ravaged by the locusts, and the storms from heaven which rained down hailstones.

86. The Egyptians' free will caused all these things according to the preceding principle, and the impartial justice of God followed their free choices and brought upon them what they deserved. As we follow closely the reading of the text at hand, let us not draw the conclusion that these distresses upon· those who deserved them came directly from God, but rather let us observe that each man makes his own plagues when through his own free will he inclines toward these painful experiences. The Apostle says the same thing when talking to such a person: *Your stubborn refusal to repent is only adding to the anger God will have toward you on that day of anger when his just judgments will be made known. He will repay each one as his works deserve.* [107]

87. What we are describing is like some destructive and bilious humor which arises in the intestines because of a dissipated life. When the physician induces vomiting by his medicines, he does not become the cause of the sickness in the body, but on the contrary it is disorderly eating habits which bring it about; medical knowledge only brought it into the open. In the same way, even if one says that painful retribution comes directly from God upon those who abuse their free will, it would only be reasonable to note that such sufferings have their origin and cause in ourselves. [108]

88. To the one who has lived without sin there is no darkness, no worm, no Gehenna, no fire, nor any other of these fearful names and things, as indeed the history goes on to say that the plagues of Egypt were not meant for the Hebrews. Since then in the same place evil comes to one but not to the other, the difference of free choices distinguishing each from the other, it is evident that nothing evil can come into existence apart from our free choice.

The Death of the Firstborn

89. Let us proceed to what follows in the text. We have learned through the things examined already that Moses (and he who exalts himself by virtue in keeping with his example), when his soul had been empowered through long application and high and lofty life, and through the illumination which came from above, considered it a loss not to lead his countrymen to the life of freedom.

90. When he came to them, he implanted in them a more intense desire for freedom by holding out worse sufferings to them. Intending to remove his countrymen from evil, he brought death upon all the firstborn in Egypt. By doing this he laid down for us the principle that it is necessary to destroy utterly the first birth of evil.[109] It is impossible to flee the Egyptian life in any other way.

91. It does not seem good to me to pass this interpretation by without further contemplation. How would a concept worthy of God be preserved in the description of what happened if one looked only to the history? The Egyptian acts unjustly, and in his place is punished his newborn child, who in his infancy cannot discern what is good and what is not.[110] His life has no experience of evil, for infancy is not capable of passion. He does not know how to distinguish between his right hand and his left.[111] The infant lifts his eyes only to his mother's nipple, and tears are the sole perceptible sign of his sadness. And if he obtains anything which his nature desires, he signifies his pleasure by smiling. If such a one now pays the penalty of his father's wickedness, where is justice? Where is piety? Where is holiness? Where is Ezekiel, who cries: *The man who has sinned is the man who must die* and *a son is not to suffer for the sins of his father?*[112] How can the history so contradict reason?

92. Therefore, as we look for the true spiritual meaning, seeking to determine whether the events took place typologi-

cally, we should be prepared to believe that the lawgiver has taught through the things said. The teaching is this: When through virtue one comes to grips with any evil, he must completely destroy the first beginnings of evil.

93. For when he slays the beginning, he destroys at the same time what follows after it. The Lord teaches the same thing in the Gospel, all but explicitly calling on us to kill the firstborn of the Egyptian evils when he commands us to abolish lust and anger and to have no more fear of the stain of adultery or the guilt of murder.[113] Neither of these things would develop of itself, but anger produces murder and lust produces adultery.

94. Since the producer of evil gives birth to lust before adultery and anger before murder, in destroying the firstborn he certainly kills along with it the offspring which follows. Take for an example a snake: When one crushes his head he kills the rest of the body at the same time.[114]

95. This would not have happened unless the blood which turns aside the destroyer had been poured out on our doors.[115] And if it is necessary to perceive the meaning presented here more fully, the history provides this perception in both the killing of the firstborn and the safeguarding of the entrance by blood. In the one the first impulse to evil is destroyed, and in the other the first entrance of evil into us is turned away by the true Lamb. For when the destroyer has come inside, we do not drive him out by our own devices, but by the Law we throw up a defense to keep him from gaining a foothold among us.

96. Safety and security consist in marking the upper doorpost and the side posts of the entrance with the blood of the lamb. While in this way Scripture gives us through figures a scientific understanding of the nature of the soul, profane learning also places it before the mind, dividing the soul into the rational, the appetitive, and the spirited.[116] Of these parts we are told that the spirit and the appetite are placed below,

supporting on each side the intellectual part of the soul, while the rational aspect is joined to both so as to keep them together and to be held up by them, being trained for courage by the spirit and elevated to the participation in the Good by the appetite.[117]

97. As long, therefore, as the soul is kept safe in this manner, maintaining its firmness by virtuous thoughts as if by bolts, all the parts cooperate with one another for good. The rational for its part furnishes safety to its supports, and in its turn receives from them an equal benefit.

98. But if this arrangement should be upset and the upper become the lower—so that if the rational falls from above, the appetitive and spirited disposition makes it the part trampled upon—then the destroyer slips inside. No opposition from the blood resists his entrance; that is to say, faith in Christ does not ally itself with those of such a disposition.

99. For he says first to anoint the upper doorpost with blood, then to touch both side doorposts in the same way. How therefore would one anoint the upper first unless it be found on top?

100. Do not be surprised at all if both things—the death of the firstborn and the pouring out of the blood—did not happen to the Israelites and on that account reject the contemplation which we have proposed concerning the destruction of evil as if it were a fabrication without any truth. For now in the difference of the names, Israelite and Egyptian, we perceive the difference between virtue and evil. Since the spiritual meaning proposes that we perceive the Israelite as virtuous, we would not reasonably require the firstfruits of virtue's offspring to be destroyed but rather those whose destruction is more advantageous than their cultivation.

101. Consequently we have been taught by God that we must destroy the firstfruits of the Egyptian children so that evil, in being destroyed at its beginning, might come to an end. And this insight agrees with the history, for the protection of

the Israelite children took place through the pouring out of blood in order that good might come to maturity. But what would come to maturity in the Egyptian people was destroyed before it matured in evil.

The Departure from Egypt

102. What follows agrees with our spiritual understanding of the text. For Scripture requires that the body of the lamb, whose blood was displayed on the doors and separated the people from the destroyer of the firstborn, become our food.

103. The demeanor of those eating this food was to be intense and earnest, not like that of those who enjoy themselves at banquets, whose hands are relaxed and whose clothes are loose and whose feet are unprepared for travel. But everything was the opposite. Their feet were covered with sandals, a belt bound the clothing at the waist, and the staff to repel dogs was held in hand.

104. And to them in this condition was presented meat without any artfully prepared sauces but cooked upon any fire that happened to be available. The guests eagerly devoured it in great haste until the entire body of the animal was consumed. They ate whatever was edible around the bones, but they did not touch the entrails. To break the bones of this animal was one of the things forbidden. Whatever might be left of the meat was consumed by the fire.

105. From all this it is evident that the letter looks to some higher understanding, since the Law does not instruct us how to eat. (Nature which implants a desire for food in us is a sufficient lawgiver with regard to these things.) The account rather signifies something different. For what does it matter to virtue or vice to eat your food this way or that, to have the belt

loose or tight, to have your feet bare or covered with shoes, to have your staff in your hand or laid aside?

106. It is clear what the traveler's equipment figuratively stands for: It commands us explicitly to recognize that our present life is transient. Already at birth we are driven by the very nature of things toward our departure, for which we must carefully prepare our hands, feet, and the rest.

107. So that the thorns of this life (the thorns would be sins)[118] may not hurt our naked and unprotected feet, let us cover them with shoes.[119] The shoes are the self-controlled and austere life which breaks and crushes the points of the thorns and prevents sin from slipping inside unnoticed.

108. The tunic flowing down over the feet and reaching to the soles would be a hindrance to anyone who would diligently finish the divine course. The tunic accordingly would be seen as the full enjoyment of the pursuits of this life, which the prudent reason, like a traveler's belt, draws in as tightly as possible. The place around which the belt passes shows that it is to be understood as prudence.[120] The staff for repelling animals is the message of hope, by which we support the weariness of the soul and ward off what threatens us.[121]

109. The food placed before us from the fire I call the warm and fervent faith which we receive without having given thought to it. We devour as much of it as is easily eaten, but we leave aside the doctrine concealed in the thoughts which are hard and tough without investigating it thoroughly or seeking to know more about it. Instead we consign this food to the fire.

110. In order that these figures may be made clear, let us explain that whichever of the divine commands are readily perceived should not be followed sluggishly or by constraint, but we should be like those who are hungry and eagerly fill up on the things set before them, so that the food may become provision for our well-being. But such thoughts as are beyond our understanding—like the questions, What is the essence of

God? What was there before the creation? What is there outside the visible world? Why do things which happen happen? and other such things as are sought out by inquiring minds[122] — these things we concede to know only by the Holy Spirit, who *reaches the depths of God*,[123] as the Apostle says.

111. Anyone instructed in the Scriptures surely knows that instead of "Spirit" Scripture often thinks of it and designates it as "fire."[124] We are also led to this understanding by the announcement of Wisdom: *Do not try to understand things that are too difficult for you*, that is to say, Do not break the bones of Scripture, *for you have no need [to see with your eyes] those things that are hidden*.[125]

The Wealth of Egypt

112. Thus Moses led the people out of Egypt, and everyone who follows in the steps of Moses in this way sets free from the Egyptian tyrant all those guided by his word. Those who follow the leader to virtue must, I think, not lack the wealth of Egypt or be deprived of the treasures of the foreigners, but having acquired all the property of their enemies, must have it for their own use. This is exactly what Moses then commanded the people to do.

113. No one who has listened to this carelessly would accept the advice of the lawgiver if he enjoined those in want to rob and so became a leader in their wrongdoing. If someone looks to the laws which follow, which from beginning to end forbid wrongdoing to one's neighbor, he could not truthfully say that the lawgiver commanded these things, even though to some it seems reasonable that the Israelites should have exacted the wages for their work from the Egyptians by this device.[126]

114. Yet there is no less ground for complaint; this justification does not purify such a command of falsehood and fraud,

for the person who borrows something and does not repay the lender is deceitful. If he borrows something not belonging to him, he does wrong because he commits fraud. But even if he should take what is rightly his own he is still correctly called a deceiver since he misleads the lender into hoping that he will be repaid.

115. The loftier meaning is therefore more fitting than the obvious one. It commands those participating through virtue in the free life also to equip themselves with the wealth of pagan learning by which foreigners to the faith beautify themselves. Our guide in virtue commands someone who "borrows" from wealthy Egyptians to receive[127] such things as moral and natural philosophy, geometry, astronomy, dialectic, and whatever else is sought by those outside the Church, since these things will be useful when in time the divine sanctuary of mystery must be beautified with the riches of reason.[128]

116. Those who treasured up for themselves such wealth handed it over to Moses as he was working on the tent of mystery, each one making his personal contribution to the construction of the holy places. It is possible to see this happening even now. For many bring to the Church of God their profane learning as a kind of gift: Such a man was the great Basil, who acquired the Egyptian wealth in every respect during his youth and dedicated this wealth to God for the adornment of the Church, the true tabernacle.[129]

The Cloudy Pillar

117. Let us return to the point where we digressed. When those who already look to virtue and follow the lawgiver in life have left the borders of the Egyptians' dominion behind, the assaults of temptations in some way pursue them and bring on distress and fears and threats of death. When frightened by

these things, those newly established in the faith lose all hope for what is good.[130] But if Moses or some leader of the people like him happens along, he will counsel them against fear and will strengthen their downcast minds with the hope of divine help.

118. This help will not come unless the heart of the leader speaks with God. Many of those who occupy a position of leadership are concerned only with outward appearances; of those hidden things which are observed only by God they have hardly a thought. But in the case of Moses it was not so. While he exhorted the Israelites to be of good courage, he did cry out, although outwardly making no sound to God, as God himself bears witness. The Scripture teaches us, I think, that the voice which is melodious and ascends to God's hearing is not the cry made with the organs of speech but the meditation sent up from a pure conscience.[131]

119. To the one who finds himself in these circumstances the brother appears limited in the help he renders for the great struggles—I mean that brother who met Moses as he was going down to Egypt at the divine bidding, whom Scripture has understood as being in the rank of angels.[132] Then occurred the manifestation of the divine nature which manifests itself in the way that one is capable of receiving.[133] What we hear from the history to have happened, then, we understand from contemplation of the Word always to happen.

120. Whenever someone flees Egypt and, after getting outside its borders, is terrified by the assaults of temptation, the guide produces unexpected salvation from on high. Whenever the enemy with his army surrounds the one being pursued, the guide is forced to make the sea passable for him.

121. In this crossing the cloud served as guide. Those before us interpreted the cloud well as the grace of the Holy Spirit,[134] who guides toward the Good those who are worthy.[135] Whoever follows him passes through the water, since the guide makes a way through it for him. In this way

LIFE OF MOSES

he is safely led to freedom, and the one who pursues him to bring him into bondage is destroyed in the water.

Crossing the Red Sea

No one who hears this should be ignorant of the mystery of the water. He who has gone down into it with the army of the enemy emerges alone, leaving the enemy's army drowning in the water.[136]

122. For who does not know that the Egyptian army— those horses, chariots and their drivers, archers, slingers, heavily armed soldiers, and the rest of the crowd in the enemies' line of battle—are the various passions of the soul by which man is enslaved?[137] For the undisciplined intellectual drives and the sensual impulses[138] to pleasure, sorrow, and covetousness are indistinguishable from the aforementioned army. Reviling is a stone straight from the sling and the spirited impulse is the quivering spear point. The passion for pleasures is to be seen in the horses who themselves with irresistible drive pull the chariot.

123. In the chariot there are three drivers whom the history calls "viziers."[139] Since you were previously instructed in the mystery of the side posts and upper doorpost, you will perceive these three, who are completely carried along by the chariot, as the tripartite division of the soul, meaning the rational, the appetitive, and the spirited.[140]

124. So all such things rush into the water with the Israelite who leads the way in the baleful passage. Then as the staff of faith leads on and the cloud provides light, the water gives life to those who find refuge in it but destroys their pursuers.[141]

125. Moreover, the history teaches us by this what kind of people they should be who come through the water, bringing nothing of the opposing army along as they emerge from the water. For if the enemy came up out of the water with

83

them, they would continue in slavery even after the water, since they would have brought up with themselves the tyrant, still alive, whom they did not drown in the deep. If anyone wishes to clarify the figure, this lays it bare: Those who pass through the mystical water in baptism must put to death in the water[142] the whole phalanx of evil—such as covetousness, unbridled desire, rapacious thinking, the passion of conceit and arrogance, wild impulse, wrath, anger, malice, envy, and all such things. Since the passions naturally pursue our nature, we must put to death in the water both the base movements of the mind and the acts which issue from them.[143]

126. Just as unleavened bread was eaten in the mystery of the Pasch (which is the name of the sacrificial victim whose blood prevents the death of the one using it), even so the Law now commands us to eat unleavened bread at the Pasch (unleavened would be unmixed with stale yeast).[144] The Law gives us to understand by this that no remnant of evil should mix with the subsequent life. Rather we should make a totally new beginning in life after these things,[145] breaking the continuity with evil by a radical change for the better.[146] Thus also he means here that after we have drowned the whole Egyptian person (that is every form of evil)[147] in the saving baptism we emerge alone, dragging along nothing foreign in our subsequent life. This is what we hear through the history, which says that in the same water the enemy and the friend are distinguished by death and life, the enemy being destroyed and the friend given life.

127. Many of those who receive the mystical baptism, in ignorance of the commandments of the Law, mix the bad leaven of the old life with the new life. Even after crossing the water they bring along the Egyptian army, which still lives with them in their doings.

128. Take for instance the one who became rich by robbery or injustice, or who acquired property through perjury,

or lived with a woman in adultery, or undertook any of the other things against life which have been forbidden before the gift of baptism. Does he think that even after his washing he may continue to enjoy those evil things which have become attached to him[148] and yet be freed from the bondage of sin, as though he cannot see that he is under the yoke of harsh masters?

129. For uncontrolled passion is a fierce and raging master to the servile reasoning, tormenting it with pleasures as though they were scourges. Covetousness is another such master who provides no relief to the bondsman, but even if the one in bondage should slave in subservience to the commands of the master and acquire for him what he desires, the servant is always driven on to more. And all the other things which are performed by evil are so many tyrants and masters. If someone should still serve them, even if he should happen to have passed through the water, according to my thinking he has not at all touched the mystical water whose function is to destroy evil tyrants.

The First Stations in the Desert

130. Let us again proceed to the next point in the text. For the person who has crossed the sea and has seen this Egyptian dead in it, as we interpret it, no longer looks to Moses alone as the staff-bearer of virtue; but in keeping with the foregoing he believes in God, even as the Scripture says, and is obedient to his servant Moses.[149] We see this happening even now with those who truly cross the water, who dedicate themselves to God and are obedient and submissive, as the Apostle says, to those who serve the Divine in the priesthood.[150]

131. After they had crossed the sea, a three days' march ensued, during which they made camp at a place where they

found water so bitter that they could not at first drink it. But wood placed in the water made the drink agreeable to those who were thirsty.

132. The history agrees with what now happens: for to the one who has left behind the Egyptian pleasures which he served before crossing the sea, life removed from these pleasures seems at first difficult and disagreeable. But if the wood be thrown into the water, that is, if one receives the mystery of the resurrection which had its beginning with the wood (you of course understand the "cross" when you hear "wood"), then the virtuous life, being sweetened by the hope of things to come, becomes sweeter and more pleasant than all the sweetness that tickles the senses with pleasure.[151]

133. The next resting place on the journey, replete with palm trees and springs, refreshed the travelers. There were twelve springs of pure and very sweet water and seventy large, high-crested date palms which had grown tall with the years. What do we discover in these things as we follow the history? That the mystery of the wood through which the water of virtue became pleasant to those athirst leads us to the twelve springs and the seventy date palms, that is, to the teaching of the Gospel.

134. The springs are the Twelve Apostles whom the Lord chose for this service and through whom he caused his word to well up. One of the Prophets foretold the welling up of grace from the Apostles when he said: *In the churches bless God the Lord, from the fountains of Israel*.[152] And the seventy date palms would be those apostles appointed in addition to the Twelve Disciples throughout the whole world; they were the same in number as the history says the palm trees were.[153]

135. But I think it is fitting to speed our journey through the text, yet making the contemplation of the rest of the camps easier for those who are more studious by offering a few remarks.[154] The campsites, where the person following the pillar of cloud is refreshed as he presses on, would be the

virtues. Passing over the intermediate resting places with a mere mention, I shall call to mind the miracle of the rock, whose resistant and hard nature became drink to those who were thirsty when its hardness dissolved into the softness of water.

136. It is not difficult to harmonize the sequence of the history with spiritual contemplation.[155] He who left the Egyptian behind dead in the water, was sweetened by the wood, was delighted in the apostolic springs, and was refreshed by the shade of the palm trees, is already capable of receiving God. For *the rock*, as the Apostle says, *is Christ*,[156] who is moisture-less[157] and resistant to unbelievers, but if one should employ the rod of faith he becomes drink to those who are thirsty and flows into those who receive him, for he says, I and my Father *shall come to him and make our home with him*.[158]

The Manna

137. There is another event which we must not rush over without contemplation. After the travelers in virtue had crossed the sea, after the water had been sweetened for them, after their refreshing rest by the springs and palms, and after their drinking from the rock, the supplies from Egypt ran completely out.[159] And thus when they had no more of the foreign food which they had laid by in Egypt, there flowed down from above food which was at the same time varied and uniform. In appearance the food was uniform, but in quality it was varied, for it conformed itself to each person's desire.

138. What then do we learn here? We learn by what purifications one should purify himself of Egypt and the foreign life so that he empties the sack of his soul of all evil nourishment prepared by the Egyptians. In this way he receives in himself with his pure soul the food which comes down from above, which was not produced for us by any sowing in

cultivated soil. Coming down from above, the bread is found upon the earth already prepared without the wheat's having been sown or ripened.

139. You no doubt perceive the true food in the figure of the history: The bread which came from heaven[160] is not some incorporeal thing. For how could something incorporeal be nourishment to a body? Neither ploughing nor sowing produced the body of this bread, but the earth which remained unchanged was found full of this divine food, of which the hungry partake. This miracle teaches in anticipation the mystery of the Virgin.[161]

140. This bread, then, that does not come from the earth is the Word. He changes his power in diverse ways to suit those who eat.[162] He knows not only to be bread but also to become milk and meat and greens and whatever else might be appropriate to and desired by the one who receives him.[163] So teaches Paul the divine Apostle who spreads such a table as this for us—making his message strong meat for the more mature and greens for the weaker and milk for little children.[164]

141. Whatever marvels the history enumerates in connection with that food are teachings for the virtuous life. For it says that everyone shared in the food equally. The strength of those who gathered made no difference; they had neither more nor less than they needed. This is, according to my view at least, advice generally applicable: that those making their living from material things should not exceed the bounds of need but should understand well that the one natural measure for all in eating is to eat as much as can be enjoyed in one day.

142. Even if much more were prepared than is needed, it is not in the stomach's nature to exceed its proper measure or to be stretched by the insatiate desire for what is prepared. But, as the history says, neither did the one who took much have an abundance (for he had nowhere to store the excess) nor did he who took little lack any (for his requirements were lessened

according to the amount which was found).

143. In this account Scripture after a fashion cries out to the covetous that the insatiable greed of those always hoarding surplus is turned into worms. Everything beyond what they need encompassed by this covetous desire becomes on the next day—that is in the future life—a worm to the person who hoards it. He who hears "worm" certainly perceives the undying worm which is made alive by covetousness.[165]

144. The fact that what is stored up continues to supply nourishment and experiences no corruption only on the Sabbath contains the following counsel: There is a time in the course of one's life when he must be grasping—at the time when what is gathered does not submit to corruption. Then, when we pass beyond the preparation of this life and come to the rest after death, it will become useful to us. The day before the Sabbath is named the Preparation for the Sabbath. This day would be the present life in which we prepare for ourselves the things of the life to come.[166]

145. In that life none of the things we engage in now are undertaken—neither agriculture, nor trade, nor military service, nor any of the other things pursued here. But living in complete rest from such works, we acquire the fruits of the seeds which we now sow in life, some incorruptible, if the seeds of life be good, and some deadly and destructive, if the cultivation of this life produce such in us. *For he who sows in the field of the spirit*, Scripture says, *will get from it a harvest of eternal life, but he who sows in the field of self-indulgence will get a harvest of corruption out of it.*[167]

146. The preparation for the better is alone properly called Preparation and is surely confirmed by the Law, and what is stored up during it is incorruptible. That which is perceived as belonging to the opposite is neither Preparation nor is so called, for no one would reasonably call privation of good Preparation, but rather a lack of preparation. Therefore,

the history prescribes for men the Preparation for the better
and leaves it to the intelligent to perceive the opposite by its
omission.

The War with Amalek

147. Just as in military conscription the commander of
the army first supplies money and then gives the signal for
battle, in the same way also the soldiers of virtue receive
mystical money and move in battle against the enemy, being
led into the conflict by Joshua, the successor of Moses.

148. Do you observe the sequence in which Scripture
proceeds? As long as man is quite weak from maltreatment by
wicked tyranny he does not ward off the enemy by himself,
because he is not able. Someone else fights on behalf of the
weak, battering the enemy with one blow after another. After
he is set free from the bondage of his oppressors, is sweetened
by the wood, is refreshed from his toil at the resting place
among the palms, comes to know the mystery of the rock, and
partakes of heavenly food, then he no longer wards off the
enemy by another's hand. Now, since he has already outgrown
the stature of a child and has laid hold of the vigor of youth, he
fights with his opponents by himself, using as a general no
longer Moses the servant of God, but God himself, whose
servant Moses became. For the Law which from the beginning
was given in type and shadow of things to come[168] remains
unfit for battle in the real conflicts. But the fulfiller of the Law
and successor of Moses serves as general; he was announced
beforehand by the name which he shared with that earlier
general.[169] (Joshua = savior)

149. If the people saw the hands of their lawgiver lifted
up, they prevailed over the enemy in battle; but if they saw
them hanging limp, they fell back. Moses' holding his hands
aloft signifies the contemplation of the Law with lofty insights;

his letting 'them hang to earth signifies the mean and lowly literal exposition and observance of the Law.

150. The priest lifted the weary hands of Moses, using as a helper a member of his family.[170] Nor is this outside the sequence of things contemplated. For the true priesthood, through the word of God joined with it, lifts high again the powers of the Law which fell to earth because of the heaviness of the Jewish understanding. The priesthood supports the falling Law at its base with a stone so that the Law, presenting a figure of outstretched hands, shows forth its own purpose to those who behold it.

151. For truly, to those who are able to see, the mystery of the cross is especially contemplated in the Law.[171] Wherefore the Gospel says somewhere that *not one dot, not one little stroke, shall disappear from the Law*,[172] signifying in these words the vertical and horizontal lines by which the form of the cross is drawn.[173] That which was seen in Moses, who is perceived in the Law's place, is appointed as the cause and monument of victory to those who look at it.

The Mountain of Divine Knowledge

152. Again the Scripture leads our understanding upward to the higher levels of virtue. For the man who received strength from the food and showed his power in fighting with his enemies and was the victor over his opponents is then led to the ineffable knowledge of God.[174] Scripture teaches us by these things the nature and the number of things one must accomplish in life before he would at some time dare to approach in his understanding the mountain of the knowledge of God, to hear the sound of the trumpets, to enter into the darkness where God is, to inscribe the tablets with divine characters, and, if these should be broken through some offense, again to present the hand-cut tables to God and to carve

with the divine finger the letters which were damaged on the first tables.

153. It would be better next, in keeping with the order of the history, to harmonize what is perceived with the spiritual sense.[175] Whoever looks to Moses and the cloud, both of whom are guides to those who progress in virtue (Moses in this place would be the legal precepts, and the cloud which leads, the proper understanding of the Law), who has been purified by crossing the water, who has put the foreigner to death and separated himself from the foreigner, who has tasted the waters of Marah (that is, the life removed far from pleasures) which although appearing bitter and unpleasant at first to those tasting it offers a sweet sensation to those accepting the wood, who has then delighted in the beauties of the palm trees and springs (which were those who preached the Gospel, who were filled with the living water which is the rock), who received the heavenly bread, who has played the man against the foreigners, and for whom the outstretched hands of the lawgiver became the cause of victory foreshadowing the mystery of the cross, he it is who then advances to the contemplation of the transcendent nature.

154. His way to such knowledge is purity, not only purity of a body sprinkled by some lustral vessels but also of the clothes washed from every stain with water.[176] This means that the one person who would approach the contemplation of Being[177] must be pure in all things so as to be pure in soul and body, washed stainless of every spot in both parts, in order that he might appear pure to the One who sees what is hidden and that visible respectability might correspond to the inward condition of the soul.[178]

155. For this reason the garments are washed at divine command before he ascends the mountain, the garments representing for us in a figure the outward respectability of life. No one would say that a visible spot on the garments hinders the progress of those ascending to God, but I think that the out-

ward pursuits of life are well named the "garment."

156. When this had been accomplished and the herd of irrational animals had been driven as far from the mountain as possible, Moses then approached the ascent to lofty perceptions. That none of the irrational animals was allowed to appear on the mountain signifies, in my opinion, that in the contemplation of the intelligibles we surpass the knowledge which originates with the senses.[179] For it is characteristic of the nature of irrational animals that they are governed by the senses alone divorced from understanding. Their sight and hearing often lead them to what stimulates their appetites. Also, all other things through which sense perception becomes active assume an important place in irrational animals.

157. The contemplation of God is not effected by sight and hearing, nor is it comprehended by any of the customary perceptions of the mind. For *no eye has seen, and no ear has heard*, nor does it belong to those things which usually enter *into the heart of man*.[180] He who would approach the knowledge of things sublime must first purify his manner of life from all sensual and irrational emotion. He must wash from his understanding every opinion derived from some preconception and withdraw himself from his customary intercourse with his own companion, that is, with his sense perceptions, which are, as it were, wedded to our nature as its companion. When he is so purified, then he assaults the mountain.[181]

158. The knowledge of God[182] is a mountain steep indeed and difficult to climb[183]—the majority of people scarcely reach its base. If one were a Moses, he would ascend higher and hear the sound of trumpets which, as the text of the history says,[184] becomes louder as one advances. For the preaching of the divine nature is truly a trumpet blast, which strikes the hearing, being already loud at the beginning but becoming yet louder at the end.

159. The Law and the Prophets trumpeted the divine mystery of the incarnation,[185] but the first sounds were too

weak to strike the disobedient ear. Therefore the Jews' deaf ears did not receive the sound of the trumpets. As the trumpets came closer, according to the text, they became louder. The last sounds, which came through the preaching of the Gospels, struck their ears, since the Spirit through his instruments sounds a noise more loudly ringing and makes a sound more vibrant in each succeeding spokesman. The instruments which ring out the Spirit's sound would be the Prophets and Apostles whose *voice*,[186] as the Psalter says, *goes out through all the earth: and their message to the ends of the world*.[187]

160. The multitude was not capable of hearing the voice from above but relied on Moses to learn by himself the secrets and to teach the people whatever doctrine he might learn through instruction from above. This is also true of the arrangement in the Church: Not all thrust themselves toward the apprehension of the mysteries, but, choosing from among themselves[188] someone who is able to hear things divine, they give ear gratefully to him, considering trustworthy whatever they might hear from someone initiated into the divine mysteries.

161. It is said, *Not all are apostles, nor all prophets*,[189] but this is not now heeded in many of the churches. For many, still in need of being purified from the way they have lived, unwashed and full of spots in their life's garment and protecting themselves only with their irrational senses, make an assault on the divine mountain. So it happens that they are stoned by their own reasonings, for heretical opinions are in effect stones which crush the inventor of evil doctrines.[190]

The Darkness

162. What does it mean that Moses entered the darkness and then saw God in it?[191] What is now recounted seems somehow to be contradictory to the first theophany, for then

the Divine was beheld in light but now he is seen in darkness.[192] Let us not think that this is at variance with the sequence of things we have contemplated spiritually. Scripture teaches by this that religious knowledge comes at first to those who receive it as light. Therefore what is perceived to be contrary to religion is darkness, and the escape from darkness comes about when one participates in light. But as the mind progresses and, through an ever greater and more perfect diligence, comes to apprehend reality, as it approaches more nearly to contemplation, it sees more clearly what of the divine nature[193] is uncontemplated.

163. For leaving behind everything that is observed, not only what sense comprehends but also what the intelligence thinks it sees,[194] it keeps on penetrating deeper[195] until by the intelligence's yearning[196] for understanding it gains access to the invisible and the incomprehensible, and there it sees God. This is the true knowledge of what is sought; this is the seeing that consists in not seeing,[197] because that which is sought transcends all knowledge, being separated on all sides by incomprehensibility as by a kind of darkness. Wherefore John the sublime, who penetrated into the luminous darkness,[198] says, *No one has ever seen God*,[199] thus asserting that knowledge of the divine essence is unattainable not only by men but also by every intelligent creature.[200]

164. When, therefore, Moses grew in knowledge, he declared that he had seen God in the darkness, that is, that he had then come to know that what is divine is beyond all knowledge and comprehension, for the text says, *Moses approached the dark cloud where God was*.[201] What God? He who *made darkness his hiding place*,[202] as David says, who also was initiated into the mysteries in the same inner sanctuary.[203]

165. When Moses arrived there, he was taught by word what he had formerly learned from darkness, so that, I think, the doctrine on this matter might be made firmer for us for being testified to by the divine voice. The divine word at the

beginning forbids that the Divine be likened to any of the things known by men,[204] since every concept which comes from some comprehensible image[205] by an approximate understanding and by guessing at the divine nature constitutes an idol of God and does not proclaim God.

166. Religious virtue is divided into two parts, into that which pertains to the Divine and that which pertains to right conduct (for purity of life is a part of religion).[206] Moses learns at first the things which must be known about God (namely, that none of those things known by human comprehension is to be ascribed to him). Then he is taught the other side of virtue, learning by what pursuits the virtuous life is perfected.

167. After this he comes to the tabernacle not made with hands. Who will follow someone who makes his way through such places and elevates his mind to such heights, who, as though he were passing from one peak to another, comes ever higher than he was through his ascent to the heights? First, he leaves behind the base of the mountain and is separated from all those too weak for the ascent. Then as he rises higher in his ascent he hears the sounds of the trumpets. Thereupon, he slips into the inner sanctuary of divine knowledge. And he does not remain there, but he passes on to the tabernacle not made with hands.[207] For truly this is the limit that someone reaches who is elevated through such ascents.

168. For it seems to me that in another sense the heavenly trumpet becomes a teacher to the one ascending as he makes his way to what is not made with hands. For the wonderful harmony of the heavens proclaims the wisdom which shines forth in the creation and sets forth the great glory of God through the things which are seen, in keeping with the statement, *the heavens declare the glory of God*.[208] It becomes the loud sounding trumpet of clear and melodious teaching, as one of the Prophets says, *The heavens trumpeted from above*.[209]

169. When he who has been purified and is sharp of hearing in his heart hears this sound (I am speaking of the

knowledge of the divine power which comes from the contemplation of reality), he is led by it to the place where his intelligence lets him slip in where God is. This is called *darkness* by the Scripture,[210] which signifies, as I said, the unknown and unseen. When he arrives there, he sees that tabernacle not made with hands, which he shows to those below by means of a material likeness.[211]

The Heavenly Tabernacle

170. What then is that tabernacle not made with hands which was shown to Moses on the mountain and to which he was commanded to look as to an archetype so that he might reproduce in a handmade structure that marvel not made with hands?[212] God says, *See that you make them according to the pattern shown you on the mountain.*[213] There were gold pillars supported by silver bases and decorated with similar silver capitals; then, there were other pillars whose capitals and bases were of bronze but whose shafts were of silver. The core of all the pillars was wood that does not rot.[214] But all around shone the brightness of these precious metals.

171. Likewise, there was an ark made of wood that does not rot, overlaid with gleaming pure gold. In addition, there was a candlestick with a single base, divided at its top into seven branches, each supporting a lamp. The candlestick was made of solid gold and not of wood overlaid with gold. There was, moreover, an altar and the throne of mercy and the so-called cherubim whose wings overshadowed the ark.[215] All these were gold, not merely presenting a superficial appearance of gold but gold through and through.

172. Furthermore, there were curtains artistically woven of diverse colors; these brilliant colors were woven together to make a beautiful fabric. The curtains divided the tabernacle into two parts: the one visible and accessible to certain of the

priests and the other secret and inaccessible. The name of the front part was the Holy Place and that of the hidden part was the Holy of Holies. In addition, there were lavers and braziers and hangings around the outer court and the curtains of hair and skins dyed red and all the other things he describes in the text. What words could accurately describe it all?

173. Of what things not made with hands are these an imitation? And what benefit does the material imitation of those things Moses saw there convey to those who look at it? It seems good to me to leave the precise meaning of these things to those who have by the Spirit the power to search *the depths of God*,[216] to someone who may be able, as the Apostle says, *in the Spirit* to speak *about mysterious things*.[217] We shall leave what we say conjecturally and by supposition on the thought at hand to the judgment of our readers. Their critical intelligence must decide whether it should be rejected or accepted.

174. Taking a hint from what has been said by Paul, who partially uncovered the mystery of these things, we say that Moses was earlier instructed by a type in the mystery of the tabernacle which encompasses the universe. This tabernacle would be *Christ who is the power and the wisdom of God*,[218] who in his own nature was not made with hands, yet capable of being made when it became necessary for this tabernacle to be erected among us. Thus, the same tabernacle is in a way both unfashioned and fashioned, uncreated in preexistence but created in having received this material composition.[219]

175. What we say is of course not obscure to those who have accurately received the mystery of our faith. For there is one thing out of all others which both existed before the ages and came into being at the end of the ages.[220] It did not need a temporal beginning (for how could what was before all times and ages be in need of a temporal origin?), but for our sakes, who had lost our existence through our thoughtlessness, it consented to be born like us so that it might bring that which had left reality back again to reality. This one is the Only

Begotten God, who encompasses everything in himself but who also pitched his own tabernacle among us.[221]

176. But if we name such a God "tabernacle," the person who loves Christ should not be disturbed at all on the grounds that the suggestion involved in the phrase diminishes the magnificence of the nature of God. For neither is any other name worthy of the nature thus signified, but all names have equally fallen short of accurate description, both those recognized as insignificant as well as those by which some great insight is indicated.[222]

177. But just as all the other names, in keeping with what is being specified, are each used piously to express the divine power—as, for example, physician, shepherd, protector, bread, vine, way, door, mansion, water, rock, spring, and whatever other designations are used of him—in the same way he is given the predicate "tabernacle" in accord with a signification fitting to God.[223] For the power which encompasses the universe, in which *lives the fulness of divinity*,[224] the common protector of all, who encompasses everything within himself, is rightly called "tabernacle."

178. The vision must correspond to the name "tabernacle,"[225] so that each thing seen leads to the contemplation of a concept appropriate to God. Now the great Apostle says that the curtain of the lower tabernacle is the flesh of Christ,[226] I think, because it is composed of various colors, of the four elements.[227] Doubtless he himself had a vision of the tabernacle when he entered the supercelestial sanctuary where the mysteries of Paradise were revealed to him by the Spirit.[228] It would be well then by paying heed to the partial interpretation, to fit the total contemplation of the tabernacle to it.

179. We can gain clarity about the figures pertaining to the tabernacle from the very words of the Apostle. For he says somewhere with reference to the Only Begotten, whom we have perceived in place of the tabernacle, that *in him were created all things, everything visible and everything invisible, Thrones, Dom-*

inations, Sovereignties, Powers,[229] or forces. Then the pillars gleaming with silver and gold, the bearing poles and rings, and those cherubim who hide the ark with their wings, and all the other things which are contained in the description of the tabernacle's construction—all of these things, if one should turn his view to things above, are the heavenly powers which are contemplated in the tabernacle and which support the universe in accord with the divine will.[230]

180. These are our true supports, *sent to help those who will be the heirs of salvation.*[231] They are slipped through the souls of those being saved as through rings and by themselves raise to the height of virtue those lying upon the earth. In saying that the cherubim cover the mysteries in the ark with their wings, the text confirms our contemplation of the tabernacle. For we have learned that this is the name of those powers which we see around the divine nature, which powers Isaiah and Ezekiel perceived.[232]

181. The ark of the covenant, covered by their wings, should not sound strange to your ears. For it is possible to read the same thing also in Isaiah, where the Prophet speaks in a figure about the wings. The same thing is called the ark of the covenant in one place and in the other place the Face;[233] in the one the ark is covered by the wings, in the other the Face is. It is as though one thing is perceived in both, which suggests to me the incomprehensibility of contemplating the ineffable secrets.[234] And if you should hear about lamps which have many branches coming out of one candlestick so that a full and brilliant light is cast all around, you would correctly conclude that they are the varied rays of the Spirit which shine brightly in this tabernacle. This is what Isaiah is speaking about when he divides the lights of the Spirit into seven.[235]

182. The throne of mercy, I think, needs no interpretation since the Apostle laid bare what is hidden when he said, *Whom God has appointed to be a throne of mercy*[236] for our souls. When I hear of the altar of offering and the altar of incense, I

understand the adoration of the heavenly beings which is per-
petually offered in this tabernacle. For he says that not only the
tongues of those *on earth and in the underworld* but also of those *in
the heavens*[237] render praise to the beginning of all things. This is
the sacrifice pleasing to God, *a verbal sacrifice*, as the Apostle
says, the fragrance of prayer.[238]

183. Even if one sees skin dyed red and hair woven,[239] the
sequence of contemplation is not broken in this way. For the
prophetic eye, attaining to a vision of divine things, will see the
saving Passion there predetermined. It is signified in both of
the elements mentioned: the redness pointing to blood and the
hair to death. Hair on the body has no feeling; hence it is rightly
a symbol of death.

The Earthly Tabernacle

184. Whenever the prophet looks to the tabernacle above,
he sees the heavenly realities through these symbols. But if one
should look at the tabernacle below (since in many places the
Church also is called Christ by Paul),[240] it would be well to
regard the names "apostles, teachers, and prophets" as referring to those servants of the divine mystery whom Scripture
also calls pillars of the Church.[241] For it is not only Peter and
John and James who are pillars of the Church, nor was only
John the Baptist *a burning light*,[242] but all those who themselves support the Church and become lights through their
own works[243] are called "pillars" and "lights." *You are the light
of the world*,[244] says the Lord to the Apostles. And again the
divine Apostle bids others to be pillars, saying *Be steadfast and
unmovable*.[245] And he made Timothy into an excellent pillar,
when he made him (as he says in his own words) a *pillar and
ground of truth*.[246]

185. In this tabernacle both the sacrifice of praise and the
incense of prayer are seen offered continually at morning and
evening. The great David allows us to perceive these things

when he directs the incense of his prayer *in an odor of sweetness to God*, performing his sacrifice through the *lifting up of his hands*.[247] When hearing about the lavers, one will certainly perceive those who wash away the blemish of sins with mystical water.[248] John was a laver, washing men in the Jordan with the baptism of repentance,[249] as was Peter, who led three thousand at the same time to the water.[250] Philip, too, was a laver of the servant of Candace,[251] and all those who administer grace are lavers to those who share in the free gift.

186. The interconnecting courts which surround the tabernacle are fittingly understood as the harmony, love, and peace of believers. David interprets it in this way when he says: *Who has granted you peace on your frontiers.*[252]

187. The skin dyed red and the coverings made of hair, which add to the decoration of the tabernacle, would be perceived respectively as the mortification of the sinful flesh (the figure of which is the skin dyed red) and the ascetic way of life. By these the tabernacle of the church is especially beautified. By nature these skins do not have in themselves a vital power, but they become bright red because of the red dye. This teaches that grace, which flourishes through the Spirit, is not found in men unless they first make themselves dead to sin. Whether or not Scripture signifies by the red dye chaste modesty, I leave for whoever wishes to decide. The woven hair, which produced a fabric rough and hard to the touch, foreshadows the self-control which is rough and consumes the habitual passions. The life of virginity demonstrates in itself all such things, as it chastises the flesh of all those who live this way.[253]

188. If the interior, which is called the Holy of Holies, is not accessible to the multitude, let us not think that this is at variance with the sequence of what has been perceived. For the truth of reality is truly a holy thing, a holy of holies, and is incomprehensible and inaccessible to the multitude. Since it is set in the secret and ineffable areas of the tabernacle of mys-

tery, the apprehension of the realities above comprehension should not be meddled with;[254] one should rather believe that what is sought does exist, not that it lies visible to all, but that it remains in the secret and ineffable areas of the intelligence.[255]

The Priestly Vestments

189. Having been instructed in these and other such things through the vision of the tabernacle, the eye of Moses' soul, purified and elevated through sights such as these, rises again to the height of other insights when he is instructed in the vestments of the priesthood.[256] Among these are the tunic, the ephod, the breast-piece shining with varied rays from precious stones, the turban for the head and the metal-leaf upon it, the breeches, the pomegranates, the bells, then above all these the rational and the doctrine[257] (and the truth discerned in both), and the shoulder-pieces tied together on both sides and fastened with the names of the patriarchs.

190. The very names for the clothing keep most folk from an accurate contemplation of their details. What sort of material garments would be called rational, doctrine, or truth? Indeed, these names clearly illustrate that it is not the perceptible clothing which is traced by the history but a certain adornment of the soul woven by virtuous pursuits.

191. The dye of the tunic is blue. Some of those who before us have contemplated the passage say that the dye signifies the air.[258] I, for my part, cannot accurately affirm whether such a color as this has anything in common with the color of the air. Nevertheless, I do not reject it. The perception does lead to the contemplation of virtue, because it requires that he who would be a priest to God also bring his own body to the altar and become a sacrifice, not by being put to death, but by being *a living sacrifice* and *rational service*.[259] He should not inflict upon his soul a heavy and fleshy garment of life, but by

the purity of his life he should make all the pursuits of life as thin as the thread of a spider web. Reweaving this bodily nature, we should be close to what rises upwards and is light and airy, in order that when we hear the last trumpet we may be found weightless and light in responding to the voice of the One who calls us. Then we shall be borne on high through the air to be together with the Lord,[260] not drawn down to earth by anything heavy. He who, in keeping with the counsel of the Psalmist, has *like a moth eaten away his soul*,[261] has put on that airy tunic which extends from his head to his feet, for the Law does not want virtue to be cut short.[262]

192. The golden bells alternating with the pomegranates represent the brilliance of good works. They are the two pursuits through which virtue is acquired, namely, faith toward the divine and conscience toward life. The great Paul adds these pomegranates and bells to Timothy's garment, saying that he should have *faith and a good conscience*.[263] So let faith sound forth pure and loud in the preaching of the holy Trinity and let life imitate the nature of the pomegranate's fruit.[264]

193. Because it is covered with a hard and sour rind, its outside is inedible, but the inside is a pleasant sight with its many neatly ordered seeds and it becomes even sweeter when it is tasted. The philosophical life, although outwardly austere and unpleasant, is yet full of good hopes when it ripens. For when our Gardener opens the pomegranate of life at the proper time and manifests the hidden beauty, then those who partake of their own fruit will enjoy the sweetness. For somewhere the divine Apostle says that *any punishment is most painful at the time, and far from pleasant* (that is the first contact with the pomegranate): *but later, in those on whom it has been used, it bears fruit in peace and goodness.*[265] This is the sweetness of the nourishment inside.

194. The Scripture commands that this tunic be tasseled.[266] The tassels of the tunic are round pendants which serve no other purpose than decoration alone. We learn from

this that virtue should not be measured only by what is required, and that we should discover something extra by our own endeavor, in order that some further adornment might be added to the garment. Thus it was with Paul, who joined his own beautiful tassels to the commandments. For whereas the Law commands that *the ministers serving in the Temple get their food from the Temple* and *those who preach the Gospel should get their living from the Gospel*,[267] Paul offers the Gospel *without charge*,[268] being himself in *hunger, and thirst, and naked*.[269] These are the beautiful tassels which adorn the tunic of the commandments by being added to it.

195. Above the long tunic were worn two pieces of cloth which reached from the shoulders down the chest and down the back and were joined to one another by a clasp on each shoulder. The clasps were stones with the names of six patriarchs engraved on each. The cloths were woven of many colors: violet was woven with purple, and scarlet was mixed with linen. Gold thread was interspersed through all this so that from the mixture of the various colors resulted a single radiant beauty.

196. From this we learn that the upper part of the outer garment, which is in a particular way an adornment of the heart, is composed of many varied virtues. Now the violet is interwoven with purple, for kingliness is joined to purity of life. Scarlet is mixed with linen because the bright and pure quality of life in some way mingles with the redness of modesty. The gold which lends radiance to these colors foreshadows the treasure reserved for such a life. The patriarchs engraved on the shoulders make a great contribution to our adornment, for men's lives are adorned by the earlier examples of good men.

197. Furthermore, there is another adornment worn on top of these beautiful cloths. Little shield-like ornaments of gold hung down from each of the shoulder pieces and held a four-cornered object of gold further brightened by twelve

stones arranged in rows. There were four rows, each containing three stones. No two of them were alike, but each was
beautified by its own particular radiance.

198. That was the outward appearance of the ornament,
and this is its meaning: The shield-like ornaments hanging
down from both shoulders symbolize the two-fold nature of
our armor against the Adversary. Therefore, as I said a short
time ago, since the life of virtue is lived in a two-fold way—by
faith and a good conscience in life—we are made safe with
respect to both by the shields' protection. We remain un-
wounded by the enemy's darts, *by being armed with the weapons of
righteousness in the right hand and in the left*.[270]

199. That four-cornered ornament which hung down
from both of the shield-like ornaments and which had on it
stones inscribed with the patriarchal names of the tribes protects the heart. Scripture instructs us in this figure that he who
repels the evil archer with these two shields will adorn his own
soul with all the virtues of the patriarchs,[271] for each stone
shines with its own brilliance on the cloth of virtue. Let the
four-cornered shape be a demonstration to you of steadfastness
in the good. Such a shape is hard to move, since it is supported
equally by the corners at each side.[272]

200. The straps by which these adornments are tied to the
arms seem to me to provide a teaching for the higher life,
namely that practical philosophy should be joined to contemplative philosophy. So the heart becomes the symbol of contemplation, and the arms, of works.

201. The head adorned with the diadem signifies the
crown reserved for those who have lived well. It is beautified
by an inscription of ineffable letters in gold leaf. Whoever has
put on such adornment wears no sandals so he will not be
encumbered in his race and hindered by the covering of dead
skins (which accords with the understanding obtained in our
contemplation concerning the mount). How then is the sandal

going to be an adornment for the foot when it is cast off at the first initiation as being an impediment to the ascent?[273]

The Tables of Stone

202. He who has progressed this far through the ascents which we have contemplated carries in his hand the tables, written by God, which contain the divine Law. But these are broken, crushed by the harsh opposition of sinners. Their sin was that they made for idolatrous worship an image in the shape of a calf. The whole image was pulverized by Moses and mixed with water, and drunk by those who had sinned so that the material which served the godlessness of men was completely destroyed.

203. The history prophetically proclaimed at that time the things which have now come to pass in our own time.[274] The error of idolatry utterly disappeared from life, being swallowed by pious mouths, which through good confession[275] bring about the destruction of the material of godlessness. The mysteries established of old by idolators became running water, completely liquid, a water swallowed by the very mouths of those who were at one time idol-mad.[276] When you see those who formerly stooped under such vanity now destroying those things in which they had trusted, does the history then not seem to you to cry out clearly that every idol will then be swallowed by the mouths of those who have left error for true religion?

204. Moses armed the Levites against their fellow countrymen. And crossing the camp from one end to the other, they killed without inquiry, their swords finding their own victims. Death came to everyone they met, without preference; no distinction was made between enemy and friend, stranger and neighbor, kinsman and foreigner. (There was one thrust of the

hand equally for everyone.) With equal energy the same thrust of the hand ran through everyone they fell upon.

205. This account provides the following useful lesson:[277] Because the Israelites in a body agreed to the evil and because the whole camp to a man participated in it, they were all without distinction scourged. It is like someone punishing a person caught in an evil act by whipping him. Whatever part of the body he may hit, he tears to shreds with the scourge, knowing that the pain inflicted on that part extends throughout the whole body. The same thing happens when the whole body united in evil is punished: The scourging inflicted on the part chastens the whole.

206. So if at any time someone observes the same evil in many, but the wrath of God is vented not against everyone but only against some, it is fitting that one perceive the correction as administered through love for mankind. While not all are struck, the blows upon some chastise all to turn them from evil.

207. This understanding still pertains to the literal account, but the spiritual meaning would profit us in the following manner. The Lawgiver says in a general proclamation to all: *If any man be on the Lord's side let him join with me*.[278] This is the Law commanding all: "If anyone wishes to be the friend of God, let him be a friend of me, the Law" (for the friend of the Law is certainly a friend of God). And he commands those gathered to him by such a proclamation to use the sword against their brother, friend, and neighbor.

208. As we observe the sequence of the contemplation, we perceive that everyone who looks to God and the Law is purified by the death of his evil habits. For not everyone is named brother or friend or neighbor in a good sense by the Scripture. It is possible for one to be both brother and foreigner, both friend and enemy, both neighbor and opponent. These we perceive as our innermost thoughts, whose life brings about our death and whose death brings about our life.[279]

209. Such an understanding agrees with our earlier investigation of Aaron,[280] when in his meeting with Moses we perceived the angel as an ally and helper who cooperated in the signs against the Egyptians. He is rightly perceived as being older, since the angelic and incorporeal nature was created before our nature, but he is clearly a brother by virtue of the kinship of his intellectual nature to ours.

210. While, then, there is a contradiction (because how is it possible to take in a good sense Moses' meeting with Aaron. who became the Israelites' servant in making an idol?), nevertheless Scripture, in a limited sense, gives an indication of the double meaning of brotherhood, that the same word does not always signify the same thing but may be taken with opposite meanings. In one case the person killing the Egyptian tyrant is the brother; in another, it is the one molding the idol for the Israelites. Thus the same name is used in both instances.

211. Against such brothers, then, Moses bares the sword. For he very clearly lays down for himself the same requirement that he demands of others. One kills such a brother by destroying sin, for everyone who destroys some evil that the Adversary has contrived in him kills in himself that one who lives through sin.[281]

212. The teaching on this matter may be more surely confirmed to us if we bring further details of the history to bear on this contemplation. It is said that at Aaron's command they took off their earrings, which provided the material for the idol. What shall we say about this? That Moses adorned the ears of the Israelites with an ornament for the ears, which is the Law, but the false brother through disobedience removes the ornament placed on their ears and makes an idol with it.

213. At the first entrance of sin[282] the advice to disobey the commandment removed the earrings. The serpent was regarded as a friend and neighbor by the first mortals when he advised them that it would be useful and beneficial to them if they transgressed the divine commandment, that is, if they

removed from their ears the earring of the commandment. Therefore, he who kills such brothers and friends and neighbors will hear from the Law that statement which the history says Moses spoke to those who killed them: *Today you have won yourselves investiture as priests of Yahweh at the cost, one of his son, another of his brother; and so he grants you a blessing today.*[283]

214. I think it is time to call attention to those who gave themselves over to sin. Thus we may learn how the tables inscribed by God with the divine Law, which fell from Moses' hands to the ground and were broken by the impact, were restored again by Moses. The tables were not wholly the same, only the writing on them was the same. Having made the tables out of earthly matter, Moses submitted them to the power of the One who would engrave his Law upon them. In this way, while he carried the Law in letters of stone, he restored grace inasmuch as God himself had impressed the words on the stone.

215. For perhaps it is possible, as we are led by these events, to come to some perception of the divine concern for us. For if the divine Apostle speaks the truth when he calls the tables "hearts,"[284] that is, the foremost part of the soul (and certainly he who *by the Spirit . . . reaches . . . the depths of God*[285] does speak the truth), then it is possible to learn from this that human nature at its beginning was unbroken and immortal. Since human nature was fashioned by the divine hands and beautified with the unwritten characters of the Law, the intention of the Law lay in our nature in turning us away from evil and in honoring the divine.[286]

216. When the sound of sin struck our ears, that sound which the first book of Scripture calls the "voice of the serpent,"[287] but the history concerning the tables calls the "voice of drunken singing,"[288] the tables fell to the earth and were broken. But again the true Lawgiver, of whom Moses was a type, cut the tables of human nature for himself from our earth. It was not marriage which produced for him his "God-

receiving"[289] flesh, but he became the stonecutter of his own flesh, which was carved by the divine finger, for *the Holy Spirit came upon the virgin and the power of the Most High overshadowed her*.[290] When this took place, our nature regained its unbroken character, becoming immortal through the letters written by his finger. The Holy Spirit is called "finger" in many places by Scripture.[291]

217. Moses was transformed to such a degree of glory that the mortal eye could not behold him.[292] Certainly he who has been instructed in the divine mystery of our faith knows how the contemplation of the spiritual sense agrees with the literal account. For when the restorer of our broken nature (you no doubt perceive in him the one who healed our brokenness) had restored the broken table of our nature to its original beauty—doing this by the finger of God, as I said—the eyes of the unworthy could no longer behold him. In his surpassing glory he becomes inaccessible to these who would look upon him.

218. For in truth, as the Gospel says, *when he shall come in his glory escorted by all the angels*,[293] he is scarcely bearable and visible to the righteous. He who is impious and follows the Judaizing heresy[294] remains without a share in that vision, for let the impious be removed, as Isaiah says, and *he shall not see the glory of the Lord*.[295]

Eternal Progress[296]

219. While following these things in the sequence of our investigation, we were led to a deeper meaning in contemplating this passage.[297] Let us return to the subject. How does someone who Scripture says saw God clearly in such divine appearances—*face to face, as a man speaks with his friend*[298]—require that God appear to him, as though he who is always visible had not yet been seen, as though Moses had not yet

attained what Scripture testifies he had indeed attained?

220. The heavenly voice now grants the petitioner's request and does not deny this additional grace. Yet again He leads him to despair[299] in that He affirms that what the petitioner seeks cannot be contained by human life. Still, God says there is a *place with himself* where there is a *rock with a hole in it*[300] into which he commands Moses to enter. Then God placed his hand over the mouth of the hole and called out to Moses as he passed by. When Moses was summoned, he came out of the hole and saw the back of the One who called him.[301] In this way he thought he saw what he was seeking, and the promise of the divine voice did not prove false.

221. If these things are looked at literally, not only will the understanding of those who seek God be dim, but their concept of him will also be inappropriate.[302] Front and back pertain only to those things which are observed to have shape. Every shape provides the limits of a body. So then he who conceives of God in some shape will not realize that he is free of a bodily nature. It is a fact that every body is composite, and that what is composite exists by the joining of its different elements. No one would say that what is composite cannot be decomposed. And what decomposes cannot be incorruptible, for corruption is the decomposition of what is composite.

222. If therefore one should think of the back of God in a literal fashion, he will necessarily be carried to such an absurd conclusion. For front and back pertain to a shape, and shape pertains to a body. A body by its very nature can be decomposed, for everything composite is capable of dissolution. But what is being decomposed cannot be incorruptible; therefore, he who is bound to the letter would consequently conceive the Divine to be corruptible. But in fact God is incorruptible and incorporeal.

223. But what understanding other than the literal interpretation fits what is written? If this part of the written

narrative compels us to seek out another understanding, it is certainly appropriate to understand the whole in the same way. Whatever we perceive in the part, we of necessity take as true for the whole, since every whole is made up of its parts. Wherefore the place with God, the rock at that place, the opening in it called a hole, Moses' entrance into it, the placing of the divine hand over its mouth, the passing by and the calling and after this the vision of the back—all this would more fittingly be contemplated in its spiritual sense.

224. What then is being signified? Bodies, once they have received the initial thrust downward, are driven downward by themselves with greater speed without any additional help as long as the surface on which they move is steadily sloping and no resistance to their downward thrust is encountered.[303] Similarly, the soul moves in the opposite direction. Once it is released from its earthly attachment, it becomes light and swift for its movement upward, soaring from below up to the heights.[304]

225. If nothing comes from above to hinder its upward thrust (for the nature of the Good attracts to itself those who look to it),[305] the soul rises ever higher and will always make its flight yet higher—by its desire of the heavenly things *straining ahead for what is still to come*,[306] as the Apostle says.

226. Made to desire and not to abandon the transcendent height by the things already attained, it makes its way upward without ceasing, ever through its prior accomplishments renewing its intensity for the flight.[307] Activity directed toward virtue causes its capacity to grow through exertion; this kind of activity alone does not slacken its intensity by the effort, but increases it.[308]

227. For this reason we also say that the great Moses, as he was becoming ever greater, at no time stopped in his ascent, nor did he set a limit for himself in his upward course. Once having set foot on the ladder which God set up (as Jacob

says),[309] he continually climbed to the step above and never ceased to rise higher, because he always found a step higher than the one he had attained.

228. He denied the specious kinship with the Egyptian queen. He avenged the Hebrew. He chose the desert way of life where there was no human being to disturb him. In himself he shepherded a flock of tame animals. He saw the brilliance of the light. Unencumbered, having taken off his sandals, he made his approach to the light. He brought his kinsmen and countrymen out to freedom. He saw the enemy drowning in the sea.

229. He made camps under the cloud. He quenched thirst with the rock. He produced bread from heaven. By stretching out his hands, he overcame the foreigner. He heard the trumpet. He entered the darkness. He slipped into the inner sanctuary of the tabernacle not made with hands. He learned the secrets of the divine priesthood. He destroyed the idol. He supplicated the divine Being. He restored the Law destroyed by the evil of the Jews.

230. He shone with glory. And although lifted up through such lofty experiences, he is still unsatisfied in his desire for more. He still thirsts for that with which he constantly filled himself to capacity, and he asks to attain as if he had never partaken, beseeching God to appear to him, not according to his capacity to partake, but according to God's true being.[310]

231. Such an experience seems to me to belong to the soul which loves what is beautiful.[311] Hope always draws the soul from the beauty which is seen to what is beyond, always kindles the desire for the hidden through what is constantly perceived.[312] Therefore, the ardent lover of beauty, although receiving what is always visible as an image of what he desires, yet longs to be filled with the very stamp of the archetype.

232. And the bold request which goes up the mountains of desire asks this: to enjoy the Beauty[313] not in mirrors and

reflections, but face to face. The divine voice granted what was requested in what was denied, showing in a few words an immeasurable depth of thought. The munificence of God assented to the fulfillment of his desire, but did not promise any cessation or satiety of the desire.[314]

233. He would not have shown himself to his servant if the sight were such as to bring the desire of the beholder to an end, since the true sight of God consists in this, that the one who looks up to God never ceases in that desire. For he says: *You cannot see my face, for man cannot see me and live.*[315]

234. Scripture does not indicate that this causes the death of those who look, for how would the face of life ever be the cause of death to those who approach it? On the contrary, the Divine is by its nature life-giving. Yet the characteristic of the divine nature is to transcend all characteristics.[316] Therefore, he who thinks God is something to be known does not have life, because he has turned from true Being to what he considers by sense perception to have being.[317]

235. True Being is true life. This Being is inaccessible to knowledge.[318] If then the life-giving nature transcends knowledge, that which is perceived certainly is not life. It is not in the nature of what is not life to be the cause of life. Thus, what Moses yearned for is satisfied by the very things which leave his desire unsatisfied.

236. He learns from what was said that the Divine is by its very nature infinite, enclosed by no boundary. If the Divine is perceived as though bounded by something, one must by all means consider along with that boundary what is beyond it. For certainly that which is bounded leaves off at some point, as air provides the boundary for all that flies and water for all that live in it. Therefore, fish are surrounded on every side by water, and birds by air. The limits of the boundaries which circumscribe the birds or the fish are obvious: The water is the limit to what swims and the air to what flies. In the same way, God, if he is conceived as bounded, would necessarily be

surrounded by something different in nature. It is only logical that what encompasses is much larger than what is contained.

237. Now it is agreed that the Divine is good in nature.[319] But what is different in nature from the Good is surely something other than the Good. What is outside the Good is perceived to be evil in nature. But it was shown that what encompasses is much larger than what is encompassed. It most certainly follows, then, that those who think God is bounded conclude that he is enclosed by evil.

238. Since what is encompassed is certainly less than what encompasses, it would follow that the stronger prevails. Therefore, he who encloses the Divine by any boundary makes out that the Good is ruled over by its opposite. But that is out of the question. Therefore, no consideration will be given to anything enclosing infinite nature. It is not in the nature of what is unenclosed to be grasped. But every desire for the Good which is attracted to that ascent constantly expands[320] as one progresses in pressing on to the Good.

239. This truly is the vision of God: never to be satisfied in the desire to see him.[321] But one must always, by looking at what he can see, rekindle his desire to see more. Thus, no limit would interrupt growth in the ascent to God, since no limit to the Good can be found nor is the increasing of desire for the Good brought to an end because it is satisfied.[322]

240. But what is that place which is seen next to God? What is the rock? And what again is the hole in the rock? What is the hand of God that covers the mouth of the rock? What is the passing by of God? What is his back which God promised to Moses when he asked to see him face to face?

241. Naturally each of these things must be highly significant and worthy of the munificence of the divine Giver. Thus this promise is believed to be more magnificent and loftier than every theophany which had previously been granted to his great servant. How then would one, from what has been said, understand this height to which Moses desires to attain after

such previous ascents and to which *he who turns everything to their good cooperates with all those who love God*[323] makes the ascent easy through his leadership? *Here is a place,* he says, *beside me.*[324]

242. The thought harmonizes readily with what has been contemplated before. In speaking of "place" he does not limit *the place* indicated by anything quantitative (for to something unquantitative there is no measure). On the contrary, by the use of the analogy of a measurable surface he leads the hearer to the unlimited and infinite. The text seems to signify some such understanding: "Whereas, Moses, your desire for *what is still to come*[325] has expanded and you have not reached satisfaction in your progress and whereas you do not see any limit to the Good, but your yearning always looks for more, the place with me is so great that the one running in it is never able to cease from his progress."[326]

243. In another Scriptural passage the progress is a standing still, for it says, *You must stand on the rock.*[327] This is the most marvelous thing of all: how the same thing is both a standing still and a moving.[328] For he who ascends certainly does not stand still, and he who stands still does not move upwards. But here the ascent takes place by means of the standing. I mean by this that the firmer and more immovable one remains in the Good, the more he progresses in the course of virtue. The man who in his reasonings is uncertain and liable to slip, since he has no firm grounding in the Good but *is tossed one way and another and carried along*[329] (as the Apostle says) and is doubtful and wavers in his opinions concerning reality, would never attain to the height of virtue.

244. He is like those who toil endlessly as they climb uphill in sand: Even though they take long steps, their footing in the sand always slips downhill,[330] so that, although there is much motion, no progress results from it. But if someone, as the Psalmist says, should pull his feet up from the mud of the pit and plant them upon the rock[331] (the rock is Christ[332] who is absolute virtue), then the more *steadfast and unmoveable*[333] (ac-

cording to the advice of Paul) he becomes in the Good the faster
he completes the course. It is like using the standing still as if it
were a wing while the heart flies upward through its stability in
the good.[334]

245. Therefore, he who showed Moses the place urges
him on in his course. When he promised that he would stand
him on the rock, he showed him the nature of that divine race.
But the opening in the rock which Scripture calls a "hole" the
divine Apostle interprets well in his own words when he speaks
of a heavenly house not made with hands which is laid up by
hope for those who have dissolved their earthly tabernacle.[335]

246. For truly he who has *run the race*, as the Apostle says,
in that wide and roomy stadium, which the divine voice calls
"place," and has *kept the faith*[336] and, as the figurative expression says, has planted his feet on the rock; such a person will be
adorned with the *crown of righteousness* from the hand of the
contest's judge.[337] This prize is described in different ways by
Scripture.[338]

247. For the same thing which is here called an opening in
the rock is elsewhere referred to as "pleasure of paradise,"[339]
"eternal tabernacle,"[340] "mansion with the Father,"[341] "bosom
of the patriarch,"[342] "land of the living,"[343] "water of refresh-
ment,"[344] "Jerusalem which is above,"[345] "kingdom of
heaven,"[346] "prize of calling,"[347] "crown of graces,"[348] "crown
of pleasure,"[349] "crown of beauty,"[350] "pillar of strength,"[351]
"pleasure on a table,"[352] "councils of God,"[353] "throne of
judgment,"[354] "place of name,"[355] "hidden tabernacle."[356]

248. We say, then, that Moses' entrance into the rock has
the same significance as these descriptions. For, since Christ is
understood by Paul as the rock, all hope of good things is
believed to be in Christ, in whom we have learned all the
treasures of good things to be.[357] He who finds any good finds
it in Christ who contains all good.

249. He who attained to this and was shadowed by the
hand of God, as the text promised (for the hand of God[358]

would be the creative power of what exists, the *only begotten God*, by whom *all things were made*,[359] who is also "place" for those who run, who is, according to his own words, the "way" of the course,[360] and who is "rock" to those who are well established and "house"[361] to those who are resting), he it is who will hear the One who summons and will see the back of the One who calls, which means he will *follow Yahweh your God*,[362] as the Law commands.

250. When the great David heard and understood this, he said to him *who dwells in the shelter of the most High; He will overshadow you with his shoulders*,[363] which is the same as being behind God (for the shoulder is on the back of the body). Concerning himself David says, *My soul clings close to you, your right hand supports me*.[364] You see how the Psalms agree with the history. For as the one says that the right hand is a help to the person who has joined himself close behind God, so the other says that the hand touches the person who waits in the rock upon the divine voice and prays that he might follow behind.

251. But when the Lord who spoke to Moses came to fulfill his own law, he likewise gave a clear explanation to his disciples, laying bare the meaning of what had previously been said in a figure when he said, *If anyone wants to be a follower of mine*[365] and not "If any man will go before me." And to the one asking about eternal life he proposes the same thing, for he says *Come, follow me*.[366] Now, he who follows sees the back.[367]

252. So Moses, who eagerly seeks to behold God, is now taught how he can behold Him: to follow God wherever he might lead is to behold God. His passing by signifies his guiding the one who follows, for someone who does not know the way cannot complete his journey safely in any other way than by following behind his guide. He who leads, then, by his guidance shows the way to the one following. He who follows will not turn aside from the right way if he always keeps the back of his leader in view.

253. For he who moves to one side or brings himself to

face his guide assumes another direction for himself than the
one his guide shows him. Therefore, he says to the one who is
led, *My face is not to be seen*,[368] that is, "Do not face your guide."
If he does so, his course will certainly be in the opposite
direction, for good does not look good in the face, but follows
it.

254. What is perceived to be its opposite is face to face
with the good, for what looks virtue in the face is evil.[369] But
virtue is not perceived in contrast to virtue. Therefore, Moses
does not look God in the face, but looks at his back; for whoever
looks at him face to face shall not live, as the divine voice
testifies, *man cannot see* the face of the Lord *and live*.[370]

255. You see how it is so great a thing to learn how to
follow God, that after those lofty ascents and awesome and
glorious theophanies virtually at the end of his life, the man
who has learned to follow behind God is scarcely considered
worthy of this grace.

Moses Envied

256. No longer does any offense which comes about
through evil withstand the one who in this manner follows
God. After these things the envy of his brothers arose against
him. Envy is the passion which causes evil, the father of death,
the first entrance of sin, the root of wickedness, the birth of
sorrow, the mother of misfortune, the basis of disobedience,
the beginning of shame. Envy banished us from Paradise,
having become a serpent to oppose Eve. Envy walled us off
from the tree of life, divested us of holy garments,[371] and in
shame led us away clothed with fig leaves.

257. Envy armed Cain contrary to nature and instituted
the death which is vindicated seven times.[372] Envy made
Joseph a slave. Envy is the death-dealing sting, the hidden
weapon, the sickness of nature, the bitter poison, the self-

willed emaciation, the bitter dart, the nail of the soul,[373] the fire in the heart, the flame burning on the inside.

258. For envy, it is not its own misfortune but another's good fortune that is unfortunate. Again, inversely, success is not one's own good fortune but the neighbor's misfortune.[374] Envy is grieved at the good deeds of men and takes advantage of their misfortunes. It is said that the vultures which devour corpses are destroyed by perfume.[375] Their nature is akin to the foul and corrupt. Anyone who is in the power of this sickness is destroyed by the happiness of his neighbors as by the application of some perfume; but if he should see any unfortunate experience he flies to it, sets his crooked beak to it, and draws forth the hidden misfortunes.

259. Envy fought against many who lived before Moses, but when it attacked this great man, it was broken like a clay pot being dashed against a rock. By this especially was shown the progress which Moses had made in his journey with God. He ran in the divine place, took his stand on the rock, was held in its opening, was covered by God's hand, and followed behind his leader, not looking him in the face, but looking at his back.

260. That he appeared higher than the bow can shoot shows that of himself he had become most blessed in following God. For envy also sends the dart against Moses, but it does not reach the height where Moses was.[376] The bowstring of evil was too slack to shoot the passion far enough to reach Moses from those who were previously ill. But Aaron and Miriam were wounded by the passion of its evil influence and became like a bow of envy, shooting words against him rather than darts.

261. Moses so refrained from becoming involved in their weakness that he even ministered to the condition of those who had become ill. Not only was he not moved to defend himself against those who caused him sorrow, but he even besought God for mercy on their behalf. He showed through what he

did, I think, that the person who is well fortified with the shield of virtue will not be stung by the tips of the darts.

262. He blunts the spears; the hardness of his armor deflects them. The armor that protects against such darts is God himself, whom the soldier of virtue puts on. For Scripture says *let your armor be the Lord Jesus*,[377] that is to say, the full armor that cannot be pierced. Being thus well protected, Moses rendered the evil archer ineffective.

263. He did not rush to defend himself against those who caused him sorrow; although they had been condemned by impartial judgment and he knew what was the naturally right thing to do, he nevertheless interceded with God for his brethren. He would not have done this if he had not been behind God, who had shown him his back as a safe guide to virtue.

Joshua and the Spies

264. Let us proceed. When the natural enemy of men found no occasion to harm Moses, he directed the battle against those more vulnerable. When the lust of gluttony had been thrown at the people like a dart, he caused in them a desire for the things of Egypt so that they preferred the meat eaten by the Egyptians to the bread of heaven.

265. But Moses, having an elevated soul and soaring above such lust, was totally devoted to the coming inheritance which had been promised by God to those who departed from Egypt (spiritually understood) and made their way to that land flowing with milk and honey. For this reason he appointed some spies to be teachers of the beauties in that land.

266. The spies, in my opinion, are: on the one hand those who offer hope of good things are the reasonings born of faith which confirm hope for the good things laid up for us; on the other hand, the reasonings of the Adversary would be those who reject better hopes and blunt faith in the things reported.

Moses considered no report of the opponents trustworthy, but accepted the man who gave a more favorable report of that land.

267. Joshua was the one who led the better mission and he made the things reported trustworthy by his own confirmation. When Moses looked at him, he had a steady firm hope for the future, finding proof of that land's abundance in the bunch of grapes which Joshua had carried back on poles. Of course, when you hear of Joshua telling about that land and about a bunch of grapes hanging on the wood, you perceive what it is that he sees which makes him secure in his hopes.

268. What is the bunch of grapes suspended from the wood but that bunch suspended from the wood in the last days, whose blood becomes a saving drink for those who believe?[378] Moses spoke to us of this ahead of time when he said in a figure: *They drank the blood of the grape*.[379] By this he signifies the saving passion.

The Brazen Serpent

269. Again the way led through the desert, and the people lost hope in the good things promised and were reduced to thirst. Moses again made water flow in the desert for them. When it is perceived spiritually, this account teaches us what the mystery of repentance is.[380] Those who turn to the stomach, the flesh, and the Egyptian pleasures, after having once tasted the rock, are sentenced to be excluded from partaking in good things.

270. But they can by repentance again find the rock which they abandoned and again open the spring of water for themselves and again take their fill. The rock gives forth water to Moses who believed that Joshua's spying is truer than his opponents', Moses who looked to the bunch of grapes which for our sakes was suspended and shed blood, and Moses who

by the wood prepared water to gush from the rock again for them.[381]

271. But the people had not yet learned to keep in step with Moses' greatness. They were still drawn down to the slavish passions and were inclined to the Egyptian pleasures. The history shows by this that human nature is especially drawn to this passion, being led to the disease along thousands of ways.

272. As a physician by his treatment prevents a disease from prevailing, so Moses does not permit the disease to cause death. Their unruly desires produced serpents which injected deadly poison into those they bit. The great lawgiver, however, rendered the real serpents powerless by the image of a serpent.

273. This would be an appropriate time to explain the figure. There is one antidote for these evil passions: the purification of our souls which takes place through the mystery of godliness. The chief act of faith in the "mystery" is to look to him who suffered the passion for us.[382] The cross is the passion, so that whoever looks to it, as the text relates, is not harmed by the poison of desire.[383]

274. To look to the cross means to render one's whole life dead and crucified to the world,[384] unmoved by evil. Truly it is as the prophet says: "They nail their own flesh with the fear of God."[385] The nail would be the self-control that holds the flesh.[386]

275. Since therefore unruly desires brought forth the deadly serpents from the earth (for every offspring of evil desire is a serpent), the Law prefigures for us what is clear in the wood. This figure is a likeness of a serpent and not a serpent itself, as the great Paul himself says, *in the likeness of sinful flesh*.[387] Sin is the real serpent, and whoever deserts to sin takes on the nature of the serpent.[388]

276. Man, then, is freed from sin through him who assumed the form of sin and became like us who had turned into

the form of the serpent. He keeps the bites from causing death, but the beasts themselves are not destroyed. By beasts I mean desires. For although the evil of death which follows sins does not prevail against those who look to the cross, the lust of flesh against spirit[389] has not completely ceased to exist.

277. In fact, the gnawings of desire are frequently active even in the faithful.[390] Nevertheless, the person who looks to the One lifted up on the wood rejects passion, diluting the poison with the fear of the commandment as with a medicine. The voice of the Lord teaches clearly that the serpent lifted up in the desert is a symbol[391] of the mystery of the cross when he says, *The Son of Man must be lifted up as Moses lifted up the serpent in the desert.*[392]

The True Priesthood

278. Again sin advanced in evil succession in its customary way, progressing consistently as in an evil series. And the lawgiver, like a physician, accommodated the remedy to what the evil had produced. When the bite of the serpents was ineffective against those who looked to the likeness of the serpent—you certainly perceive the figure through what has been said—another stratagem was contrived by him who with infinite variety devises such things against us.

279. It is possible even now to see this happening on many occasions. For when some individuals punish the passion of desire by living a disciplined life, they thrust themselves into the priesthood, and with human zeal and selfish ambition they arrogate to themselves God's ministry.[393] He whom the history accuses of producing evil in men leads them to the subsequent sin.

280. When those who were lusting believed in the one lifted up on the wood, the earth stopped bringing forth serpents to bite them, and they then thought themselves to be

above the venomous bites. It is then, when lustful desire leaves them, that the disease of arrogance enters in its place. Judging that to keep to their assigned place was too lowly a thing, they thrust themselves into the honor of the priesthood and contentiously thrust out those who had obtained this ministry from God.[394] They were swallowed up by the yawning chasm and were destroyed. All of those left on the earth were burned to ashes by lightning.[395]

The Scripture teaches in the history, I think, that when one arrogantly exalts himself he ends by falling even below the earth. And perhaps, if viewed through these events, arrogance might not unreasonably be defined as a downward ascent.

281. Do not be surprised if popular opinion leads to the opposite notion, for the masses think that the word "arrogance" means "being above others." But the truth of the narrative confirms our definition. For if those who elevate themselves above others in some way go downward, as the earth opens a chasm for them, no one should argue with the definition of "arrogance" as "an abject fall."

282. Moses instructs those who see this to be moderate and not to be puffed up by their right conduct but always to keep a good disposition in the present. Overcoming one's pleasures does not mean being no longer liable to be seized by another kind of passion, for every passion is a fall as long as it is a passion. The diversity in passions does not mean a different kind of fall. The man who slipped on slippery passion has fallen, as has the man who was tripped by arrogance. The intelligent man should prefer no kind of fall, but every fall should be equally avoided as long as it is a fall.

283. So if you should now see someone purifying himself to some degree of the disease of pleasure and with great zeal considering himself above others as he thrusts himself into the priesthood, realize that this man whom you see is someone who is falling to earth by his lofty arrogance. For in what follows the Law teaches that the priesthood is something divine and not

human. It teaches this in the following manner.

284. Having marked the rods which he received from each tribe with the name of those who gave them, Moses placed them on the altar. The result was that one rod became a testimony to the heavenly ordination,[396] for it was distinguished over the others by a divine miracle. This happened: The rods of the others remained as they were; but the rod of the priest took root by itself (not through any extraneous moisture but through the power which was placed in it by God), and brought forth branches and fruit, and the fruit ripened. The fruit was a nut.

285. By this event all the people were instructed in discipline. In the fruit that Aaron's rod produced it is fitting to perceive the kind of life that must characterize the priesthood—namely, a life self-controlled, tough and dried in appearance, but containing on the inside (hidden and invisible) what can be eaten. It becomes visible when the food ripens and the hard shell is stripped off and the wood-like covering of the meat is removed.[397]

286. If you should discover the life of the priest we are discussing to be quince-like, fragrant and rose-colored, like the lives of many who are adorned with linen and purple and who fatten themselves at rich tables and who drink pure wine and anoint themselves with the best myrrh[398] and who make use of whatever seems pleasant to those who have a taste for a life of luxury, then you would with good cause apply to this situation the word of the Gospel: "When I look at your fruit, I do not recognize the priestly tree by it."[399] The priesthood has one fruit and this kind of life another. The fruit of the one is self-control, that of the other is self-indulgence. The fruit of the priesthood does not mature from earthly moisture, but this kind of fruit has many streams of pleasure which flow from underneath, by which life's fruit is brought to a state of ripeness like this.[400]

The Royal Way

287. When the people are purified of this passion, then they cross through the foreign life. As the Law leads them along the royal highway,[401] they deviate from it in no way at all. It is easy for a traveler to turn aside. Suppose two precipices form a high narrow pass; from its middle the person crossing it veers at his peril in either direction (for the chasm on either side swallows the person who turns aside). In the same way the Law requires the person who keeps in step with it not to leave the way which is, as the Lord says, *narrow and hard*, to the left or to the right.[402]

288. This teaching lays down that virtue is discerned in the mean.[403] Accordingly, all evil naturally operates in a deficiency of or an excess of virtue. In the case of courage, cowardice is the lack of virtue and rashness is its excess. What is pure of each of these is seen to lie between these corresponding evils and is virtue. In the same way all other things which strive for the better also somehow take the middle road between the neighboring evils.

289. Wisdom holds to the mean between shrewdness and simplicity. Neither the wisdom of the serpent nor the simplicity of the dove[404] is to be praised, if one should choose either of these with respect to itself alone. Rather it is the disposition which closely unites these two by the mean that is virtue. The person who lacks moderation[405] is a libertine, and he who goes beyond moderation has his *conscience branded*,[406] as the Apostle says. For the one has given himself up without restraint to pleasures, and the other defiles marriage as if it were adultery. The disposition observed in the mean between these two is moderation.

290. Since, as the Lord says, this *world lies in wickedness*,[407] and everything opposed to virtue (which is wickedness) is foreign to those who follow the Law, the man who in his life makes his way through this world will safely conclude this

necessary journey of virtue if he truly keeps to the highway which is hardened and smoothed[408] by virtue and will under no circumstances be turned aside to any byways because of evil.

Balaam and the Daughters of Moab

291. Since, as has been said, the assault of the Adversary accompanies the ascent of virtue and seeks out corresponding opportunities to subvert toward evil, as the people improve in the godly life, the Adversary launches another attack such as experts in warfare use. These latter, when they estimate that their adversary has superior power in open battle, lay their plans for an ambush. In the same way evil's general no longer brings his power to bear openly against those empowered by the law and virtue, but he carries out his assault secretly by laying ambushes for them.

292. He calls in magic as his ally against those whom he assaults. The history says this magic is a diviner and augur who derived his presumably harmful power from the working of demons to use it against the adversaries and was paid by the ruler of the Midianites to curse those who live to God, but actually he turned the curse into a blessing. We perceive through the sequence of the things previously contemplated that magic is ineffective against those who live in virtue; on the contrary, those fortified by divine help prevail over every onslaught.

293. The history gives witness of divination by observing birds when it says of the one mentioned that he possessed powers of divination and received counsel from birds. Before this it testifies that he was taught things about his immediate undertaking[409] by the braying of his ass. Because he usually received advice by the sounds made by irrational animals under demonic influence,[410] Scripture clearly describes the utterance of the ass. It shows in this way that those who had previously

been overtaken by deceit of demons have come to the point that, instead of reasoning, they accept teaching which comes to them from paying attention to the sound of irrational animals. By paying attention to the ass, he was instructed by those very things which had deceived him and learned that the power of those against whom he was hired was invincible.

294. In the Gospel history also the Legion, the horde of demons, was ready to oppose the authority of the Lord. When he who has power over all things drew near, Legion hailed his superior power and did not hide the truth that this was the divine nature which at the appropriate time punishes those who have sinned.[411] For the voice of the demons says, *We know who you are, the Holy One of God*, and that, *You have come here to torture us before the time*.[412] The same thing happened earlier when the demonic power which accompanied the diviner taught Balaam that the people of God are invincible.

295. But, as we bring the history into harmony with our earlier investigations, we say that whoever wishes to utter a curse against those who live in virtue can bring forth no harmful and maledictory sound at all, but that the curse turns into a blessing. What we mean is this: Railing reproach does not touch those who live virtuously.

296. For how can the man without possessions be reviled for covetousness? How can someone go around preaching on profligacy to the man who lives a retiring and secluded life? Or about temper to the mild man? Or about luxury to the man of moderate habits? Or about any other blameable things to those who are renowned for their opposites? Their goal is to present their life blameless, in order that, as the Apostle says, *any opponent will be at a loss, with no accusation to make against us*.[413] Wherefore the voice of the one who has been called in to deliver the curse says, *How shall I curse one whom God does not curse?*[414] That is to say, "How shall I revile someone who has given no ground for reviling, whose life is impervious to evil because he looks to God?"

297. When the inventor of evil failed in this, he still did not stop completely conniving against those he was assaulting. But, resorting to that trickery characteristic of him, he through pleasure again enticed nature to evil.[415] Pleasure is truly like evil's bait; when it is thrown out lightly, it draws gluttonous souls to the fish hook of destruction.[416] Especially through licentious pleasure is nature, when it is not on guard, drawn aside to evil. This is indeed what took place on that occasion.

298. For those who prevailed over the enemy's arms, who proved every assault made with iron weapons weaker than their own power, and who by their might turned their enemies' line of battle, were themselves wounded by feminine darts of pleasure. Those who were stronger than men were conquered by women.[417] As soon as the women appeared to them, showing off comeliness instead of weapons, they forgot their manly strength and dissipated their vigor in pleasure.

299. It was only to be expected that some among them would be filled with lust[418] for unlawful intercourse with foreigners. But intimacy with evil meant estrangement from the assistance of the Good; immediately God began to war against them. The zealous Phineas, however, did not wait to have sin purged by heavenly decision; he himself became at once judge and jury.

300. Having been moved to wrath against the men who were filled with lust, he did the work of a priest by purging the sin with blood, not the blood of some guiltless animal which had no part in the stain of licentiousness, but the blood of those who were joined with one another in evil. The spear, by piercing the two bodies conjointly, stayed divine justice, mixing pleasure with the death of those who sinned.[419]

301. The history, it seems to me, offers some advice profitable to men. It teaches us that of the many passions which afflict men's thinking there is none so strong as the disease of pleasure. That those Israelites, who were manifestly stronger than the Egyptian cavalry and had prevailed over the Amale-

kites and had shown themselves awesome to the next nation and then had prevailed over the troops of the Midianites, were enslaved by this sickness at the very moment they saw the foreign women only shows, as I have said, that pleasure is an enemy of ours that is hard to fight and difficult to overcome.

302. By vanquishing by her very appearance those who had not been conquered by weapons, pleasure raised a trophy of dishonor against them and held up their shame to public scorn. Pleasure showed that she makes men beasts.[420] The irrational animal impulse to licentiousness made them forget their human nature; they did not hide their excess but adorned themselves with the dishonor of passion and beautified themselves with the stain of shame as they wallowed, like pigs, in the slimy mire of uncleanness, openly for everyone to see.

303. What, then, are we taught by this account? This: that now having learned what great power for evil the disease of pleasure possesses, we should conduct our lives as far removed from it as possible; otherwise the disease may find some opening against us, like fire whose very proximity causes an evil flame. Solomon teaches this in Wisdom when he says that one should not walk upon hot coals with bare feet or hide fire in his bosom.[421] So also it is in our power to remain unaffected by passion[422] as long as we stay far away from the thing that enflames. If we come close enough to step on this burning heat, the fire of desire will burn in our breast and so it will follow that we are burned both in our feet and our breast.

304. In order that we might be kept far from such evil, the Lord in the Gospel with his own voice cuts out the very root of evil—namely, the desire which arises through sight—when he teaches that the person who welcomes passion by his taking a look gives an opening to the disease harmful to himself.[423] For the evils of the passions, like a plague, when once they have gained possession of the critical parts, stop only at death.

The Perfection of the Servant

305. I think there is no need to prolong the discourse by presenting to the reader the whole life of Moses as an example of virtue. For to anyone straining to the higher life what has been said provides amply for true wisdom. To anyone who shows weakness in toiling[424] for virtue there would be no gain even if many more things should be written than what has been said.[425]

306. Nevertheless, let us not forget our definition in the prologue.[426] There we affirmed that the perfect life was such that no description of its perfection hinders its progress; the continual development of life to what is better is the soul's way to perfection. We would do well, by bringing our discourse up to the end of Moses's life, to show the certainty of the definition of perfection which we have proposed.

307. For he who elevates his life beyond earthly things through such ascents never fails to become even loftier than he was until, as I think, like an eagle in all things his life may be seen above and beyond the cloud whirling around the ether of spiritual ascent.[427]

308. He was born when the Egyptians considered a Hebrew birth an offense.[428] When the tyrant ruling at that time punished by his law every boy who was born, Moses triumphed over the murderous law, being saved at first by his parents and then by the very persons who laid down the law. And those who desired his death by law actually exercised great care not only for his life but also for his highly esteemed education by introducing the youth to all wisdom.

309. After this he stood above human honor and beyond royal dignity, considering it to be stronger and more royal to keep watch for virtue and to be beautified with its adornment than to be a spearman and to wear royal adornment.

310. Then he saved his countryman and struck down the Egyptian; in this we see by our interpretative contemplation both the friend and the enemy of the soul. Next, he made his retirement the teacher of lofty matters, and in this way his understanding was enlightened by the light which shone from the bush. And then he made haste to share with his countrymen the good things which came to him from God.

311. On that occasion he demonstrated his power in two ways, by warding off his opponents with ingenious blows one after the other and by doing good to his countrymen. He led this people through the sea on foot without making a fleet of ships for himself; instead, he made their faith a ship for crossing through the water. He made the bottom of the sea dry land for the Hebrews and the dry land sea for the Egyptians.

312. He sang the victory song. He was led by the pillar. He was enlightened by the heavenly fire. He prepared a table out of the food which came down to him from above. He drew water[429] from the rock. He stretched forth his hands to destroy the Amalekites. He ascended the mountain. He entered the darkness. He heard the trumpet. He approached the divine nature. He was enclosed by the heavenly tabernacle. He adorned the priesthood. He built the tabernacle. He ordered life by the laws. He successfully waged his last wars in the manner we have described.

313. As the last of his right actions he punished licentiousness through the priesthood. This was signified by the wrath that Phineas showed against passion. After all these things he went to the mountain of rest. He did not set foot on the land below for which the people were longing by reason of the promise. He who preferred to live by what flowed from above no longer tasted earthly food. But having come to the very top of the mountain, he, like a good sculptor who has fashioned well the whole statue of his own life,[430] did not simply bring his creation to an end but he placed the finishing touch on his work.[431]

314. What does the history say about this? That *Moses the servant of Yahweh died as Yahweh decreed, and no one has ever found his grave, his eyes were undimmed, and his face unimpaired*.[432] From this we learn that, when one has accomplished such noble actions, he is considered worthy of this sublime name, to be called *servant of Yahweh*,[433] which is the same as saying that he is better than all others. For one would not serve God unless he had become superior to everyone in the world. This for him is the end[434] of the virtuous life, an end wrought by the word of God. History speaks of "death," a living death,[435] which is not followed by the grave, or fills the tomb, or brings dimness to the eyes and aging to the person.

315. What then are we taught through what has been said? To have but one purpose in life: to be called servants of God by virtue of the lives we live. For when you conquer all enemies (the Egyptian, the Amalekite, the Idumaean, the Midianite), cross the water, are enlightened by the cloud, are sweetened by the wood, drink from the rock, taste of the food from above, make your ascent up the mountain through purity and sanctity; and when you arrive there, you are instructed in the divine mystery by the sound of the trumpets, and in the impenetrable darkness draw near to God by your faith, and there are taught the mysteries of the tabernacle and the dignity of the priesthood.

316. And when you, as a sculptor, carve in your own heart the divine oracles which you receive from God;[436] and when you destroy the golden idol[437] (that is, if you wipe from your life the desire of covetousness); and when you are elevated to such heights that you appear invincible to the magic of Balaam (by "magic" you will perceive the crafty deceit of this life[438] through which men drugged as though by some philtre of Circe[439] are changed into the form of irrational animals and leave their proper nature); and when you come through all these things, and the staff of the priesthood blossoms in you, drawing no moisture at all from the earth but having its own

unique power for producing fruit (that is the nut whose first taste is bitter and tough but whose inside is sweet and edible); when you destroy everything which opposes your worth, as Dathan was swallowed in the earth and Core was consumed by the fire—then you will draw near to the goal.

317. I mean by "goal" that for the sake of which everything is done, for example: The goal of agriculture is the enjoyment of its fruits; the goal of building a house is living in it; the goal of commerce is wealth; and the goal of striving in contests is the prize. In the same way, too, the goal of the sublime way of life is being called a servant of God. Along with this honor is contemplated an end which is not covered by a tomb; it refers to the life lived simply and free from evil appendages.[440]

318. Scripture describes another characteristic of this service to God: The eye is not dimmed nor does the person age. For how can an eye which is always in the light be dimmed by the darkness from which it is always separated? And the person who by every means achieves incorruption in his whole life admits no corruption in himself. For he who has truly come to be in the image of God[441] and who has in no way turned aside from the divine character bears in himself its distinguishing marks and shows in all things his conformity to the archetype; he beautifies his own soul with what is incorruptible, unchangeable, and shares in no evil at all.[442]

Conclusion

319. These things concerning the perfection of the virtuous life, O Caesarius,[443] man of God, we have briefly written for you, tracing in outline like a pattern of beauty the life of the great Moses so that each one of us might copy the image of the beauty which has been shown to us by imitating his way of life. What more trustworthy witness of the fact that Moses did

attain the perfection which was possible would be found than the divine voice which said to him: *I have known you more than all others?*[444] It is also shown in the fact that he is named the "friend of God"[445] by God himself, and by preferring to perish with all the rest if the Divine One did not through his good will forgive their errors, he stayed God's wrath against the Israelites. God averted judgment so as not to grieve his friend.[446] All such things are a clear testimony and demonstration of the fact that the life of Moses did ascend the highest mount of perfection.[447]

320. Since the goal of the virtuous way of life was the very thing we have been seeking, and this goal has been found in what we have said, it is time for you, noble friend, to look to that example and, by transferring to your own life what is contemplated through spiritual interpretation of the things spoken literally, to be known by God and to become his friend. This is true perfection: not to avoid a wicked life because like slaves we servilely fear punishment, nor to do good because we hope for rewards, as if cashing in on the virtuous life by some business-like and contractual arrangement. On the contrary, disregarding all those things for which we hope and which have been reserved by promise, we regard falling from God's friendship as the only thing dreadful and we consider becoming God's friend the only thing worthy of honor and desire.[448] This, as I have said, is the perfection of life.

321. As your understanding is lifted up to what is magnificent and divine, whatever you may find (and I know full well that you will find many things) will most certainly be for the common benefit in Christ Jesus. Amen.

Bibliography

Editions and Translations

Blum, Manfred. *Gregor von Nyssa, Der Aufstieg des Moses.* Sophia 4. Freiburg, 1963.

Daniélou, Jean. *Grégoire de Nysse, La Vie de Moïse.* Sources Chrétiennes 1 bis. Paris, 1955.

Migne, J.P. *Patrologiae Graecae* 44. Paris, 1863.

Musurillo, Herbertus. *Gregorii Nysseni, De Vita Moysis. Gregorii Nysseni Opera* 7, 1, ed. W. Jaeger and Hermannus Langerbeck. Leiden, 1964.

Studies

Balás, David L. ΜΕΤΟΥΣΙΑ ΘΕΟΥ. *Man's Participation in God's Perfections according to Saint Gregory of Nyssa. Studia Anselmiana,* 55. Rome, 1966.

Balthasar, H. v., *Presence et Pensée. Essai sur la philosophie religieuse de Grégoire de Nysse.* Paris, 1942.

Bebis, George S. "Gregory of Nyssa's 'De Vita Moysis': A Philosophical and Theological Analysis." *Greek Orthodox Theological Review* 12 (1967): 369-393.

Cazelles, H., et al. *Moïse, L'homme de l'alliance*. Paris, 1955.

Cherniss, H.F. *The Platonism of Gregory of Nyssa* (University of California Publications in Classical Philology XI). Berkeley, 1930.

Daniélou, Jean. *Platonisme et Théologie Mystique*. Théologie 2. Paris, 1944.

Daniélou, Jean, and Herbert Musurillo. *From Glory to Glory: Texts from Gregory of Nyssa's Mystical Writings*. London, 1961.

Ivánka, E. v., *Hellenisches und Christliches im frühbyzantinischen Geistesleben*. Vienna, 1948.

Jaeger, W., *Two Rediscovered Works of Ancient Christian Literature: Gregory of Nyssa and Macarius*. Leiden, 1954.

Konstantinou, Evangelos G., *Die Tugendlehre Gregors von Nyssa im Verhältnis zu der Antike–Philosophischen und Judisch-Christlichen Tradition*. Würzburg, 1966.

Leys, R., *L'image de Dieu chez Saint Grégoire de Nysse. Esquisse d'une doctrine*. Paris, 1951.

Merki, H., ʿΟμοίωσις Θεῷ. *Von der platonischen Angleichung an Gott zur Gottähnlichkeit bei Gregor von Nyssa* (*Paradosis* VII). Freiburg, 1952.

Mühlenberg, E., *Die Unendlichkeit Gottes bei Gregor von Nyssa. Gregors Kritik am Gottesbegriff der klassischen Metaphysik*. (*Forschungen zur Kirchen- und Dogmengeschichte*, 16). Göttingen, 1966.

Völker, W., *Gregor von Nyssa als Mystiker*. Wiesbaden, 1955.

Notes

Abbreviations

ACW   *Ancient Christian Writers*, ed. J. Quasten and J.C. Plumpe (Westminster, Md., 1946-)

Balás   David L. Balás, ΜΕΤΟΥΣΙΑ ΘΕΟΥ *Man's Participation in God's Perfections according to Saint Gregory of Nyssa* (Studia Anselmiana 55, Rome, 1966).

Daniélou   Jean Daniélou, *Gregoire de Nysse, La Vie de Moïse* (Sources Chrétiennes 1, Paris, 1955).

Daniélou, *Platonisme*   Jean Daniélou, *Platonisme et Théologie Mystique* (Théologie 2, Paris, 1944).

DOP   *Dumbarton Oaks Papers* (Cambridge, Mass., 1941-).

Glory to Glory   Jean Daniélou and Herbertus Musurillo, *From Glory to Glory: Texts from Gregory of Nyssa's Mystical Writings* (London, 1961).

Jaeger   Werner Jaeger, ed., *Gregorii Nysseni Opera* (Leiden, 1960-). Gregory references are to volume, page, and lines of this edition where available.

Jaeger, *Two*   Werner Jaeger, *Two Rediscovered Works of Ancient Christian*

Rediscovered Works	*Literature: Gregory of Nyssa and Macarius* (Leiden, 1954).
MG	*Patrologia graeca*, ed. J.P. Migne (Paris, 1857-1866).
ML	*Patrologia Latina*, ed. J.P. Migne (Paris, 1844-1855).
Moïse	H. Cazelles et al., *Moïse, L'homme de l'alliance* (Paris, 1955).
Musurillo	Herbertus Musurillo, *Gregorii Nysseni De Vita Moysis* (Leiden, 1964).
PGL	G.W.H. Lampe, *A Patristic Greek Lexicon* (Oxford, 1961-).
PO	*Patrologia Orientalis*, ed. R. Graffin and F. Nau (Paris, 1903).
Pat. Syr.	*Patrologia Syriaca*, ed. R. Graffin (Paris, 1894-1926).
SC	*Sources Chrétiennes*, ed. H. de Lubac and J. Daniélou (Paris, 1942-).

Introduction

1. The most thorough treatment of Gregory's life before his appointment to the episcopate is by Michel Aubineau in the Introduction to his edition and translation of *On Virginity* for SC 119:29-82. For Gregory's life in general see Hilda Graef in ACW 18:3ff.; Jean Daniélou in *From Glory to Glory*, pp. 3-10; J. Quasten, *Patrology*, Vol. 3 (Utrecht, 1960), pp. 254ff.; Hans von Campenhausen, *The Fathers of the Greek Church* (New York, 1955), pp. 107-116.

2. This is the conclusion of Daniélou, p. ix, and Jaeger, *Two Rediscovered Works*, pp. 119, 130.

3. I, 2, but see Bk. I, n. 6 for other works where Gregory makes allusion to his old age.

4. II, 256ff.; 278f.

5. See the discussion of the Holy Spirit, pp. 15f. of this work.

6. Daniélou, p. ix; cf. Jaeger, *Two Rediscovered Works*, pp. 116ff.

7. *Gregorii Nysseni Opera*, ed. W. Jaeger, Vol. 8, 1 (Leiden, 1963).

8. Mary Emily Keenan, "*De Professione Christiana* and *De Perfectione*: A Study of the Ascetical Doctrine of Saint Gregory of Nyssa," DOP 5 (1950): 170f. Cf. remarks by R. Leys, "La théologie spirituelle de Grégoire de Nysse," *Studia Patristica* 2 (1957): 498.

9. Jaeger, *Two Rediscovered Works*, pp. 32, 115, and *passim*.

10. *Ibid.*, pp. 27-32, 132ff.

11. Daniélou, p. ix, and Jaeger, *Two Rediscovered Works*, pp. 117, 141f.

12. I, 2 and Bk. I, n. 4.

13. Manuscript evidence in Daniélou, p. 134 and Musurillo, p. 143. One manuscript names Olympius in the title and others name Gregory's brother Peter—Musurillo, p. 3.

14. Musurillo, *Glory to Glory*, p. 289.

15. Musurillo, "History and Symbol," *Theological Studies* 18 (1957): 357-386.

16. Jaeger, *Two Rediscovered Works*, p. 20; J. Leipoldt, *Griechische Philosophie und frühchristliche Askese* (Berlin, 1961); Dorothy Emmet, "Theoria and the Way of Life," *Journal of Theological Studies* New Series XVII (April 1966): 38-52. For the changes in the meaning of 'philosophy' see Anne-Marie Malingrey, *"Philosophia." Etude d'un groupe de mots dans la litterature grecque, des Presocratiques au IVe siècle après J.-C.* (Paris, 1961).

17. Quasten, *op. cit.*, pp. 283ff. and bibliography cited. Especially note H. Merki, 'Ομοίωσις Θεῷ. *Von der platonischen Angleichung an Gott zur Gottähnlichkeit bei Gregor von Nyssa* (Paradosis 7, Freiburg, 1952); Endre von Ivánka, "Vom Platonismus zur Theorie der Mystik (Zur Erkenntnislehre Gregors von Nyssa)," *Scholastik* 11 (1936): 163-195. According to F. Überweg and B. Geyer, *Grundriss der Philosophie* II: *Die patristische und scholastische Philosophie* (Berlin, 1928), p. 84, nobody before Gregory had sought to establish the Christian faith rationally in so comprehensive a manner as he did. O. Bardenhewer, *Geschichte der altkirchlichen Literatur* III (Freiburg, 1912), believes that Gregory was perhaps better versed in pagan philosophy than any other Christian writer of the 4th century. K. Gronau's assessment of the importance of Posidonius for Gregory has not been accepted generally (cf. *Poseidonios und die jüdisch-christiliche Genesisexegese*, Leipzig-Berlin, 1914).

18. The passages where Gregory mentions Greek philosophies by name, usually in an unfavorable way, are assembled by Harold Fredrik Cherniss, *The Platonism of Gregory of Nyssa* (University of California Publications in Classical Philology 11, Berkeley, Calif., 1930), pp. 1-12. Cf. A.C. Weiswurm, *The Nature of Human Knowledge according to St. Gregory of Nyssa* (Washington, 1952), pp. 16ff.

19. On the other hand, his disclaimers in *Ep.* 13, addressed to Libanius, may be professional modesty—Vol. 8, 2, pp. 44-46 (MG 46.1048A-1049B).

20. In the notes reference will be made to Gregory's appropriation of philosophical ideas and terminology from all the earlier schools which by the 4th century had become the stock and trade of educated men.

21. For details see Daniélou, p. xxviiff., and the notes. Cf. Cherniss, *op. cit.*; R. Arnou, "Platonisme des Pères," *Dictionnaire de Théologie Catholique* 12 (Paris, 1935): 2258-2392.

22. Daniélou, pp. xi-xiv.

23. R.M. Grant, *The Letter and the Spirit* (London, 1957); R.P.C. Hanson, *Allegory and Event* (Richmond, 1959).

24. The Jewish, Christian, and Moslem interpretations of Moses have been surveyed in the special issue of *Cahiers Sion* published under the title *Moïse: l'homme de l'alliance* (Paris, 1955). For the high exaltation of Moses, see Philo, *De sacr.* 3.8; J. Bonsirven, *Palestinian Judaism in the Time of Jesus Christ* (New York, 1964), pp. 80-82; Moses Hadas, *Hellenistic Culture* (New York, 1959), p. 172.

25. Jaeger, *Two Rediscovered Works*, p. 78, notes the evidence that medieval scribes observed the influence of Philo on Gregory. Daniélou, pp. xiv-xv, notes specific parallels of the *Vita Moysis* with Philo.

26. Trans. by F.H. Colson in the *Loeb Classical Library* (Cambridge, Mass., 1935).

27. Fr. Leo, *Die griechisch-römische Biographie* (Leipzig, 1901). Gregory does not follow the form of the Hellenistic biography but has the same "didactic" interest.

28. Cf. also Philo, *De praemiis* 9.53-56. In the *De Ios.* and *De Abrah.* Philo first describes the literal story drawing edifying lessons from it, then he allegorizes, but he alternates throughout. Cf. *De Abrah.* 18.88 where he refers to "both our expositions, the literal as applied to the man and the allegorical as applied to the soul."

29. Our notes will be full on Philo's treatment of the same events in order to facilitate comparison.

30. Bernard Botte, "La vie de Moïse par Philon," *Moïse*, p. 60.

31. Trans. by Ralph Marcus from the Armenian in *Loeb Classical Library* (Cambridge, Mass., 1953).

32. Philo preferred ὑπόνοια for allegory—see Hanson, *op. cit.*, p. 40. Cf. *De Ios.* 6. 28, "After this literal account of the story, it will be well to explain the underlying (ὑπόνοια) meaning."

33. See especially II, 196 on the tabernacle and priest's garments and the notes for Philo's treatment.

34. Cf. *Midrash Rabbah, Exodus*, trans. S.M. Lehrman (London, 1951) and the haggadic portions (about three-fifths) of *Mekilta de Rabbi Ishmael*, trans. J.Z. Lauterbach (Philadelphia, 1949).

35. *Strom.* 1.23-26.

36. Grant, *op. cit.*, p. 91.

37. Brought together by Daniélou, p. xviii. Gregory's general indebtedness to Origen is well-known—see J.H. Srawley, *The Catechetical Oration of Gregory of Nyssa* (Cambridge, 1956), pp. xix-xxv; William Moore, *Select Writings and Letters of Gregory, Bishop of Nyssa* in *Nicene and Post-Nicene Fathers*,

Vol. 5, pp. 14-23. P. Godet, "Grégoire de Nysse," *Dictionnaire de Théologie Catholique* Vol. 6 (Paris, 1920): 1847-52.

38. Origen begins this section of suggestions for an Exodus allegory by saying, "This descent of the holy fathers into Egypt will appear as granted to this world by the providence of God for the illumination of others, and for the instruction of the human race, that so by this means the souls of others might be assisted in the work of enlightenment." But he refers to the nation, not Moses.

39. Daniélou, *Origène* (Paris, 1948), pp.260ff.

40. Henri de Lubac, " ' Typologie' et 'Allegorisme,' " *Rech. de Sc. Rel.* 34 (1947): 180-226; H.N. Bate, "Some Technical Terms of Greek Exegesis," *Journal of Theological Studies* 24 (October 1922): 59-66.

41. Οὐχ ἱστοπικὸν διήγησιν, 'αλλὰ θεωρίαν νοητήνϑ *Comm. Joh. Frg.* 20.

42. R.M. Grant, *The Earliest Lives of Jesus* (New York, 1961), pp. 120f.

43. Daniélou, "*Akolouthia* chez Grégoire de Nysse," *Rev. des Sci. Rel.* 27 (1953): 236ff; Alexander Kerrigan, *St. Cyril of Alexandria: Interpreter of the Old Testament* (Rome, 1952), pp. 36ff.

44. Bate, *op. cit.*, pp. 62f. A. Vaccari, "La ΘΕΩΡΙΑ nella scuola esegetica di Antiochia," *Biblica* 1 (1920): 14ff.

45. Bate, *op. cit.*, pp. 61ff. See Book I, note 27.

46. De Lubac, *op. cit.*, pp. 181ff.

47. In the *Life of Moses* Gregory also uses ἀναγωγή (II, 223), ϑὑπόνοια (II, 219), and τεοπικός ("a more tropical *theoria*," II, 43) in reference to the nonliteral meaning. The different meanings of *theoria* in Gregory are given by Daniélou, *Platonisme. . .* , p. 148. Cf. Walther Völker, *Gregor von Nyssa als Mystiker* (Wiesbaden, 1955), pp. 146-148, 172ff.

48. Kerrigan, *op. cit.*, pp. 117f., 122.

49. *Ibid.*, pp. 115, 191. Of interest for Gregory's method is Cyril's statement in the prologue to his *Comm. in Isa.* that he intends to expound "the literal text *(historia)* accurately" and give "the interpretation of the spiritual *theoria*" (MG70.9A; cf. 69.16A for *Glaph. in Gen.* 1). He suggests that the things of the old covenant are not valueless when they lead to *theoria*—*De ador. in sp. et verit.* 1.3 (MG 68.137A). Cyril represents a narrowing down from Gregory's interests in his concern for dogma—"all spiritual *theoria* looks toward Christ's mystery" (Frg. 2, 2 Cor. 3.12; *Comm. St. Joh.* Pusey 3,365,25). The few references we have found suggest that someone versed in Cyril of Alexandria would find many points of continuity with Gregory.

50. In addition to the general works cited in note 21, cf. Jaeger, *Two*

Rediscovered Works, pp. 120-124, on Clement of Alexandria, and Kerrigan, *op. cit.*, pp. 135ff.

51. Elsewhere Gregory appeals to inaccuracies in the literal statement as a justification for allegory—*C. Eun.* 3.1.37f., Vol. 2, pp. 16, 20ff. (MG 45.577C-D).

52. Daniélou, pp. xvi-xvii, and in *Moïse*, pp. 276-282.

53. *Moïse*, pp. 245-314.

54. Justin, *Dial.* 131-132; Hippolytus, *Ben. Mos.* (PO 27, 171ff.); Ps. Clem., *Recog.* 1:35; Aphraates, *Demons.* 21 (Pat. Syr. 1, pp. 958-62); Hilary, *De Mys.* 1.16ff.; Clement of Alexandria, *Strom.* 1.23-26.

55. Auguste Luneau in *Moïse*, pp. 283-303. Hence we have fewer references to Latin authors in the notes.

56. Cf. II, 173.

57. Daniélou, *Platonisme*. . . ; Bouyer, *The Spirituality of the New Testament and the Fathers* (Paris, 1963), pp. 351-368; H. V. Balthasar, *Présence et Pensée. Essai sur la philosophie religieuse de Grégoire de Nysse* (Paris, 1942); W. Völker, *Gregor von Nyssa als Mystiker* (Wiesbaden, 1955); J.T. Muckle, "The Doctrine of St. Gregory of Nyssa on Man as the Image of God," *Mediaeval Studies* 7 (1945): 77-84; Endre v. Ivánka, *Hellenisches und Christliches im frühbyzantinischen Geistesleben* (Vienna, 1948).

58. Consult the notes on the passages referred to for parallels in other works of Gregory and for fuller discussion.

59. See the works by Daniélou, Muckle, Ivánka, and Völker referred to in note 57. Discussions of Gregory's mysticism center around his understanding of ecstasy. For a modification of Daniélou's view of Gregory (*Platonisme*. . . , pp. 261-73, discusses ecstasy), see Ekkehard Mühlenberg, *Die Unendlichkeit Gottes bei Gregor von Nyssa*, Forschungen zur Kirchen- und Dogmengeschichte 16 (Göttingen, 1966), pp. 155ff. He insists that the psychological attempt at meaning is contradicted by progress in knowledge implied in ecstasy. Völker, *op. cit.*, pp. 202-215, sees Gregory's view of ecstasy in the context of his piety. Ecstasy unites within itself an intellectual and an emotional side. It speaks the language of Plato, but permeates the whole with a Christian spirit and finally fits itself into the framework of negative theology. Gregory gives what he had inherited from Origen a form that the Areopagite could use in his building of a speculative structure.

60. See Aubineau, SC 119: 143-213; Muckle, *loc. cit.*; R. Leys, "La théologie spirituelle de Grégorie de Nysse," *Studia Patristica* 2 (1957): 495-511.

61. Daniélou's writings urge this as Gregory's major new contribution and adopts the Greek word ἐπέκτασις to express it: *Platonisme*. . . , pp. 291-307; *Glory to Glory*, pp. 46-71; *Eranos Jahrbuch*, 23 (1954): 409-418; *Dictionnaire de Spiritualité* II: 1882-85.

NOTES

62. *Or.* 38 (MG 36.317B); cf. II, 237ff.

63. Daniélou, *"Akolouthia,"* *Rev. des Sci. Rel.* 27 (1953): 236ff.

64. The artificiality of imposing the later "three ways" of mysticism on Gregory is the major criticism leveled at Daniélou's *Platonisme* . . . ; see Muckle, *op. cit.*, p. 84, and I. Hausherr's review in *Revue d'ascétique et de mystique* 22 (1946): 310-314.

65. See note 37.

66. Brooks Otis, "Cappadocian Thought as a Coherent System," *DOP* 12 (1958): 108, 115. On Origen's "satiety" with God, in contrast to Gregory's "continual progress," cf. M. Harl, "Recherches sur l'Origénisme d' Origène: la 'satiété: (κόεος) de la contemplation comme motif de la chute des âmes," *Studia Patristica* 8 (Berlin, 1966): 373-405. For the reality of temptation in the *Life of Moses*, see Daniélou, *Platonisme* . . . , pp. 87ff.

67. *Two Rediscovered Works*, esp. pp. 174ff. But see J. Gribomont, "Le *De Instituto Christiano* et le Messalianisme de Grégoire de Nysse," *Studia Patristica* 5 (1962): 312ff.

68. Mühlenberg, *op. cit.*; W. Völker, "Zur Gotteslehre Gregors von Nyssa," *Vigiliae Christianae* 9 (1955): 103-128.

69. Johann Lenz, *Jesus Christus nach der Lehre des hl. Gregor von Nyssa* (Trier, 1925).

70. W.W. Jaeger, *Gregor von Nyssa's Lehre vom Heiligen Geist* (Leiden, 1966). Ludger Kleinheidt, *Sancti Gregorii episcopi Nysseni doctrina de Angelis* (Freiburg, 1860).

71. F. Hilt, *Des hl. Gregors von Nyssa Lehre vom Menschen systematisch dargestellt* (Köln, 1890). See Book II, note 29 for further references.

72. J. Gaith, *La conception de la liberté chez Grégoire de Nysse*, Etudes de phil. médiév. 43 (Paris, 1953). See Book II, note 5.

73. Gregory's thoughts on baptism do not show the originality his treatment of some other things do, and in the *Vita Moysis* what he has to say fits his treatment in his other works—*Or. cat.* 33-36, 38-40 (MG 44.84-92, 97-105); *In bapt. Christi* (MG 46.577-600); *Adv. eos qui bapt. diff.* (MG 46.416-432).

74. See Book II, note 102.

75. T.A. Goggin, *The Times of Saint Gregory of Nyssa As Reflected in the Letters and the Contra Eunomium* (Washington, 1947), pp. 145-177.

76. Before Christianity had its own cycle of saints, the holy men of the Old Testament served as examples—Auguste Luneau in *Moïse*, p. 288. See M. Simon, "Les saints d'Israel dans la devotion de l'Eglise ancienne," *Rev. Hist. Phil. Rel.* 34 (1954): 98-128.

77. Daniélou in *Moïse*, p. 269.

78. *C. Eun.* 2.322, Vol. 1, p. 320, 9-12 (MG 45.1017D).

79. MG 46.857C.

80. *C. Eun.* 2.85-92, Vol. 1, pp. 251, 22—253, 30 (MG 45.940A-941B).
81. MG 46.713A-B.
82. Daniélou in *Moïse*, pp. 269ff.
83. *In inscrip. Ps.* 1.7, Vol. 5, pp. 43, 21—45, 20 (MG 44.456C-457B); *De castig.* (MG 46.316A-C); *In laud. frat. Bas.* (MG 46.808D-813A)— compared to *Vita Moysis* by J.A. Stein, *Encomium of St. Gregory of Nyssa On his Brother St. Basil* (Washington, 1928), pp. 20-23.
84. *In Cant.* 11, Vol. 6, p. 322, 9-12 (MG 44.1000C). The three incidents referred to have been variously identified: (1) Exod. 19.18 or 3.2; (2) Exod. 20.21 or 24.15-18; (3) Exod. 24.15-18 or 20.21. If the first set of passages is taken, then Gregory has in mind different statements made in connection with the Sinai theophany; the difficulty is that in the LXX the darkness is mentioned in 20.21 and the cloud in 24.18 so the order is wrong. If the effort is made to identify three separate incidents, the identity of the third one still poses a problem, and yet this must be the most important one for Gregory. Without reference to the *Canticles* text, Dorothy Emmet, *op. cit.*, p. 43 (following Daniélou, *Platonisme* . . . , pp. 17-23) proposes three stages in the *Life of Moses*: (1) purification and illumination—burning bush; (2) separation from the world—passing through the cloud in traversing the desert; (3) entering the darkness of Sinai. Number 2 does not seem to have this importance in the *Life of Moses*. If the *Canticles* passage is to be brought into relation to *Vit. Mos.*, we would propose that the "light" is the burning bush, the "cloud" is the Sinai theophany (taking 20-24 as a whole), and the "darkness" is the seeing of the "back" of God while the hand of God shadowed Moses in the cleft of the rock (Exod. 33.20-33). Although the word "darkness" does not occur in the latter, this could be Gregory's interpretation. This scheme corresponds to the events that are the basis of the three principal passages on the knowledge of God in the *Life of Moses* (see above p. 14) and which are elaborated on in the passage cited in the next note. P. Marechal *Etudes sur la Psychologie des mystiques* (Paris, 1937), II, pp. 108f., writes on Moses' three theophanies.
85. *In Cant.* 12, Vol. 6, pp. 354, 8—356, 16 (MG 44.1025A-D).
86. Heb. 11.25.
87. Exod. 33.13 modified.
88. Exod. 33.17, LXX.
89. See the bibliography for publication information on the editions and translations of the *Vita Moysis*.
90. Aubineau, SC 119: 218.
91. For information on the manuscripts, see Daniélou, pp. xxxii-xxxv; Musurillo, pp. v-xix.

Book I

1. Reading ἐπικλάζοντες. The reading of the text, ἐποκλάζοντες, occurs in II, 57.

2. The same comparison occurs in Gregory of Nazianzus, *Or.* 42, *In laudem Bas.* 15 (MG 36.513D-516A).

3. Phil. 3.14. The racecourse is a favorite imagery in the work; cf. the phrase "to devote your soul to the race of virtue" in the Introduction to *De instituto Christiano* Vol. 8, 1, p. 43, 13.

4. *De perfectione* has a similar Introduction, being written in response to a request for direction in attaining perfection "by the life according to virtue," Vol. 8, 1, p. 173 (MG 46.252A). There Gregory proposes Paul as a leader as he does Moses in this treatise. The *De instituto Christiano* was written in response to a request from a group of monks for Gregory's ideas on the goal of the virtuous life and the way by which this might be attained—Vol. 8, 1, p. 41, 10ff.

5. On spiritual fatherhood see I. Hausherr, *Direction spirituelle en Orient autrefois*, Orientalia Christiana Analecta 144 (Rome, 1955), pp. 17-39.

6. Gregory also refers to his old age in *De inf. qui praem. abr.* (MG 46.161B); *C. Eun.* 2.605, Vol. 1, p. 403, 6-7 (MG 45.1112D); *Ref. conf. Eun.* 208, Vol. 2, p. 401, 3 (MG 45.561B).

7. The customary way to begin a *logos* was to ask for divine guidance. Cf. *In Hex.* (MG 44.68C-D). We have rendered it "treatise."

8. See note 83 for κατανοέω.

9. Ps. 13.5, LXX (would be 14.5 of the Hebrew, but missing from Masoretic text).

10. Cf. *In Cant.* 6, Vol. 6, p. 173, 11ff. (MG 44.885C-D). See Aristotle, *Categories* 4b 20ff.

11. Phil. 3.13. This text is the theme of the whole treatise, namely that perfection is a continual progress. See Introduction, pp. 12-13, especially n. 61.

12. Cf. *In Ps.* 1.8, Vol. 5, p. 63, 4-5 (MG 44.480A), "the non-existence of the good becomes sin." *In Eccl.* 7, Vol. 5, pp. 406, 16—407, 3 (MG 44.725A), similarly has evil opposite to good and nonbeing to Being. For Gregory's use of limitation by contraries see also *Or. cat.* 6 (MG 45.28C); *C. Eun.* 1.167-68, Vol. 1, p. 77 (MG 45.301C).

13. Cf. Aristotle, *Nicomachean Ethics* 1157a30.

14. "The nature of good is true being"—*De an. et res.* (MG 46.93B). Cf. *Ep. can.* (MG 45.224D-225A) where Gregory affirms that the truly beautiful is only in virtue and in that nature which is virtue's source. That

NOTES

there is no intermediate state between virtue and vice was a Stoic doctrine
(J. von Arnim, *Stoicorum veterum fragmenta* 1. 566), but is also in Philo (*Ebr.*
7; *Sac.* 135) and Origen (*Comm. Jno.* 20.13). That God is virtue was repug-
nant to Platonists (Albinus, *Didas.* 28) and may be derived from the Stoic
principle that human and divine virtue are the same (von Arnim, *op. cit.*
1.564; 3.245ff.), but see Plato, *Theaet.* 176b.

15. See II, 305-306. The present passage is discussed by Balás, pp.
154f.

16. The basis of the perpetual progress in virtue is the divine infinity.
Cf. II, 236. See Plotinus, *Enn.* 6, 7, 32. Since the good is unlimited, there is
no limit to the advance in the good—*Cat. or.* 21 (MG 45.60A); *C. Eun.*
1.290, Vol. 1, p. 112, 15-20 (MG 340D); *De an. et res.* (MG 46.96C-97A); *De
hom. op.* 21 (MG 44.201B-C). For the constant increase in the desire for
God, cf. *In Cant.* 1, Vol. 6, p. 31, 6-9 (MG 44.777B); 12, Vol. 6, p. 366,
11-20 (MG 44.1036A). On the general subject see Ekkehard Mühlenberg,
Die Unendlichkeit Gottes bei Gregor von Nyssa, Forschungen zur Kirchen—und
Dogmengeschichte 16 (Göttingen, 1966), esp. pp. 159ff.

17. Matt. 5.48.

18. This thesis that perfection is to be found in progress itself is
developed in *De perf.*, especially the conclusion, Vol. 8, 1, pp. 213, 14—
214, 6 (MG 46.285C-D). The contrast of this philosophy of growth to the
Greek conception according to which change involves imperfection is developed by Daniélou, "La Colombe et la ténèbre dans la mystique byzantine ancienne," *Eranos Jahrbuch* 23 (1954): 400-405.

19. Isa. 51.2.

20. On the symbolism of the sea, see H. Rahner, "Antenna Crucis,
II, Das Meer der Welt," *Zeitschr. Kath. Theol.* 66 (1942): 89-118.

21. Palladius, *Hist. Laus.*, Prol., 2 and 15 offers stories of both sexes
for models.

22. Philo, *De sacrif.* 27.90.

23. On the place of the saints of the Old Testament in the early
Church, see Introduction, n. 76. On Abraham as a model of virtue in the
fathers, see Daniélou, "Abraham dans la tradition chrétienne," *Cahiers
Sioniens* (1951): 160-179. Abraham and Sarah are referred to by Gregory in
De deitate filii et sp. sanc. (MG 46.569). For other Gregory references to
Abraham, cf. Int., n. 78, 80, 81.

24. Ps. 75.2,3.

25. κατὰ τὴν πεόχειέον ἔννοιαν. This formulation seems to be
different for Gregory from the κοιναὶ ἔννοιαι, those common truths of the
faith on which he dwells, which he borrowed from Stoicism and Neo-
platonism, and which he makes the framework of his religious philosophy.

NOTES

See Jules Gross, *La divinisation du chrétien d'après les Pères grecs* (Paris, 1938), p. 219.

26. See Introduction, n. 82 and 83 for other passages where Gregory proposes Moses as a pattern of virtue.

27. For the background of "understanding" (διάνοια) in Greek treatment of allegories, see R.M. Grant, *The Letter and the Spirit* (London, 1957), pp. 125f.; for "history" (ἱστοεία), see Introduction at note 42.

28. Exod. 2.2ff.

29. Josephus, *Ant.* 2.9.226-31. Jewish traditions surrounding the birth of Moses are given by Renée Bloch, "Moïse dans la tradition rabbinique," *Moïse*, pp. 115f.

30. Exod. 2.3, LXX.

31. A similar wording in *C. Eun.* 2.285, Vol. 1, p. 310, 13ff. (MG 45.1008A).

32. *Midrash Rabbah, Exodus* 1.25, has the infant Moses reject a series of Egyptian nurses before the princess tries a Hebrew nurse.

33. Acts 7.20-22; Philo, *Vit. Mos.* 1.5.21-24. Cf. also Clement of Alexandria, *Strom.* 1.23, where he summarizes Hellenistic Jewish tradition; elsewhere in Gregory, *In laud. frat. Bas.* (MG 46.789B; 808D). It has been suggested that this midrash might go back to a Near Eastern tradition according to which a foundling is brought up as a scribe — Brevard Childs, "The Birth of Moses," *Journal of Biblical Literature* 84 (June, 1965): 114.

For Christians and classical education, see H.I. Marrou, *A History of Education in Antiquity*, trans. George Lamb (New York, 1956), pp. 419-438. Gregory uses the phrase τὴν ἔξωθεν παίδευσιν for the education carried on "outside" the Church (cf. II, 13). We have translated "pagan," or "profane," according to the context. For the word, see H. Karpp, "Christennamen," *RAC* 2; 1137f.; Ilona Opelt, "Griechische und Lateinische Bezeichnungen der Nichtchristen. Ein terminologisoher Versuch," *Vig. Christ.* 19 (1965): 1-22. For Gregory's attitude toward pagan education, see Introduction, pp. 4f. and Bk. II, n. 57; cf. T.A. Goggin, *The Times of Gregory of Nyssa as Reflected in the Letters and the Contra Eunomium* (Washington, 1947), pp. 99ff.; W. Jaeger, *Early Christianity and Greek Paideia* (Cambridge, Mass., 1961), pp. 86ff.

34. See W.C. van Unnik, *Tarsus or Jerusalem* (London, 1962) for the use of τεοφή and παίδευσις for stages in ancient education.

35. Cf. *In inscrip.* Ps. 1.7, Vol. 5, p. 43, 24-26 (MG 44.456C); *In laud. frat. Bas.* (MG 46.808D-809A); Philo, *Vit. Mos.* 1.7.32.

36. Exod. 2.11-14.

37. Exod. 2.15-21. The interpretation of Moses in Midian follows Philo, *Vit. Mos.* 1.9.46-50. Cf. Bk. II, n. 23. For the ascetic life as

philosophy, cf. *Vita S. Mac.*, Vol. 8, 1, p. 377, 4 (MG 46.965B) and *passim*; *De inst. Chris.* Vol. 8, 1, p. 41, 20f.

38. Philo, *Vit. Mos.* 1.11.59 is very close. The treatment of the whole episode begins with 10.51.

39. Exod. 3.2-5.

40. Is this detail influenced by Acts 9.3 and 22.6? Philo says that the form in the midst of the flame was a "light shining brighter than fire," *Vit. Mos.* 1.12.66. Gregory adds details to accent the miraculous—Daniélou, "Moïse exemple et figure chez Grégoire de Nysse," *Moïse*, p. 273.

41. Philo, *Vit. Mos.* 1.12.65.

42. For the sandals made of "dead skins" see Bk. II, n. 29.

43. Exod. 4.1-7.

44. Exod. 4.19-27.

45. Exod. 4.29-31.

46. That the command was to increase the levy of bricks does not correspond to Exod. 5.4ff.

47. Exod. 7.10-12. Philo, *Vit. Mos.* 1.16.91ff. uses similar language.

48. Exod. 7.17ff.

49. Wisd. 19.18; Philo, *Vit. Mos.* 1.17.96-97. Cf. *ibid.*, 1.26.143, "Earth, water, air, fire, the constituent parts of that nature which it is impossible to escape, joined in the attack. And the strangest thing of all was that the same elements in the same place and at the same time brought destruction to one people and safety to the other." The comparison of the plagues to a military campaign is in *Midrash Rabbah, Exodus* 15.27.

50. Exod. 7.20-22.

51. Exod. 8.1-15.

52. Exod. 10.21-23.

53. The Greek has σκινῖπες; the type of insect is not certain.

54. Gregory does not follow the biblical order of the plagues in Exod. 8-10 (cf. Ps. 105(D-R 104).29-36). He has yet another order in II, 63-88. Philo's topical arrangement is different still—*Vit. Mos.* 1.17.96-24.139. Gregory has another summary of the plagues in *In Cant.* 3, Vol. 6, p. 77, 8ff. (MG 44.813B-C).

55. Exod. 11.46; 12.29-31.

56. Heb. 11.28.

57. Exod. 12.35f., 15; 13.17-19.

58. See Bk. II, n. 126.

59. Exod. 14.5-15. For the Red Sea episode, cf. Philo, *Vit. Mos.* 1.30.169-32.180 and 2.45.246-46.257.

60. Exod. 14.15, based on the absence of any mention in the biblical text of Moses' crying to God although it says that God "heard his cry," as he

NOTES

explains in *C. Eun.* 2.267-68, Vol. 1, p. 304, 21ff. (MG 45.1002A); cf. II, 118. Philo, *Quis rer. div.* 4.14.

61. Exod. 13.21-22. Cf. Philo, *Vit. Mos.* 1.29.166.

62. Gregory treats the formation of clouds also in *In Hex.* (MG 44.97D); *C. Eun.* 1.300, Vol. 1, p. 115, 12f. (MG 45.344B); 3.39, Vol. 2, p. 17, 8ff. (MG 45.577D).

63. The word δᾳδουχεῖν, borrowed from the language of the mysteries, is found in Gregory for the pillar of fire in *In Christi res* 4 (MG 46.681B-C), with which compare *In Cant.* 15, Vol. 6, p. 432, 12 (MG 44.1089A). On the Christian use of mystery terminology see A.D. Nock, *Early Gentile Christianity and its Hellenistic Background* (New York, 1964 reprint), pp. 30ff., 67f., 117-124, 132-143; "The Vocabulary of the New Testament," *Journal of Biblical Literature* 52 (1933): 134; "Mysterion," *Harvard Studies in Classical Philology* 60 (1951): 201-204. Cf. n. 74.

64. Exod. 14.16-22.

65. Philo, *Vit. Mos.* 1.32.177-180.

66. Exod. 14.23-31.

67. On τεόπαιον, see Christine Mohrmann, "A propos de deux mots controversés de la latinité chrétienne: tropaeum-nomen," *Vig. Christ.* 8 (1954): 155-173; Jean Bernardi, "Le mot τεόπαιον applique aux martyrs," *Vig. Christ.* 8 (1954): 174f.

68. Exod. 15.22-25.

69. Num. 9.15-23 supplies the thought.

70. Exod. 15.27. Cf. Bk. II, n. 153 for Philo.

71. Exod. 17.1-7. Philo, *Vit. Mos.* 1.38.210-213. See Bk. II, n. 156.

72. Exod. 16 is the basis for sections 36-38. Gregory has inverted the order of the manna and the water from the rock. For the manna, cf. Philo, *Vit. Mos.* 1.35.191-37.209 and 2.47.258-62.

73. Exod. 17.8-16. Philo, *Vit. Mos.* 1.39.214-19.

74. Exod. 19.10ff. The Sinai theophany is omitted in Philo's *Vita Mosis* but is treated in *De decalogo* 11.44-49. *De decalogo* 10.41 uses mystery terminology for Moses' receiving the Law, and Moses is a priest of the mysteries who leads the people in their initiation in the *Vita Mosis* 2.15.71-75. On Moses as an initiate into the mysteries, cf. Daniélou, *Moïse*, pp. 274f.; see E.R. Goodenough, *By Light Light* (New Haven, 1935), pp. 199-234. The terminology of mystery initiation was employed by Hellenistic philosophers to express learning philosophical doctrines.

75. Gregory frequently refers to "stains" or "defilements"—*De inst. Chris.* Vol. 8, 1, pp. 44, 5; 48, 2; 48, 18; 64, 5; *In Cant.* 5, Vol. 6, p. 162, 8 (MG 44.877C).

76. Gregory makes a distinction between the rational and the irra-

153

NOTES

tional (animals), a distinction not made in the biblical text.

77. Cf. Heb. 12:18-21 for the description in sections 43-44. In *Or. Dom.* 2 (MG 44.1137A) he draws on the Hebrews passage to contrast Moses at Sinai with Christ, the new Lawgiver, who brings divine grace.

78. The experience of the sound of the trumpets (Exod. 19.19) made a strong impression on Gregory. Aristobulus spoke of the trumpet at Sinai sounded "by God without any aid," Eusebius, *Praep. Evang.* 8.10. Cf. for Gregory's statement Philo, *De decal.* 9.32-35. Origen gives the same explanation of God's voice at Jesus' baptism—*C. Cels.* 2.72; 6.62. See the note by Henry Chadwick, *Origen: Contra Celsum* (Cambridge, 1953), p. 121, on unvibrated air.

79. Exodus 34.29ff. is apparently the basis for Gregory's statement, but he does not follow the biblical account. Paul's use of the Exodus passage in 2 Cor. 3 stays closer to the biblical text. The role of mediator is what Gregory underlines in one of the primary texts where he treats of Moses— *In inscrip. Ps.* 1.7, Vol. 5, p. 45, 7ff. (MG 44.457B-C). See II, 319. Philo discusses Moses as legislator in *Vit. Mos.* 2.9.51-10.53. On Christ as mediator, see *Ref. conf. Eun.* 142-44, Vol. 2, pp. 373, 16—374, 24 (MG 45.532D-533A). On Moses as mediator in Judaism, cf. *Ass. Mos.* 1.14.

80. See the mystery terminology discussion, Bk. I, n. 63 and 74, and Bk. II, n. 203.

81. Gregory follows the Philonian exegesis in which darkness signifies the incomprehensibility of the divine essence and its transcendence of all conceptual knowledge. Cf. especially *In Cant.* 6, Vol. 6, p. 181, 4ff. (MG 44.892C-D). See II, 162ff. and notes there.

82. Exod. 20.3-7.

83. For ὑπόληψις and other cognitive terms, see Aubineau, SC 119: 173, and Weiswurm, *Nature of Human Knowledge*, p. 163.

84. We know that God is but not what he is—cf. Balás, p. 128. *De an. et res.* (MG 46.40C); *C. Eun.* 2.13, 71, 98, Vol. 1, p. 230, 26-30, p. 248, 1-3, and p. 255, 9-14 (MG 45.916A, 933D, and 944A-B); *In Cant.* 11, Vol. 6, p. 335, 1 (MG 44.1009C-D); *De mort.* (MG 46.513C). See Bk. II, n. 208. Walther Völker, "Zur Gotteslehre Gregors von Nyssa," *Vig. Chris.* 9 (1955): 103-128.

85. Cf. Lev. 19.18. For the widespread use of this passage, and its relation to the Golden Rule, see Albrecht Dihle, *Die Goldene Regel*, Studienhefte zur Altertumswissenschaft, 7 (Göttingen, 1962).

86. Cf. Rom. 13.10.

87. Exod. 20.12-17.

88. Exod. 25-27 gives the instructions for building the tabernacle and its furnishings. Gregory's treatment follows Philo, *Vit. Mos.* 2.15.74. See Bk. II, n. 212.

NOTES

89. A similar summary listing in Heb. 9.2ff.

90. Exod. 25.9, 40; 31.1ff.; 35:30-38.31.

91. For the Jewish background of ἀχειροποίητος and its introduction into the Christian vocabulary, see Marcel Simon, *Saint Stephen and the Hellentists* (London, 1958), pp. 89ff., 95ff.; idem, "Retour du Christ et reconstruction du Temple dans la penseé chrétienne primitive," in *Aux Sources de la Tradition Chretienne. Mélanges Goguel* (Neuchatel-Paris, 1950), pp. 251ff.

92. Exod. 28. Philo, *Vit. Mos.* 2.23.109-27.140. See Bk. II, n. 256. For an effort to picture the appearance of the priest's vestments, see *Illustrated World of the Bible Library* (New York, 1958), Vol. 1, p. 166. For discussion see Edgar Haulotte, *Symbolique du vêtement selon la bible*, Théologie 65 (Paris, 1966), pp. 44-59, 167-175.

93. Gold thread is new in the priestly garments and was not used in the tabernacle.

94. Gregory's account is not altogether clear, hence in the succeeding sections our translation is more interpretative than usual. Gregory substitutes for ἐπωμίς the "ephod," ἐπωμίδες, the "shoulder pieces," which held it together, and uses πορπαί for the latter. He reads "emerald" with the LXX whereas the Hebrew has "onyx." For Philo's wording, see *Quaest. Ex.* 2.108 with the note by Ralph Marcus, *Philo Supplement* II (Loeb Classical Library), p. 157.

95. Gregory draws on Exod. 39.15-19 (36.22-27, LXX), the account of the making of the garments, which adds details not in the instructions for making them in chapter 28.

96. This "ornament" is the "rational" of the Douay, the "pectoral" of the Jerusalem Bible.

97. Cf. Epiphanius, *De gemmis*, ed. and trans. from the Georgian version by R.P. Blake, *Studies and Documents* 2 (London, 1934).

98. The words were "Holy to the Lord," Exod. 28.36.

99. Exod. 32.15f.

100. Exod. 32. Philo. *Vit. Mos.* 2.31.159-33.173.

101. Literally "became outside nature" or "departed from nature." Cf. I, 60. For Gregory's "mysticism" see Introduction n. 59. The phrase "having gone outside himself" is used of prophetic inspiration, *In Ascensionem* (MG 46.693A). See Völker, *Gregor von Nyssa*, 203f. on leaving the body. "Nature" here designates the terrestial condition of man—cf. *In S. Steph.* (MG 46.713B-C); *De beat.* 7 (MG 44.1280C)—a sense actually less frequent in Gregory than that which designates man in his original and ideal condition. See Bk. II, n. 29 for bibliography on his doctrine of man, and Bk. II, n. 194 for similar expressions.

102. Exod. 32.26-29.

NOTES

103. Exod. 34.1.

104. Exod. 36.8-40.31 and note especially 39.43 and 40.14.

105. Num. 12.1-15.

106. Num. 11.4-34. In his use of material from Numbers Gregory does not follow the biblical order.

107. Num. 13-14. Philo, *Vit. Mos.* 1.40.220-42.236.

108. Num. 20.2-3.

109. See I, 35.

110. This incident was already a tradition in the Old Testament; for the wording, cf. Deut. 8.15; Ps. 113.8; Wisd. 11.4; Philo, *Leg. alleg.* 2.21 and 84. For the translation "jutting" or "abrupt" rock, note the representations in early Christian art where the rock always has the appearance of a steep ledge. Indeed, of all the episodes from Moses' life represented in early Christian art the striking of the rock is the most common. For reproductions see *Dictionnaire d'archéologie chrétienne et de liturgie* 11, col. 1661ff., and C.F. Rogers, "Baptism and Christian Archaeology," *Studia Biblica et Ecclesiastica* 5 (1903): 247-253. Cf. J. Leroy, "Images de Moïse dans la tradition juive et chrétienne," *Moïse*, pp. 363f. References to the incident are common in Christian literature—Justin, *Dial.* 131; Tert., *De bapt.* 9; Ps. Clem., *Recog.* 1.35; *Didas.* 26.50 (Connolly, p. 220); Eusebius, *H. E.* 7.21.5; Jerome, *Brev. in Ps.* 77. See further, Bk. II, n. 156 and 381.

111. Num. 21.6-9. Cf. 1 Cor. 10.9f. Philo, *Leg. alleg.* 2.19.76-78 compares the serpents of this passage to pleasures.

112. Num. 16. Philo, *Vit. Mos.* 2.50.280-285.

113. Num. 17. Philo, *Vit. Mos.* 2.33.178-34.186.

114. Num. 20.14-22, especially v. 17. Gregory's compression of the narrative has distorted the biblical account. The fighting comes in connection with a similar request of Sehon, king of the Amorites, in Num. 21.21-25. The passage through Edom in Philo, *Vit. Mos.* 1.43.239-44.249; the fighting with Sehon, 1.47.258-262.

115. Num. 22.2ff. Philo's treatment of Balaam and Balak in *Vit. Mos.* 1.48.263-52.291.

116. On augury, which belonged to the "artificial" type of divination, see Cicero, *De divinatione* I, 72-92. Cf. Philo, *Vit. Mos.* 1.51.282 on the passage, and II, 293.

117. The attribution of the power of sorcerers to demons is not in the biblical account but is a common theme in ancient Christianity. See Daniélou, "Demon," *Dictionnaire de spiritualité* 3: 153-160.

118. Num. 24.2ff.

119. Num. 25. See chapter 31 for the defeat of the Midianites. Philo, *Vit. Mos.* 1.53.292-58.318.

120. Deut. 34.

121. Also noted in *In laud. frat. Bas.* (MG 46.813A).
122. Simonides, *Frg.* 4, 5 (Bergk; 26, 5 Page).
123. Cf. *In inscrip. Ps.* 1.7, Vol. 5, p. 45, 2-4 (MG 44.457B).

Book II

1. Exod. 1.16.
2. Gregory refers to the Greek idea of flux; see Bk. I, n. 18. He often stresses that human beings are always changing—*De virg.* 6, Vol. 8, 1, pp. 280-281 (MG 352A-D); *Or. cat.* 21 (MG 45.60A-B); *De op. hom.* 16 (MG 44.184C). This mutability of our nature is used by Gregory to show the possibility of "ever changing for the better by growth in the good"—*In Cant.* 6, Vol. 6, p. 174, 8-9 (MG 44.885D); cf. *De perf.* Vol. 8, 1, p. 212, 17—214, 6 (MG 46.285A-D), where the changeableness of our nature becomes a pinion in our flight to higher things. B.D. Jackson's article "Sources of Origen's Doctrine of Freedom," *Church History* 35 (March 1966): 13-23, points to certain Platonic doctrines, notably *Laws* 903d.
3. This interpretation of female and male birth is found in Philo, *Quaest. Ex.* 1.7-8; *Leg. alleg.* 3.1.3; cf. 3.87.243; and in Origen, *In Ex. hom.* 2.1-3.
4. Aristotle, *De generatione et corruptione*.
5. The importance of free will (both "choice" and "free will" have been used in translating προαίρεσις) for Gregory's spirituality has been brought out by Jaeger, *Two Rediscovered Works*, pp. 85-107; cf. J.T. Muckle, "The Doctrine of St. Gregory of Nyssa on Man as the Image of God," *Mediaeval Studies* 7 (1945): 66-69; Harold Fredrik Cherniss, *The Platonism of Gregory of Nyssa* (Berkeley, 1930), pp. 52f. Cf. "We can arrive without difficulty at whatever we wish by our thoughts"—*De prof. Chris.*, Vol. 8, 1, p. 140, 9f. (MG 46.248C-D).
6. Birth applied to the development of virtue is in Philo, *Leg. alleg.* 3.63.180; *Cher.* 12.42-15.52; *De Abrah.* 20.99-101; and in the Hermetica (Festugière, *La révelation d'Hermes*, 2, pp. 550f.). Aristotle, *Eth. Nic.* 4.7 has the generation of man by himself. See also Origen, *In Num. hom.* 20.2. Gregory develops the idea often—*In Eccl.* 6, Vol. 5, p. 380, 3ff. (MG 44.701D); *Or. cat.* 39 (MG 45.97D).
7. See text at Bk. I, n. 29.
8. The control by the λογισμοί is a continual theme throughout the book. The word in Gregory customarily means the "rational faculties," but in II, 16 it refers to philosophical reasonings. For the philosophical use of the term see Albinus, *Eisag.* 6 (p. 150, 27 Hermann); Athenagoras, *Embassy* 8.1; 9, 1; cf. also Philo, *De vita contemplativa* 5, 40; *Quis rer. div.* 53.265ff.

9. For the use of αἴνιγμα by the Greek allegorists, see R.M. Grant, *The Letter and the Spirit*, pp. 120f.

10. Maximus of Tyre, *Dissert*. 40.5; Marcus Aurelius 5.23; Methodius, *Symp*. 2.

11. Exod. 2.3. This is a Philonic type of exegesis. Elsewhere—*In bapt. Christi* (MG 46.589C-D)—Gregory follows Origen in giving a baptismal interpretation to the passage (*In Ex. hom.* 2.4).

12. Exod. 2.10 mentions only the adoption. The "History," I, 17, has the adoption take place out of the princess's good will; that it was due to her sterility was a part of Jewish tradition—Artapan in Eusebius, *Praep. Evang.* 9.29; cf. Philo, *Vit. Mos.* 1.4.13. See Bk. I, n. 33 on ἔξωθεν. Origen interpreted the daughter of Pharaoh as the church of the Gentiles (*In Ex. hom.* 2.4). Here as often we see Gregory working with a particular kind of exegetical tradition but applying it in his own way.

13. See Plutarch, *Mor.* 479E.

14. For the figure, Philo compares "ignorance and lack of education" to "childlessness and infertility of soul"—*Quaest. Ex.* 2.19. Isa. 26.18 may be the source of the imagery.

15. The same imagery in Philo, *Leg. alleg.* 1.24.75-76. See *In inscrip. Ps.* 2.15, Vol. 5, p. 164, 4ff. (MG 44.596A-B); *Or. in laud. Greg. Thaum.* (MG 46.901A). On *theognosia* see Bk. II, n. 174.

16. Same contrast in Philo, *Leg. alleg.* 3.87.244-45.

17. Exod. 2.7-9.

18. Gregory develops this symbolism in *In laud. frat. Bas.* (MG 46.809A). On the Church as mother see Joseph C. Plumpe, *Mater Ecclesia* (Washington, 1943). On milk as the Church's teaching, see Clement Alexandria, *Paed.* 1.6.42, where Clement says that the Church as Virgin Mother has no milk of her own so she must offer only the Word as spiritual milk.

19. Note the idea of "fathers" of the Church versus those on the "outside" (profane). See Bk. I, n. 5.

20. Philo, *Leg. alleg.* 3.12.37-38; *Fug.* 26.148. Gregory uses εὐσέβεια, on which cf. n. 62.

21. "He who is found to be in the midst of two lives acts as a mediator between them, in order to give the victory to the purer one by destroying the inferior one"—*In Cant.* 12, Vol. 6, p. 351, 6 (MG 44.1021D), with which cf. p. 344, 15ff. (MG 44.1017B). See also *De perf.*, Vol. 8, 1, p. 180, 9-22 (MG 46.257C-D) for a close parallel to this paragraph. *In laud. frat. Bas.* (MG 46.809A-B) interprets the killing of the Egyptian by Moses as the victory of the spirit over the flesh.

22. See I, 5. Cf. Philo, *Quaest. Ex.* 2.17.

23. Basil applies the Midian episode to his withdrawal after his

student days at Athens—*Comm. in Isa.*, Proem. (MG 30.129A), an event to which Gregory also refers—*In laud. frat. Bas.* (MG 46.809B-C); cf. *In inscrip. Ps.* 1.7, Vol. 5, pp. 43, 26—44, 3 (MG 44.456C).

24. The image of the mind as shepherd of sheep is in Philo, *Sacr.* 10.45 (his *Vit. Mos.* 1.11.60 treats Moses' experience as a shepherd as a training ground for kingship—followed by Clement Alexandria, *Strom.* 1.23) and in Origen, *Hom. Jer.* 5.6, where the irrational movements of the soul are sheep and Christ is the good shepherd. The shepherds of Bethlehem suggest the same imagery in *In diem nat. Christi* (MG 46.1137B). The motif of living at peace with even wild animals is prominent in Christian monasticism; the theme is placed in full perspective by George Williams, *Wilderness and Paradise in Christian Thought* (New York, 1962).

25. The domination of the *nous* is Platonic, but modified here by the Stoic idea of "leading."

26. The Hebrew word in Exod. 3.2, 3 refers to a thorny bush; cf. Philo, *Vit. Mos.* 1.12.65; Clement Alexandria, *Paed.* 2.8.75. In Judaism the burning bush was a symbol of Israel and the thorns represent the sufferings of Israel—R. Bloch, *Moïse*, p. 103 (cf. *Midrash Rabbah, Exodus* 2:5 and Philo, *Vit. Mos.* 1.12.67). (For thorns as a symbol of sin see Bk. II, n. 118.) For Hippolytus, *Ben. Mos.* (PO 27, pp. 172f.), God "speaks with the saints in a church as in a bush"; for Hilary too (*Tract. Mys.* 1.30) the bush is the Church persecuted, but not destroyed. The burning bush was an epiphany of an angel, not God Himself, in the Septuagint and Hellenistic Jewish interpretation of the "angel of the Lord' of the Hebrew text (Philo, *Vit. Mos.* 1.12.66; Eusebius, *Praep. Evang.* 9.29). This stress on an angel distinct from the person of God is also found in Justin, *Dial.* 59.2 (cf. 127.4); Clement Alexandria, *Prot.* 1.8.3 and *Paed.* 2.8.75; Irenaeus, *Adv. haer.* 4.20.1 (Harvey, 2, p. 173). This prepares for Gregory's incarnation interpretation—see next note.

27. John 8.12 and 14.6. The importance of the incarnation for Gregory should be noted. The thorny bush is given an incarnation interpretation also in *De perf.* Vol. 8, 1, p. 206, 18f. (MG 46.280B-C). Many of the same types of the incarnation and virgin birth as Gregory employs in this treatise are present in the Byzantine rite—Jean Blanc, "La fête de Moïse dans le rite byzantin," *Moïse*, pp. 345-353. The *Adv. Apoll. ad Theoph.* (MG 45.1273B-C) seems to say that if everyone were a great contemplative like Moses there would be no need for the incarnation, but there is a more positive assessment of the incarnation as showing the manifold divine wisdom in *In Cant.* 8, Vol. 6, pp. 255f. (MG 44.948D-949A)—cf. A.H. Armstrong, "Platonic Elements in St. Gregory of Nyssa's Doctrine of Man," *Dominican Studies* 1 (April 1948): 119ff.

28. Gregory appears to be the first to make the bush a figure of

NOTES

Mary's virginity unaffected by the birth of Jesus. See also *In diem nat. Christi* (MG 46.1136B-C) for the burning bush as "the mystery of the virgin" and Cyril of Alexandria, *Adv. anthropom.* 26 (MG 76.1129A).

29. Gregory alludes to the "garments of skin" of Gen. 3.21, which hold an important place in his teaching. Cf. "Circumcision means the casting off of the dead skins which we put on when we had been stripped of the supernatural life after the transgression," *De beat.* 8 (MG 44.1292B; trans. from ACW 18: 166, and see *ibid.*, p. 184, n. 43 to *De or. dom.* 2). Gregory refers to the "garments of skins" in *In Inscrip. Ps.* 1.7, Vol. 5, p. 44, 3-5 (MG 44.456C); *Or. cat.* 8 (MG 45.33C-D); *De virg.* 12 and 13, Vol. 8, 1, pp. 302, 9f. and 303, 15 (MG 46.373D and 376B); *De an. et res.* (MG 46.148C-149A); *De mort.* (MG 46.524D); *De Mel. epis.* (MG 46.861B); *In Cant.* 11, Vol. 6, pp. 327, 14f. and 329, 17f. (MG 44.1004D and 1005C). Shortly after the last passage Gregory gives a baptismal interpretation to the removing of the sandals (p. 331, 4; MG 1008A); cf. Daniélou, *Platonisme* . . . , pp. 27-31. See further n. 260. The phrase "placed around our nature" is significant for Gregory's anthropology—the real self is something other than the fleshly existence. Human nature is made up of a series of layers which must be removed, and this removal is a continuous process according to *In Cant.* 12, Vol. 6, p. 360, 5-14 (MG 44.1029B-C). From these passages it is clear that the "garments of skin" are not bodily existence *per se*, for man had a body in Paradise, but animality or biological existence. The garments include the passions, sexuality, and especially mortality, which are added to the human nature made in the image of God. The importance of Gen. 3.21 for Gregory may in part be due to the fact that χιτών was used for the body by Neoplatonists. Cf. Proclus, *Elements of Theology* 209; Plotinus, *Enn.* 1.6.7. See E.R. Dodds, *Proclus: The Elements of Theology* (Oxford, 1962), p. 307, for the Orphic-Pythagorean origin of the term and its use by the Valentinian Gnostics. J. Quasten, "A Pythagorean Idea in Jerome," *Am. J. of Philol.* 63 (1942): 207-215 shows that animal skins were a sign of death. See also A.H. Armstrong, "Platonic Elements in St. Gregory of Nyssa's Doctrine of Man," *Dominican Studies* 1 (April 1948): 123-125. For Gregory's doctrine of man, especially with reference to the tunics of skin, see further Ladner, "The Philosophical Anthropology of Saint Gregory of Nyssa," *DOP* 12 (1958): 88ff.; Daniélou, *Platonisme* . . . , pp. 56-60; *idem*, "La colombe et la ténèbre dans la mystique byzantine ancienne," *Eranos Jahrbuch* 23 (1954): 390ff.; *idem*, *Glory to Glory*, pp. 11-14; J.T. Muckle, "The Doctrine of St. Gregory of Nyssa on Man as the Image of God," *Mediaeval Studies* 7 (1945): 55-84; R. Leys, *L'image de Dieu chez Saint Grégoire de Nysse* (Paris, 1951); F. Hilt, *Des hl. Gregors von Nyssa Lehre vom Menschen systematisch dargestellt* (Köln, 1890); W. Völker, *Gregor von Nyssa als Mystiker*, pp. 57-74;

NOTES

R. Gillet, "L'homme divinisateur cosmique dans la pensée de saint Grégoire de Nysse," *Studia Patristica* 6 (1962): 62-83.
Genesis 3.21 had received various interpretations. Origen in *Sel. in Gen.* 42 (MG 12.101A-B; Lommatsch 8, p. 58) refers to three interpretations, to each of which he finds an objection: (1) the literal interpretation is unworthy of God; (2) to say the garments are bodies is not safe and true in view of Gen. 2.23; (3) if the tunics are death, how does God and not sin make the covering and would not this interpretation demand that before sin entered the world flesh and blood were not corruptible? The rabbis understood the verse literally. Philo (*Quaest. Gen.* 1.53) and the Gnostics (Irenaeus, *Adv. haer.* 1.1.10—Harvey, 1, pp. 49-50; Clement Alexandria, *Strom.* 3.14.95; *Exc. ex Theod.* 55.1; Tert. *De res. mort.* 7) take the verse as referring to the clothing of man with the present human body. This interpretation is charged to Origen by Methodius (*De res.* 1.4.2; 1,23.3), Epiphanius (Jerome, *Ep.* 51.4,5), and Theodoret (*Quaest. in Gen.* 39). But in some passages Origen takes the coats as symbols of mortality—*C. Cels.* 4.40; *Comm. Jno.* 6.42; *In Lev. hom.* 6, with which cf. Plato, *Phaedrus* 246b-c. See LeMoine G. Lewis, *The Commentary: Jewish and Pagan Background of Origen's Commentaries with Emphasis on the Commentary on Genesis* (Ph.D. diss., Harvard University, 1958), pp. 161ff. Methodius too says they are mortality from the irrational nature (*De res.* 1.39); cf. Gregory Nazianzus, *Or.* 38.12, and Asterius, *Hom. XXII In Ps. XI, Hom. III* (Richard, p. 173).

30. The "knowledge of the truth" is the way of salvation in *De inst. christ.* Vol. 8, 1, p. 41, 3.

31. From this sentence through section 25 is commented on by Balás, pp. 100-120. The whole passage is loaded with crucial terms for Gregory.

32. Neoplatonic usage (Plotinus, *Enn.* 3.6.6) and the context of an incarnation interpretation of the burning bush suggest that by "real Being" Gregory refers to the second hypostasis of the Godhead. This and succeeding statements are strong affirmations of the full deity of Jesus Christ for which Gregory had argued so strenuously in the *Contra Eunomium*.

33. The formulation τὸ ὄν, ὃ τῇ αὐτοῦ φύσει τὸ εἶναι ἔχει appears to be inspired by Aristotle, *Metaph.* XII (Λ), 6; 1071b, 19-20. Cf. J. Gross, *La divinisation du chrétien d'après les péres grecs* (Paris, 1938), p. 220, n. 1; Endre von Ivánka, "Vom Platonismus zur Theorie der Mystik," *Scholastik* 11 (1936): 163-195.

34. There are several examples in the treatise of these definitions, *horismoi* (e.g. II, 281, 306), a "Platonic" feature (*Sophist* 260c). On Gregory's epistemology see Weiswurm, *Nature of Human Knowledge*, especially pp. 77ff. on truth and certitude. Cf. also Cherniss, *op. cit.*, p. 50 and his references to Plato for this discussion of falsehood and truth.

35. Exod. 3.14 in the LXX provided the ontological base for Gregory's thought. The definition of God as ὁ ὄντως ὤν is rather frequent in Gregory—see references in Balás, p. 108. In Plato, *Tim.* 38c; *Phaed.* 247d; *Soph.* 260c. Exod. 3.14 was a basic text in the development of Christian philosophy—Etienne Gilson, *The Spirit of Medieval Philosophy* (London, 1936), chapter 3. We find it used in Justin, *Apol.* 1.63; Athenagoras, *Leg.* 4.6; Irenaeus, *Adv. haer.* 3.6.2; Clement Alexandria, *Prot.* 6.69; *Paed.* 1.8.71; Origen, *De princ.* 1.3.6. Note Philo, *Vit. Mos.* 1.14.75: "First tell them that I am He who is, that they may learn the difference between what is and what is not, and also the further lesson that no name at all can properly be used of Me, to Whom alone existence belongs."

36. This is a thoroughly Platonic statement; see Balás, p. 108.

37. These are Platonic expressions (e.g., *Symp.* 211ab; *Repub.* 380d). For the thought cf. *De an. et res.* (MG 46.93C-97A).

38. Cf. *In bapt. Christi* (MG 46.584B); *Ep.* 3, Vol. 8, 2, p. 23, 25ff. (MG 46.1020C); and n. 118.

39. John 1.9 and 14.6.

40. The tyranny of the passions is Platonic (*Repub.* 577d). For Gregory true freedom is ἀπάθεια. See Daniélou, *Platonisme* . . . , pp. 71-83, 92-103.

41. Here are two more figures of the incarnation—the rod and the arm, cf. Ambrose, *De off.* 3.15.94-95 and Cyril Jer., *cat. Lect.* 12.28. Tertullian sees in the transformation of the hand a figure of the resurrection (*De res. mort.* 28), and Hilary sees in it an illustration of the two senses of Scripture (*Tract. Myst.* 16, a work which finds types of Christianity in the patriarchs). Cyril of Alexandria follows Gregory—*Glaph. in Ex.* 2.300 (MG 69, 2.474D). For the rod see n. 46.

42. Ps. 76.11 LXX. Cf. *C. Eun.* 3.4.24, Vol. 2, p. 143, 5ff. (MG 45.720C-D). For the next sentence cf. *Ref. conf. Eun.* 181, Vol. 2, pp. 388, 24—389, 4 (MG 45.549A).

43. John 1.18 in mss. of the Alexandrian text.

44. Ps. 76.11. Irenaeus spoke of the "two hands of God"—*Adv. haer.* 4.34.1 (Harvey, 2, p. 213)—see John Lawson, *The Biblical Theology of St. Irenaeus* (London, 1948), chapter 10.

45. Cf. Irenaeus, *Adv. haer.* 5.pref. (Harvey, 2, p. 314) and Athanasius, *De incarn. Verbi* 54.

46. The change of the rod into a snake as a figure of the incarnation appears in Irenaeus, *Adv. haer.* 3.28 (Harvey, 2, p. 118), and is used later by Cyril Alexandria, *Glaph. in Ex.* 2.299 (MG 69, 2.469D-472C). The rod is the Virgin in Irenaeus, *Proof* 59 (ACW 16: 87). Justin, *Dial.* 86 (cf. 100.4 and 126.1), identifies the rod with Christ as well as with the cross. Hilary, *Tract.*

NOTES

Mys. 1.31, applies the rod to Christ considered by the Jews as Beelzebub but manifested for what he is by the resurrection. (Note that what an Eastern theologian sees as the incarnation a Western sees as the resurrection.)

47. John 3.14. The episode referred to is discussed in II, 269ff.
48. John 8.44; Apoc. 20.2; Gen. 3.1.
49. 2 Cor. 5.21.
50. Heb. 11.1.
51. Gregory here used the word πεείνοια, which is important for him. It describes a knowledge that is superior to that derived from observation of material things. Yet it is not quite the same as the knowledge that comes from contemplation of God, for it is still dependent on human intelligence (cf. II, 162 and notes 193f.) and conjecture (cf. II, 165). Athenagoras uses the word in the same way: The masses who cannot contemplate the truth because they are enmeshed in material things do not even have an approximate knowledge (ἀπερινόητος) of the Creator (*Embassy* 27:2). The philosophers and the poets who do distinguish between what is sensible and intelligible, but who conjecture on their own initiative, are able to attain to an approximate knowledge (περινοῆσαι) but not to find true reality (*Embassy* 7:2). Even Plato had only an approximate knowledge of God (περινοήσας θεόν, *Embassy* 23:7), apparently because he had not received his knowledge by inspiration, as the Prophets had. See A. Puech, *Les apologistes grecs du IIE Siècle de notre ère* (Paris, 1912), p. 180, n. 1, for the suggestion that περινοῆσαι indicates a lack of certainty in one's knowledge of God. See note 193 and II, 165.

52. Exod. 7.1.
53. Cf. *C. Eun.* 3.8, Vol. 2, p. 261, 28f. (MG 45.852C).
54. Exod. 5.2. Pharaoh is "atheistic and pleasure-loving disposition" according to Philo, *Leg. alleg.* 3.212. Gregory, for whom the contest with Pharaoh is between good and evil, will continue Philo's line of thought. For the rabbis the issue was idolatry—*Midrash Rabbah, Exodus* 8.2. Methodius says, "Pharaoh was the symbol of the Devil"—*Sym.* 4.2.

55. The imagery of the athlete is frequently applied to the ascetic in Christian literature. See the ἀγών words in PGL. Cf. II, 44. See V.C. Pfitzner, *Paul and the Agon Motif* (*Novum Testamentum* Supplement 14, 1967). In Gregory cf. *In Eccl.* 1, Vol. 5, p. 278, 7ff. (MG 44.617C); *In S. Steph.* (MG 46.704A-C). For the motif in a martyr context, see references n. 337.

56. In Philo the marriages of the patriarchs are allegorized in the same way; thus Agar, the concubine of Abraham, symbolizes pagan education (*Congr.* 14.71), as Sephora does here. Origen similarly sees in the marriages with foreigners and concubines the symbol of the use of pagan

163

learning (*In Gen. hom.* 11.2). Irenaeus, on the contrary, sees in the Ethiopian wife of Moses the church of the Gentiles—*Adv. haer.* 4.34.12 (Harvey, 2, p. 224).

57. Note the two kinds of philosophy. Cf. "ethical philosophy" and "theoretical" in *In inscrip. Ps.* II, 3 (MG 44.496A). Jaeger sees in this defense of Greek philosophy an apology for the Origenist tradition which came under attack about 390—*Two Rediscovered Works* 120, pp. 133-136. On Gregory's attitude see the Introduction, pp. 3-5.

58. A moral or spiritual interpretation of circumcision is already present in the Bible—Deut. 10.16; Jer. 4.4; 9.26; Rom. 2.28f. Philo, *Quaest. Ex.* 2.2 gives a moral interpretation. For Gregory see the passage from *De beat.* 8 quoted in n. 29.

59. For Gregory's use of "sequence," or "connection," see Daniélou, "*Akolouthia* chez Grégoire de Nysse," *Rev. des Sci. Rel.* 27 (1953): 219-249.

60. The γονή is the reproductive organ, and Gregory is consistently carrying through his figure. For discussions of Gregory's use of this figure, see H. v. Balthasar, *Présence et Pensée. Essai sur philosophie religieuse de Grégoire de Nysse* (Paris, 1942), p. 52, n. 5; F. Floeri, "Le sens de la division des sexes chez Grégoire de Nysse," *Rev. des Sci. Rel.* 27 (1953): 108, n. 1; R. Leys, *op. cit.*, 106-111.

61. Gregory affirms the immortality of the soul in *De an. et res.* (MG 46.45C-48C; 52A); *Adv. Apoll.* 30 and 50, Vol. 3, 1, pp. 178, 19—179, 7; 218, 24-31 (MG 46.1189C-D; 1248B-C). Cf. Harry Wolfson, "Immortality and Resurrection in the Philosophy of the Church Fathers," in *Immortality and Resurrection*, ed. Krister Stendahl (New York, 1965), and F. Refoulé, "Immortalité de l'âme et résurrection de la chair," *Rev. de l'Hist. des Rel.* 163 (1963): 11ff.

62. Note the language of "piety," εὐσέβεια, used by the Cappadocians in the Arian controversy for correct theological doctrines—*Or. Cat.* 1 (MG 45.13A); *C. Eun.* 2.12, Vol. 1, p. 230, 19 (MG 45.913D). For other references see PGL *s.v.* (but correct the Gregory reference to what we have given).

63. Gregory has developed his critique of the Platonic metempsychosis in *De an. et res.* (MG 46.108B-116A) and *De hom. op.* 28 (MG 44.232A-233B), in each case prefixing a description of the theory drawn from the *Phaedrus* 248c ff.

64. The Stoic conception of God, according to the fathers. For Stoic influence on Gregory, see K. Gronau, *Poseidonios und die jüdisch-christliche Genesisexegese* (Leipzig-Berlin, 1914), pp. 112-256.

65. The Platonic doctrine of the eternity of matter is refuted in *De hom. op.* 24 (MG 44.212D-213C). See R.A. Norris, *God and World in Early Christian Theology* (New York, 1965) for the problem of creation in Justin,

Irenaeus, Tertullian, and Origen, and Harry A. Wolfson, "Patristic Arguments against the Eternity of the World," *Harvard Theological Review* 59 (October 1966): 351.

66. The Stoic doctrine of *heimarmene* is refuted in *Contra fatum* (MG 45.145D-173D).

67. See Claude Tresmontant, *La metaphysique du christianisme* (Paris, 1961), on the problems of the immortality of the soul and the creation of the universe, the central problems posed by Greek philosophy for the early Church.

68. See I, 18 and II, 13ff.

69. Note the exegetical language: literally, a "more tropical theoria." For the "purpose" of a writing, see n. 74.

It is characteristic of Gregory to combine human endeavor with God's aid, which comes in to perfect that effort. See Jaeger, *Two Rediscovered Works*, pp. 85-110, 138-39, especially 92f. Gregory's synergism is best expressed in the *De inst. Christ.*; cf. the statement quoted in n. 135.

70. Epiphanius, "The apostles handed on some things in Scripture and some in tradition," *Haer.* 61.6 (MG 41.1048B); Chrysostom, *In Ep. II ad Thess. hom.* 4.14 (MG 62.488).

71. Cf. II, 179, 180. Gregory connects providence with the doctrine of angels. Ps. Plutarch, *De fato*, shows that the subject was of great interest to Platonists. The aim of the doctrine constructed in this treatise was to make the doctrine compatible with the free will of man. (See P. de Lacy and B. Einarson, Plutarch's Moralia VII, *Loeb Classical Library* [Cambridge, 1959], pp. 303ff.) A similar doctrine, probably derived from the *De fato*, is also found in Nemesius ànd Chalcidius. See D. Amand, *Fatalisme et liberté dans l'antiquité grecque* (Louvain, 1945). For the function of angels in providence, see Athenagoras, *Embassy* 10, 24, 25 (cf. H. Wey, *Die Funktionen der bösen Geister bei den griechischen Apologeten des zweiten Jahrhunderts nach Christus* [Winthertur, 1957], pp. 37ff.). The guardian angel is already in Hermas, *Vis.* 5.1-4. See Daniélou, *The Angels and their Mission according to the Fathers of the Church* (Westminster, Md., 1957), pp. 68-82. The "two spirits" is in Hermas *Mand.* 5.1.1-4, Rabbinic speculation (G.F. Moore, *Judaism*, 1, pp. 479-493), the Dead Sea Scrolls (1QS 3-4); cf. the angels of God and of Satan in *Barnabas* 18. Philo, *Quaes. Ex.* 1.23, states, "Into every soul at its very birth there enter two powers, the salutary and the destructive." See article on "Demon," *Dict. Spir.* 3: 160-168.

72. Cf. *Sentences of Sextus* 450, "mind of man is mirror of God." The figure of the mirror appears in Athanasius in similar contexts of contemplation—see Regis Bernard, *L'image de Dieu d'après S. Athanase* (Paris, 1952), pp. 72ff. It is already to be found in Plato. See A.J. Festugière, *Contemplation et vie contemplative chez Platon* (Paris, 1936), pp.

105-122, and Leys, *op. cit.*, p. 51. It becomes central in Gregory where it is related to the liberty of the soul and participation in the Divine. Perhaps best on the mirror is *In Cant.* 5, Vol. 6, p. 150, 9-13 (MG 44.868D); and for this passage connecting the mirror of the soul with free will, *In Cant.* 4, p. 104, 1ff. (MG 44.833B). For rust on the mirror which must be scraped off in order to reflect the good, *De beat.* 6 (MG 44.1272B-C). The idea is related to the teaching of the *De virg.* by Aubineau in his edition for SC 119: 187f. See P. Horn, "Le 'Miroir,' la 'Nuée': Deux manières de voir dieu d'après S. Grégoire de Nysse," *Revue d'ascétique et de mystique* 8 (1927): 113ff. and contrast R. Leys, "La théologie spirituelle de Grégoire de Nysse," *Studia Patristica* 2 (1957): 510. Daniélou, *Platonisme . . .*, pp. 210-222; and Muckle, *op. cit.*, pp. 73ff.

73. Contemplation has the intelligible, τὸ νοητόν for its object. Cf. Plato, *Phaedo* 65de; *Phaedrus* 247c.

74. This passage is important for Gregory's method. For him the interpretation of the details of a work may be made according to the purpose proposed by the interpreter. His criterion is what edifies. See *In inscrip. Ps.* 1, Vol. 5, pp. 24-25 (MG 44.432A-B); *In Eccl.* 1, Vol. 5, p. 279, 10ff. (MG 44.620A); cf. *In Hexaem.* (MG 44.69D). *In Eccl.* 7, Vol. 5, p. 395, 4f. (MG 44.716A-B), declares that there is "one purpose (σκόπος) of divinely given laws." Alexander Kerrigan, *St. Cyril of Alexandria: Interpreter of the Old Testament* (Rome, 1952), pp. 89-90, has shown that this principle comes from Iamblichus. On pp. 367ff. he cites exact parallels to Gregory in sections 48-50 (*Glaph. in Gen.* 3 and 4—MG 69.146A and 192B).

75. Sections II, 208ff.

76. On the immateriality of the soul see Weiswurm, *op. cit.*, pp. 55ff. and Harold Fredrik Cherniss, *The Platonism of Gregory of Nyssa*, pp. 12-25. Note Philo, *Quaest. Ex.* 2.13, "An angel is an intellectual soul or rather wholly mind, wholly incorporeal, made to be a minister of God, and appointed over certain needs and the service of the race of mortals."

77. 2 Cor. 12.7.

78. Prov. 17.17, LXX.

79. Jer. 9.4 (9.3, LXX). See *In Eccl.* 8, Vol. 5, p. 432, 2ff. (MG 44.745C).

80. See II, 208ff. On ἀκολουθία, see n. 59.

81. Exod. 5.6ff. Philo, *Vit. Mos.* 1.7.34ff.

82. Exod. 5.21.

83. Origen, *In Ex. hom.* 2.1. The making of clay represents the cycle of desire, ever seeking satisfaction in pleasure but never attaining it—cf. *In Eccl.* 1, Vol. 5, pp. 284-88 (MG 44.624B-625D). *De Beat.* 4 (MG 44.1244B-1245B) explains how fleshly desires may find their satisfaction and thus cease to bring enjoyment; however, desire is soon rekindled, although the

NOTES

flesh has no new delights to offer. Virtue, on the other hand, has ever new
experiences to offer. Daniélou in *Glory to Glory*, pp. 48ff., contrasts the lack
of satisfaction in the earthly process of filling up and emptying with the
satisfaction of the continuous progress in perfection; see n. 310.

84. See II, 96 on the parts of the soul.

85. Cf. the imagery of the sand dune, II, 243f. The same idea is in
Maximus of Tyre, *Disc.* 5.6.

86. Exod. 5.4, 16-18; Matt. 3.12 and 1 Cor. 3.12.

87. Eph. 6.11.

88. II, 31ff.

89. See Cherniss, *op. cit.*, pp. 51f.; Sallustius, *Concerning the Gods and
the Universe* 12 (Nock, p. 22).

90. For διέφθορος αἷμα see Hippocrates, *Mul.* 2.134.

91. The theme of βόρβορος, "mire" or "mud," is Platonic—*Phaedo*,
69c; *Repub.* 7, 533d; Plot., *Enn.* 1.6.5; 18.13; 6.7.31. Cf. in Gregory the
"mud (πηλός) of pleasure," *In Cant.* 11, Vol. 6, p. 332, 2 (MG 44.1008C);
man "fell into the mire of sin," *De virg.* 12, Vol. 8, 1, p. 299, 28 (MG
46.372B); and "smearing passions like mud on the pearl of the soul," *De perf.*
Vol. 8, 1, p. 212, 2-3 (MG 46.284C). See Michel Aubineau, "Le thème du
'Bourbier' dans la littérature grecque profane et chrétienne," *Rech. Sci. Rel.*
47 (1959): 185-214, and H. Merki, ὁμοίωσις θεῷ von der platonischen
Angleichung am Gott zur Gottähnlichkeit bei Gregor von Nyssa (Paradosis 7,
Freiburg, 1952), p. 117, who discusses the idea as it appears in Plotinus,
Enn. 1.6.5. According to Aubineau's classification, Gregory's application
of the theme in II, 72 is more moral-proverbial than philosophical, or at least
is a fusion of the two strands and in II, 302 is certainly moral-proverbial in
the reference to the mire of pigs. Cf. MG 44.832D-833A on frogs. In the
present passage Gregory would seem to accept "spontaneous generation."

92. For the licentious pictures, cf. Clement Alexandria, *Coh. ad
Graec.* 4.

93. Exod. 9.12; Rom. 9.17-18. The hardening of Pharaoh's heart is
treated by Irenaeus, *Adv. haer.* 4.45 (Harvey 2, pp. 241f.) and often by
Origen (cf. R.P.C. Hanson, *Allegory and Event* [Richmond, 1959] 215ff. and
W.J.P. Boyd, "Origen on Pharaoh's Hardened Heart," *Studia Patristica* 7
[1966]: 434ff.)—*De princ.* 3.1.8-11; *Comm. Rom.* 7.16; *In Ex. hom.* 4.2.
Origen takes the text literally; God makes Pharaoh an instrument for the
chastisement of the Jews and he will be saved in another existence. Gregory, however, makes free will the cause of the hardening—cf. *In Eccl.* 2,
Vol. 5, p. 302, 10ff. (MG 44.640B)—but he elsewhere approaches the view
of Origen—*De inf. qui praem. abrip.* (MG 46.189A-C).

94. Rom. 1.28, 26.

95. Cf. *Or. cat.* 31 (MG 45.77C).

96. Cf. the similar illustration, *De virg.* 12, Vol. 8, 1, p. 298, 21ff. (MG 46.369D).

97. Exod. 8.5 has the stretching forth of Moses' hands in bringing on the plague of frogs, but at their destruction only prayer is mentioned (8.12f.).

98. The outstretched hands as a symbol of the cross are treated further in II, 150-151; see n. 171.

99. Cf. Exod. 7.18 for the "stinking," ἐποζεσαντος

100. Rom. 6.21.

101. See Bk. I, n. 17.

102. This passage, which teaches the ἀποκατάστασις, or "final restoration" (eternal salvation), is replaced in one family of manuscripts, but the authenticity is certain. See the discussion in Daniélou, p. 54; Musurillo, p. 57; and Daniélou, "L'apocatastase chez saint Grégoire de Nysse," *Rech. Sci. Rel.* 30 (1940): 328-347. Moreover, section 84 demands this passage. Universal salvation was taught by Origen—*De princ.* 2.10.8; 3.6.3; *C. Cels.* 8.72—and appears in Gregory also in *Or. cat.* 26 and 35 (MG 45.68D-69C; 92C); *De hom. op.* 21 (MG 44.201C); *De an. et res.* (MG 46.88A, 100A-101A, 157-160); *De mort.* (MG 46.524-525). Unlike Origen's succession of worlds Gregory seems to find one purgation sufficient. There are passages where Gregory implies a permanent lost condition—*In inscrip. Ps.* 2.16, Vol. 5, pp. 174-75 (MG 44.605-608); *De paup. amand.* (MG 46.461A). The last sentence of *In Cant.* would seem to express his hope: "When all men look to the same goal of desire and become one and no evil remains in anyone, God will be everything to everyone, to those who through unity with one another are united by participation in the good in Christ Jesus our Lord, to Whom be the glory, and the might for ever and ever. Amen" (Vol. 6, p. 469, 4ff.; MG 44.1117D-1120A). Gregory's philosophy, his theology, and his spirituality are all caught up in this statement.

103. Exod. 10.21.

104. Matt. 8.12. The rabbis identified the darkness over Egypt with Gehenna—*Midrash Rabbah, Exodus* 14.2.

105. Exod. 9.8; Matt. 13.42.

106. Cf. *In Cant.* 3, Vol. 6, p. 77, 21 (MG 44.813C). The interpretation of the "furnace" too as Gehenna was Jewish—*Mekilta de Rabbi Ishmael, Tractate Bahodesh* 9.

107. Rom. 2.5f. The same citation in connection with the same ideas appears in Origen, *De princ.* 3.1.11.

108. The comparison of chastisement inflicted by God with the remedy given by a physician and the medicinal interpretation of chastisement comes from Origen, *Comm. Matt.* 15.11. Gregory makes frequent reference

to medical matters. Cf. II, 272 and 278 in this treatise. Goggin, *op. cit.*, pp. 22-25, 137-144.

109. Origen, *In Ex. hom.* 4.8.

110. Cf. Demosthenes, *De cor.* 128.

111. Cf. Jonah 4.11.

112. Ezek. 18.20.

113. Matt. 5.22, 28.

114. Cf. *In Eccl.* 4, Vol. 5, p. 349, 5ff. (MG 44.676C-D); *De or. dom.* 4 (MG 44.1172B).

115. Exod. 12.23.

116. Λογιστικόν, ἐπιθυμητικόν βυμοειδές. The latter word especially is difficult to render in English; in these psychological contexts "spirited" translates it and is not to be confused with "spirit." The appetitive part of the soul refers to the bodily passions or sensuous desire; the spirited part refers to the ardent, spirited will or the nonphysical passions which in their negative aspect are irascible and are included in the Pauline "flesh." This threefold classification comes from Plato, *Repub.* 439d, 588b; *Phaedrus* 246b. For its Christian appropriation, cf. Clement Alexandria, *Paed.* 3.1. For the good use of the passions, see n. 117. The structure of the soul in Gregory is discussed by Daniélou, *Platonisme* . . . , pp. 61-71; Cherniss, *op. cit.*, pp. 12-25; Muckle, *op. cit.*, pp. 55ff.; Aubineau, SC 119: 98-100; J.P. Cavarnos, "Gregory of Nyssa on the Nature of the Soul," *Greek Orthodox Theological Review* 1 (March 1955): 13-41; and *idem, St. Gregory of Nyssa on the Origin and Destiny of the Soul* (Institute for Byzantine and Modern Greek Studies, 1956). Gregory follows an Aristotelian classification of souls into vegetative, sensitive, and rational in *De hom. op.* 8.4f. (MG 44.145C) where he discusses the order in which different forms of life appeared. The Platonic analysis of the present passage appears in *Ep. can.* 2 (MG 45.224A) and *Adv. Apoll.* 8 (MG 45. 1140A-B) and is the basis of the treatise *De an. et res.* The relating of the lintel and the side posts to the three parts of the soul appears in Philo, *Quaest. Ex.* 1.12, under a little different form. (Cf. *De conf. ling.* 7.21.) It is identical in Origen, *Sel. Ex.* (MG 12.285A); Ps. Chrysostom, *Peri Pascha* 2.8 (Nautin, SC, 36, p. 83; cf. pp. 40f.), Theodoret, *Quaest. Ex.* 12.24 (MG 80.252-253A). Gregory's wording in the following lines is adapted to fit the imagery of the doorway. Cf. II, 123.

117. The lower inclinations may be turned to the good; see Cherniss, *op. cit.*, esp. pp. 17-20, and Aubineau, SC 119: 158, 168, 176. For the necessity of control of the lower parts by the rational, cf. *De an. et res.* (MG 46. 60D-61C); *De virg.* 18, Vol. 8, 1, pp. 318f. (MG 46.389C-392B); *In inscrip. Ps.* 1.8, Vol. 5, pp. 61-62 (MG 44.477B-C); *De beat.* 2 (MG 44.1216B).

118. See n. 26. The thorns are a result of sin according to Gen. 3.18. For Gregory they are sins—*In inscrip. Ps.* 2.15, Vol. 5, p. 165, 4-7 (MG 44.596C); *De beat.* 5 (MG 44.1257A)—temptations—*In Cant.* 4, Vol. 6, p. 115, 11 (MG 44.841C)—demons—*In Cant.* Vol. 6, 4, p. 114, 19f. (MG 44.841B)—and sinful humanity assumed by Christ—above II, 26; *De perf.*, Vol. 8, 1, p. 206, 16ff. (MG 46.280B-D).

119. Philo, *Quaest. Ex.* 1.19.

120. "Prudence" or "moderation" (σωφεοσύνη) was the Platonic cardinal virtue for the control of the appetitive part of the soul. This usage and Gregory's interpretation are based on the literal meaning of the word, referring to the middle section of the body. See now H. North, *Sophrosyne: Self-knowledge and Self-restraint in Greek Literature* (Ithaca, 1965).

121. Cf. 1 Pet. 1.13. Philo, *Quaest. Ex.* 1.19 takes the staff as a "symbol of kingship and instrument of discipline," but gives the same interpretation of girding the loins. In II, 124 the staff is faith. Hope as a staff appears in *De virg.* 18, Vol. 8, 1, p. 318, 19 (MG 46.389D). See also the Ps. Chrys., *Hom. Pas.* 3.11, edited by Nautin, SC 36: 111. "To ward off dogs" may be inferred from Exod. 11.7; cf. *Mekilta de Rabbi Ishmael, Tractate Pisha* 7.

122. Criticism of curiosity or meddlesomeness, which is the meaning of πολυπεαγμοσὺνη here, is frequent in Gregory—*In Eccl.* 7, Vol. 5, p. 416, 1ff. (MG 44.732C-D); *In Cant.* 11, Vol. 6, p. 339, 17 (MG 44.1013C). For this characteristic, see Plutarch, *De curiositate*. See note 196.

123. 1 Cor. 2.10.

124. For Spirit as fire, cf. Cyril of Jerusalem, *Cat.* 17.14 and *De rebapt.* 17, "What is said of fire is said of the Holy Spirit." See P. Lundberg, *La typologie baptismale dans l'ancienne église* (Uppsala, 1942), p. 32. In Gregory, *In bapt. Christi* (MG 46.592D).

125. Eccus. 3.22, 23 (21, 22, LXX). See also *In Cant.* 6, Vol. 6, p. 193, 12ff. (MG 44.901B). The same incident of eating in haste is referred to by Gregory of Nazianzus, *Or.* 45.17 (MG 36.645C-D). The exegesis comes from Origen, *In Lev. hom.* 4.10.

126. The explanation that the Israelites were securing their rightful wages appears in Philo, *Vit. Mos.* 1.25.141; Clement Alexandria, *Strom.* 1.23.157; Irenaeus, *Adv. haer.* 4.46 (Harvey 2, pp. 248f.); and Tertullian, *Adv. Marc.* 4.24.4. In I, 29 Gregory alludes to the "pretext of a loan," but here he asserts that only the spiritual sense is acceptable.

127. The change from λαβόντα to ὑποδέξασθαι reflects Gregory's concern that pagan learning be accepted with discrimination.

128. Clement Alexandria, *Strom.* 1.3, had explained Hagar, the Egyptian, as secular culture. The idea of "spoiling the Egyptians" comes from Origen, *Ep. ad Greg. Thaum.* (MG 11.88-89); cf. Augustine, *De doct. Christ.* 2.40.61 for the spoils of Egypt adorning the temple. For this older allegori-

cal exposition of Gen. 44 utilized here by Gregory see H. Fuchs, *Die frühchristliche Kirche und die antike Bildung* (Antike 5, 1929), p. 111; Merki, *op. cit.*, p. 93, n. 2; B. Altaner, "Augustinus und Irenaeus," *Theol. Quartalschrift* (1949): 162ff. For the tabernacle see ahead, II, 170ff.

129. This is developed in the *In laud. frat. Bas.* (MG 46.789B; cf. 809A); cf. *Vita S. Greg. Thaum.* (MG 46.901B-D).

130. For the catechumenate as the time of proving symbolized by the Hebrews before crossing the Red Sea, see Origen, *In Ex. hom.* 5.5.

131. 1 Tim. 1.5. Origen, *In Ex. hom.* 5.4, explains that it is by the Holy Spirit that God hears the silent cries of the saints. See Bk. I, n. 60.

132. See discussion in II, 42ff. The Scriptural text behind Gregory's identification is not clear.

133. See n. 163.

134. Origen, *In Ex. hom.* 5.1; Basil, *De Sp. Sanc.* 14.31 (MG 32.124B); Ambrose, *De sacram.* 1.6; Theodoret, *Q. in Ex.* 27 (MG 80.257A), a passage which contains a succinct summary of the Exodus typology.

135. The Holy Spirit's role in the life of virtue is not prominent in this treatise, a defect remedied in *De inst. Chris.* The gift of the Holy Spirit "to those who are worthy" is characteristic of Gregory—cf. II, 44 and note there. In *De inst. Chris.* Vol. 8, 1, p. 41, 21-24, Gregory speaks of "what exercises those who desire to climb the peak of the highest virtue must undertake in order to prepare their soul to become a worthy receptable of the Holy Spirit."

136. Following 1 Cor. 10.2 the crossing of the Red Sea became a common symbol of baptism, e.g., Tertullian, *De bapt.* 9; Ambrose, *De sacram.* 1.6.20-22; *De mys.* 3.12. See F. Dölger, "Der Durchzug durch das Rote Meer als Sinnbild der christlichen Taufe," *Antike und Christentum* (1930), and Lundberg, *op. cit.*, pp. 116-145. For the nonbaptismal interpretation see Aubineau, pp. 113f.

137. The army of the Egyptians represents the passions in Philo, *Ebr.* 29.111, but the demons in Tertullian, *De bapt.* 9, and Cyril, *Cat. mys.* (MG 33.1068A-B). Origen gives both interpretations, *In Ex. hom.* 5.5. Gregory in the present passage follows Philo; elsewhere he gives the interpretation of demons—*In bapt. Christi* (MG 46.589D)—or unites the two—*In Cant.* 3, Vol. 6, p. 76, 12—77, 8 (MG 44.813A-B).

138. Note Gregory's description of the two lower parts of the soul. Cf. n. 116, and the following section.

139. Τριστάτας—Exod. 14.7 and 15.4, LXX. *The Mekilta de Rabbi Ishmael, Tractate Beshallah* 2 offers as one interpretation of the Hebrew *shalishim* ("captains") that it refers to a third man in the chariot.

140. See n. 116. Contrast Plato's description in *Phaedrus*, 253c. Gregory varies the details of his phychological discussion to suit the

occasion—Cherniss, *loc. cit.* The Platonic myth had already been linked with biblical passages by Philo, *De agr.* 16.73; *De mig. Abrah.* 11.62; Clement of Alexandria, *Strom.* 5.8; Origen, *In Ex. hom.* 6.2.

141. Baptism occurs in varying combinations with faith, the Spirit, and wood (the blood of the Cross) in the early Church. For example, regeneration according to Justin is through "water, faith, and wood"— *Dial.* 138. See further, Everett Ferguson, "Baptismal Motifs in the Ancient Church," *Restoration Quarterly* 7 (1963): 209. The staff is "hope" earlier (II, 108), but it is "faith" from here on (see II, 136). The rod of Moses is the "word of the Lord" in Origen's *In Ex. hom.* 5.5, but it is commonly the cross, as in 4.6 and in Theodoret, *Q. in Ex.* 27 (MG 80.257A).

142. We follow the reading of Daniélou's apparatus. Cf. *In Cant.* 3, Vol. 6, p. 76, 18ff. (MG 44.813A-D).

143. See also II, 129 end; *In Cant.* 3, Vol. 6, p. 77, 4ff. (MG 44.813B); *Or. cat.* 40 (MG 45.101B-104C). Gregory accents the conversion which must accompany baptism.

144. 1 Cor. 5.7f. See Justin, *Dial.* 14.3, for leaven interpreted as the practice of wicked things.

145. In this passage βίος is earthly life and ζωή is spiritual life, a common distinction but not consistently observed in Gregory—see ACW 18: 191, n. 96.

146. Daniélou, *"Akolouthia," Rev. Sc. Rel.* 27 (1953): 233.

147. Cf. 1 Thess. 5.22.

148. Plato, *Tim.* 86de; Sophocles, *OC* 1198; cf. *Or. cat.* 40 (MG 45.101D).

149. Exod. 14.31.

150. Heb. 13.17 is apparently referred to.

151. The wood which sweetens the waters is already in Philo the hope of immortality—*De migr.* 8.36-37. For the wood as the cross, see Justin, *Dial.* 86, a passage containing a series of wood and water (cross and baptism) types (see Everett Ferguson, "The Typology of Baptism in the Early Church," *Restoration Quarterly* 8 [1965]: 44) and Cyril Jer., *Cat. Lect.* 13.20. Aphraates, *Demons.* 21.10 (*Pat. Syr.* I, 959) likens the cross that sweetens our bitterness to the wood that sweetened the water. The baptismal interpretation of the water is known by Gregory—*Adv. eos qui diff. bapt.* (MG 46.420D)—but is not stated here; Cf. Tertullian, *Adv. Jud.* 13.12; *De bapt.* 9; Ambrose, *De mys.* 3.14. Origen says the Law is bitter, but the wood of Christ shows how to understand it and make it sweet—*In Ex. hom.* 7.1-2.

152. Ps. 68.26.

153. Philo, *Vit. Mos.* 1.34.188, compares the twelve springs to the twelve tribes and the seventy trees to the seventy heads of nations. The *Mekilta de Rabbi Ishmael, Tractate Vayassa'* 2, equates the twelve springs with

the twelve tribes and the seventy palms with the seventy elders; to be "camped by the water" is to be occupied with the words of Torah, and earlier (section 1), the absence of water before coming to Marah is said to be understood by "allegorists" as meaning that the people did not find the words of Torah. The springs of water are given a baptismal interpretation in Justin, *Dial*. 86, but the twelve springs are the teaching of the twelve apostles in Irenaeus, *Proof* 46 (ACW: 77f.), and the trees are the seventy disciples in Tertullian, *Adv. Marc*. 4.24; cf. Origen, *In Ex. hom*. 7.3. Daniélou, *From Shadows to Reality* (London, 1960), pp. 172-174, finds this more common in Christianity than the baptismal interpretation. The variation between seventy and seventy-two in the mss. of Luke 10.1 to which Gregory here aludes is reflected in the patristic reference to the palm trees of our text. One notes the seventy-two translators of the Greek Old Testament were known as the "Seventy." Num. 11.16 provides for seventy elders, but the size of the later Sanhedrin and *Beth-din* depended on whether the high priest (later *nasi*) was included in the count (*Mishna, Sanhedrin* 1.6). The Babylonian Talmud (*Sanh*. 16b-17a) reflects a problem between seventy and seventy-two. On the problem see Bruce Metzger, "Seventy or Seventy-Two Disciples," *Historical and Literary Studies, Pagan, Jewish, and Christian* (Leiden, 1968), pp. 67-76.

154. Origen developed the significance of the camping places in his *In Num. hom*. 27.

155. See II, 153.

156. 1 Cor. 10.4. See Bk. I, n. 110. In Philo (*Quod. det. pot*. 31) the water from the rock is Wisdom (=*logos*.). The water from the rock is the teaching of the apostles in Irenaeus, *Proof* 46 (ACW: 77f.), and specifically Peter in Aphraates, *Demons*. 21.10. Origen takes striking the rock as bringing forth the word of God, but notes that Christ, struck on the cross, made to flow the springs of the new covenant—*In Ex. hom*. 11.1. Note Gregory's concern to attach his interpretation to Scripture, a feature of his later works—cf. Jaeger, *Two Rediscovered Works*, pp. 120ff.

157. We translate ἀνικμος "moistureless," differing from the other translators who render it "inaccessible." For "moistureless," see Aristotle, *Probl*. 906b 19; Plutarch, *De primo frigido* 951B.

158. John 14.23.

159. Exod. 16.2f.

160. John 6.51. See Peder Borgen, *Bread from Heaven* (*Novum Testamentum* Supplement 10, 1965), for the exegetical tradition already used by Philo and the Gospel of John.

161. Philo saw in the manna a figure of the divine Word (*Quis. rer. div.* 15.79; *Quod. det.* 31.118). Origen also interpreted the manna of the word of God (*In Ex. hom*. 7.5). Gregory sees here another figure of the incarnate

NOTES

Word born of the Virgin; cf. Origen, *In Ex. hom.* 7.8. One recalls the theme of Irenaeus, *Adv. haer.* 3.30 (Harvey, 2, p. 120), of the birth of Adam from the virgin earth as a figure of the virgin birth. A soteriological interpretation of Christ as Bread, the "firstfruits of the dough," may be seen in *In Cant.* 14, Vol. 6, p. 427, 20ff. (MG 44.1085B-C).

162. Wisd. 16.21.

163. This tradition of the diverse taste of the manna according to the one eating it is suggested by Wisd. 16.20, and is frequent in Jewish *haggada*—cf. *Midrash Rabbah, Exodus* 5.9 and 25.3, and *Mekilta de Rabbi Ishmael, Tractate Vayassa'* 5 and *Tractate Amalek* 3. One finds it in Philo, according to Basil, *Ep.* 190.3 (MG 32.700C). Origen considers the tradition by way of Rom. 14.2 (*In Ex. hom.* 7.8). In Gregory, cf. *In Eccl.* 8, Vol. 5, p. 423, 4ff. (MG 44.740A). That the language of God's revelation is accommodated to our capacity to understand is developed in *C. Eun.* II.242, Vol. 1, p. 297, 2ff. (MG 45.992C-D).

164. Heb. 5.12ff.; Rom. 14.1f.; 1 Cor. 3.2.

165. Mark 9.48 (Isa. 66.24).

166. This contrast of the six days which are the present life to the Sabbath as the eternal life comes from Origen, *In Ex. hom.* 7.5-6. In a general way it is ancient—Irenaeus, *Adv. haer.* 4.27.1 (Harvey, 2, p. 190). A Christian typology of the week has roots in apocalyptic and Alexandrian Judaism, united in Barnabas 15.5. See Daniélou, "La typologie millénariste de la semaine," *Vig. Chris.* 2 (1948): 1-17. Elsewhere Gregory considers the seven days as the time of this life and the "eighth" day as the world to come—cf. *In inscrip. Ps.* 2.5, Vol. 5, p. 83, 21—84, 13 (MG 44.504D-505A); *In sex. Ps.* Vol. 5, 188, 14—189, 29 (MG 44.609B-612A). This latter contrast is more common in the ancient Church—see Daniélou, *The Bible and the Liturgy* (Notre Dame, 1956), pp. 255-86.

167. Gal. 6.8.

168. Cf. Heb. 8.5.

169. The names Joshua and Jesus are the same in Greek, hence Joshua is a traditional figure of Jesus (Barnabas 12.8). Philo had already observed that " 'Joshua' is to be interpreted as 'salvation,' " in *Quaest. Ex.* 2.43 (cf. *De mut. nom.* 21.121). The opposition of Moses and the Old Testament to Joshua and the New Testament is in Justin, *Dial.* 113 and 75; Irenaeus, *Proof* 27 and 46 (ACW: 65f., 78); and holds a great place in Origen, *In Jes. hom.* 12.

170. Aaron's helper was Hur, not a member of his family. The *Mekilta de Rabbi Ishmael, Tractate Amalek* 1, attributes the efficacy of Moses' prayer not to the merit of Moses before God but to the faith of the people: When the hands were up the people were strong in the words of Torah, and when the hands were lowered this meant that Israel would lower their zeal for Torah.

In view of the typology in the following sentences, it is to be noted that this passage in the *Mekilta* already relates the outstretched hands of Moses against Amalek to the brazen serpent (see II, 273f.). It is characteristic that where the rabbis see types of the Law in the events of the Exodus, Christians see types of Christ—J. Bonsirven, *Palestinian Judaism in the Time of Jesus Christ* (New York, 1964), p. 79.

171. The application to the spiritual sense of Scripture (cf. the rabbinic interpretation cited in the preceding note and Philo, *Leg. alleg.* 3.66.186) is in the line of Origen, *In Ex. hom.* 11.4. Actually Origen gives several different interpretations to the event—Hanson, *op. cit.*, p. 252. The extended hands of Moses are a common figure of the cross—Barnabas 12.2; Justin *Dial.* 91; 112; 131; Irenaeus, *Proof* 46 (ACW: 78); *Sibylline Oracles* 8: 250-253; Tertullian, *Adv. Marc.* 3.18; *Adv. Jud.* 10.10; Cyprian, *Ad Fort.* 8; Jerome, *Ep.* 60.17; Aphraates, *Demons.* 21.10. See Daniélou, *The Theology of Jewish Christianity* (London, 1964), pp. 270ff. This is one of several traditional figures of the cross in Gregory—cf. *In Christi res.* (MG 46.601D).

172. Matt. 5.18, not quoted verbally.

173. The *iota* (i) and the *tittle* (a cross stroke) combined formed a *T*, an image of the cross. For references see Hugo Rahner, "Antenna Crucis," 5 "Das mystische Tau," *Zeitschrift für Katholische Theologie* 75 (1953): 385-410. See for example *Didasc. Apost.* 26.49 (Connolly, p. 218). Gregory often gives this interpretation of Matt. 5.18—*In Christi res.* 1 (MG 46.624D-625A); *C. Eun.* 3.3.40, Vol. 2, p. 121 (MG 45.696B-C).

174. On *theognosia* see Louis Bouyer, *The Spirituality of the New Testament and the Fathers* (Paris, 1960), pp. 362-65, and Daniélou, *Platonisme . . .*, 189f.

175. See II, 136.

176. Exod. 19.10.

177. The expression, "the contemplation *(theoria)* of Being" is frequent in Origen. See Völker, *Das Vollkommenheitsideal des Origenes* (Tübingen, 1931), p. 93. The variant reading "intelligibles," for "Being," appears in the text of II, 156. The same variant between "Being" and "intelligibles" occurs in II, 169, where we translate "contemplation of reality." Cf. II, 157 for "contemplation of God." See further n. 179.

178. Philo, *Quaest. Ex.* 1.2. Cf. *In Cant.* 1, Vol. 6, p. 25, 10ff. (MG 44.773A) and 3, Vol. 6, p. 71, 8ff. (MG 44.809A).

179. We have used "the intelligibles" to translate τὰ νοητά which in the Platonic tradition describes that reality which is perceived by mind and reason alone, the perception of which results in scientific knowledge (ἐπιστήμη). Based on Plato, *Phaedrus* 247CD and *Timaeus* 27D-28A, this understanding of philosophical knowledge is already applied by Albinus to the knowledge of God. Cf. *Didask.* II, 2; III, 5; IV, 6 Louis. For earlier

Christian appropriation of these Platonic categories, see Abraham J. Malherbe, "The Structure of Athenagoras, *Supplicatio pro Christianis*," *Vigiliae Christianae* 23 (1969): esp. 7ff.

180. 1 Cor. 2.9; Isa. 64.4. *De beat.* 2 gives the same sense as the text (MG 44.1209D). The passage is referred to God's gifts reserved for man in *De prof. Christ.*, Vol. 8, 1, p. 142, 1f. (MG 46.249C).

181. Plotinus, *Enn.* 1.6.4.

182. θεολογία here describes the contemplation of things divine. The term would be reserved, in the terminology of the Greek mystics, for the highest degree of the contemplative ascent. Cf. J. Marechal, *Études sur la psychologie des mystiques* II (Paris, 1937), p. 104, n. 1. For the earlier use of word see P. Natorp. "Thema und Disposition der aristotelischen Metaphysik I," *Philosophische Monatshefte* 14 (1887/88): 58ff.; A.J. Festugière, *La révelation d'Hermes Trismégiste. II. Le Dieu cosmique* (Paris, 1949), pp. 598-605. For early Christian use see F. Kattenbusch, "Die Entstehung einer christlicher Theologie. Zur Geschichte der Ausdruck θεολογία, θεολογεῖν, θεολόγος," *Zeitsch. f. Theol. u. Kirche* 2 (1930): 161-205.

183. Cf. Jaeger, *Two Rediscovered Works*, p. 78, for the frequency in Gregory of the idea that the approach to God is a toilsome ascent. Cf. Gregory Nazianzus, *Or.* 28.2 (MG 36.28B-D) for going up the mountain as Moses did for contemplation.

184. Exod. 19.19. In this passage the *logos* is the *historia*.

185. Οἰκονομία is a regular word of the incarnation, see PGL *s.v.* J. Reumann, *The Use of Οἰκονομία and Related Terms in Greek Sources to about A.D. 100, as a Background for Patristic Applications* (Ph.D. diss., University of Pennsylvania, 1957). In Gregory cf. *Ep.* 3, Vol. 8, 2, p. 25, 23 (MG 46.1021C) and frequently in the *Or. cat.*

186. The description of inspired men as musical instruments already occurs earlier. Cf. Plutarch, *De def. or.* 436F; Philo, *De spec. leg.* 1.9.65; Athenogoras, *Embassy* 9:1.

187. Ps. 18.5.

188. The evidence for congregational election of bishops in the 4th century is assembled in Everett Ferguson, *Ordination in the Ancient Church* (Ph.D. diss., Harvard University, 1959), pp. 236-342. A particularly vivid account, with all the atmosphere of a modern political campaign, is found in the *Vit. Greg. Thaum.* (MG 46.933ff.), the pertinent passages of which are translated in the dissertation, pp. 229-32.

189. 1 Cor. 12.29.

190. See *In Cant.* 1, Vol. 6, p. 26, 4-6 (MG 44.773B). Gregory also criticizes the ambitions of ecclesiastics in II, 279.

191. Exod. 20.21. For the divine transcendence, cf. *In Eccl.* 7, Vol. 5,

p. 415, 1ff. (MG 44.732B). The darkness into which Moses entered represented the ultimate inaccessibility of God already in Clement Alexandria, *Strom.* 2.2.6 and 5.12.78. The Cappadacians followed Clement instead of Origen on this point—Brooks Otis, "Cappadocian Thought as a Coherent System," DOP 12 (1958): 108. For the theme of darkness in Gregory's spirituality see Daniélou, *Platonisme* . . . , pp. 190-199; *Glory to Glory*, pp. 26ff.; and "Mystique de la ténèbre chez Grégoire de Nysse," *Dictionnaire de Spiritualité* 2; 1872ff.; G. Horn, "Le 'Miroir,' la 'Nuée': Deux manières de voir dieu d'après S. Grégoire de Nysse," *Revue d'ascétique et de mystique* 8 (1927): 113-131. See n. 200.

192. Gregory is inspired here by Philo, *De post. Cain.* 4.12-5.16, a passage which also has the quest of God; cf. *Vit. Mos.* 1.28.158 and *De mut.* 2, 7. The same teaching is in *In Cant.* 11, Vol. 6, p. 322, 9 (MG 44.1000D).

193. Gregory seems to be saying that the more philosophical one becomes the nearer he approaches to *theoria*. At this point one is still περινοίᾳ (see note 51 and II, 165), not ἐν θεωείᾳ. The whole passage reflects the theme of progress.

194. One must leave behind not only sensation but also the ordinary intelligence—see *In Cant.* 6, Vol. 6, p. 183, 2-3 (MG 44.893B) and *C. Eun.* 2, Vol. 1, p. 252, 16ff. (MG 45.940C-D), a passage which also stresses the continual progress. Cf. the descriptions "going beyond oneself"—*De virg.* 10, Vol. 8, 1, p. 290, 4 (MG 46.361B); going "out of human nature"—*Vita Macr.*, Vol. 8, 1, p. 390, 7 (MG 46.977B); "to abandon the senses," or "to abandon human nature"—*In Cant.* 6, Vol. 6, p. 181, 13 (MG 44.892D) and 11, Vol. 6, p. 323, 3 (MG 44.1000D); "giddy from the heights"—*De beat.* 6 (MG 44.1264B-C); and the reference to Paul in the "third heaven"—*C. Eun.* 3.1.16, Vol. 2, p. 9, 12ff. Cf. n. 198. See Daniélou, *Platonisme* . . . , pp. 261-273; Völker, *Gregor von Nyssa*, pp. 203ff.

195. The "going out of oneself" is at the same time an interiorization—*In Cant.* 12, Vol. 6, p. 366, 14ff. (MG 44.1036A).

196. See note 122. Here he's positive and elsewhere negative on *polypragmosune*. *C. Eun.* 2.92, Vol. 1, p. 253, 28f. (MG 45.941B), states that it was after Abraham abandoned the "curiosity of knowledge *(gnosis)*" that he believed on God and was justified.

197. This is a fundamental text which closely approximates Philo, *De post. Cain.* 5.15. The theme of the true sight of God will appear again in II, 234f. and 253f. See also *In Eccl.* 7, Vol. 5, p. 411, 13 (MG 44.729A) for the Divine to be above knowledge. See Weiswurm, *op. cit.*, p. 216 for a note on this passage.

198. On the use of this oxymoron, see Hans Lewy, *Sobria Ebrietas. Untersuchungen zur Geschichte der antiken Mystik* (Giessen, 1929), pp. 31 n. 1 and 41 n. 3; H. Koch, "Das mystische Schauen bei Gregor von Nyssa,"

Theol. Quartalschrift 80 (1898): 405f., 415f. *In Cant.* 11, Vol. 6, p. 324, 10f. (MG 44.1001B) speaks of a "certain sense of his presence" given in the darkness. Gregory delights in these paradoxes: "sober inebriation"—*In Cant.* 10, Vol. 6, p. 308, 5ff. (MG 44.989B-C), cf. Philo, *Vit. Mos.* 1.34.187; "watchful sleep"—*In Cant.* 10, Vol. 6, pp. 311-314 (MG 44.992C-993D) (studied by R. Joly, "Sur deux thèmes mystiques de Grégoire de Nysse," *Byzantion* 36 [1966]: 137-143); "passionless love"—*In Cant.* 1, Vol. 6, pp. 23, 9f. and 27, 5ff. (MG 44.772A and 773C-D); "wise folly"—*In Cant.* 10, Vol. 6, p. 309, 11-14 (MG 44.989D); "stationary movement"—II, 243; and "living death"—II, 314. See Daniélou in *Dict. Spirit.* 2: 1872-1885, in *Platonisme* . . . , pp. 274ff., and in *Glory to Glory*, pp. 34-46; and Louis Bouyer, *The Spirituality of the New Testament and the Fathers* (New York, 1960), p. 362. H. Langerbeck, "Zur Interpretation Gregors von Nyssa," *Theol. Literaturzeitung* 82 (1957): 83, objects against the view that such formulations are merely rhetorical and represent a stylistic taste for antithetic formulas. He fears that such an understanding will reduce the *theologia negativa* to a stylistic play.

199. John 1.18.

200. His argument is based on the literal meaning of John 1.18, "no one," not "no man." God is invisible to the angels themselves, according to John Chrysostom, *Hom. de incompr. Dei natura* 6 (MG 48.725A). The incomprehensibility of God often recurs—*De perf.*, Vol. 8, 1, p. 188 (MG 46.264D-265A). This is based on the infinity of the divine nature—Weiswurm, *op. cit.*, pp. 154-59. Cf. Basil *Ep.* 234 (MG 32.868C-872A) and Bk. I, n. 84.

201. Exod. 20.21.

202. Ps. 17.12. Cf. on this section *In Cant.* 6, Vol. 6, pp. 176-183 (MG 44.888C-893C) and with the same citation of Ps. 17.12, set in the middle of a key passage.

203. On ἄδυτον see Plotinus, *Enn.* 6.9.11, 25. Cf. *De beat.* 7 (MG 44.1277B); *De or. dom.* 3 (MG 44.1149C-1152A) where the *adyton* is the "hidden storeroom of the heart"; I, 46 and Bk. I, n. 74. The word is discussed by Daniélou, *Platonisme* . . . , pp. 182-189.

204. Exod. 20.2.

205. See note 51. "When St. Gregory uses the word φαντασία, he does not, in most cases, employ it to signify the faculty of imagination, but the image which the senses cause in the rational principle"—Weiswurm, *op. cit.*, pp. 107f. For examples of this philosophical usage, cf. B.D. Jackson, *loc. cit.* This statement taken with II, 163 shows that Gregory interprets the first commandment as prohibiting even an intellectual representation of God, as coming ultimately from sense experience. On Gregory's understanding of knowledge, see H. v. Balthasar, *Présence et Pensée*, pp. 60-67.

206. This fact was not commonly recognized by the Greeks of the pre-Christian centuries. See A.D. Nock, *Conversion* (Oxford, 1933), pp. 215ff.

207. Heb. 9.11.

208. Ps. 19.1. If the essence of God is inaccessible, his existence is manifested by his action in the world—*In Cant.* 1, Vol. 6, p. 36, 12ff. (MG 44.781D) and 11, Vol. 6, p. 334, 15ff. (MG 44.1009D); *De beat.* 6 (MG 44.1268C-1269A); *C. Eun.* 2, Vol. 1, pp. 256-57 (MG 45.944D-945C); *De inf. qui praem. abr.* (MG 46.181A-C). See Bk. I, n. 84. This was a first step of the ascent to God, accessible to the pagan wise men—*De beat.* 6 (MG 44.1269D); it was taken by Abraham when he was still in Chaldaea—*C. Eun.* 2, Vol. 1, p. 252, 24ff. (MG 45.940D). Cf. Philo, *Quaest. Ex.* 2.67, "The most lucid and most prophetic mind receives the knowledge and science of the Existent One not from the Existent One Himself, for it will not contain His greatness, but from His chief and ministering powers." See Cherniss, *op. cit.*, pp. 33-49, for knowledge of the material world as a first stage which must finally be abandoned for reflection on the real world. See Aubineau, SC 119: 185, and Endre von Ivánka, "Von Platonismus zur Theorie der Mystik," *Scholastik* 11 (1936): 178-185.

209. Ecclus. 46.17, but not according to the LXX; cf. Homer, *Il.* 21, 388.

210. Exod. 20.21. In 24.15, 18 Moses enters the "cloud."

211. Exod. 25-27. Philo, *Quaest. Ex.* 2.52 and 82.

212. The symbolism of the tabernacle occupies a considerable place in Philo, who interprets it mainly in terms of natural science but with some philosophy and psychology—*Vit. Mos.* 2.15.71-27.140 and *Quaest. Ex.* 2.51-106. See also Clement Alexandria, *Strom.* 5.6.32-40; Origen, *In Ex. hom.* 9; Ps. Justin, *Coh. ad Graecos* (MG 6.296B-C); Gregory Nazianzus, *Or.* 28.31 (MG 36.72A). The Epistle of Barnabas 16 recognizes only a spiritual tabernacle. *Midrash Rabbah Exodus* 50.5 interprets the tabernacle of the Messianic Age.

213. Exod. 25.40.

214. Is. 40.20 for the wood that will not rot.

215. Heb. 9.5.

216. 1 Cor. 2.10.

217. 1 Cor. 14.2. Gregory declares that the *theoria* of the secrets of Scripture belongs only to "those who fathom its depths by the Holy Spirit and who know how to speak in the spirit of the divine mysteries"—*C. Eun.* 3.1.42, Vol. 2, p. 18, 11ff. (MG 45.580B). Cf. Origen, *In Ex. hom.* 4.5.

218. 1 Cor. 1.24.

219. For Philo the celestial tabernacle is the intelligible world of archetypal ideas (*Quaest. Ex.* 2.52, 59, 83) and the earthly tabernacle is the

universe (*Spec. leg.* 1.12.66; *Quaest. Ex.* 2.83). It is rather typical of Gregory, but yet peculiar to him, that he takes the two tabernacles of the two natures in Christ, a subject beginning to exercise the attention of the Church at the end of the 4th century. Methodius, *Sym.* 5.7, compares the tabernacle to the Church; *De res.* 1.14 to the resurrection body.

220. Col. 1.17.

221. John 1.14. The incarnation is compared to a building in *C. Eun.* 3.1, Vol. 2, p. 19, 6-12 (MG 45.580D) and to the construction of the true tabernacle in *In Cant.* 13, Vol. 6, p. 381, 1ff. (MG 44.1045D) and in *Ep.* 3, Vol. 8, 2, p. 25, 8ff. (MG 46.1021C). *In Nativitatem* (MG 46.1128-29) shows the steps of the progressive manifestation of the tabernacle: the tabernacle of the Jews, the incarnation, baptism, and the resurrection of the body. See Daniélou, *The Bible and the Liturgy*, pp. 333-347.

222. Literally, "by which some great concept originating in sense impression." On the thought cf. *De beat.* 2 (MG 44.1209B) and see Weiswurm, *op. cit.*, p. 182.

223. The names of Christ is a catechetical theme—see Justin, *Dial.* 4; 34; 126; Melito, *Peri Pascha*, pp. 103-105; Origen, *Comm. Joh.* 1.9.52; Cyril, *Cat. Lect.* 10 (MG 33.660-90); Gregory Nazianzus, *Or.* 1.6-7 (MG 35.400B-C). Gregory has devoted the treatise *On Perfection* to the names of Christ. For similar listings see *In Eccl.* 2, Vol. 5, pp. 298, 10ff. (MG 44.636B); *De prof. Chris.*, Vol. 8, 1, pp. 134-35 (MG 46.241C-244B); *Adv. Maced.* 5, Vol. 3, 1, p. 92, 23-24 (MG 45.1305D); *Ref. conf. Eun.* 124, Vol. 2, p. 365, 14ff. (MG 45.524B); *C. Eun.* 3, 1, 127, Vol. 2, p. 46, 21ff. (MG 45.609C-D); 3, 8, 9-10, Vol. 2, pp. 241, 21-242, 8 (MG 45. 829D).

224. Col. 2.9. For the theme of God's penetrating and containing the universe, see Balás, pp. 116f.

225. The Stoic notion of the *logos* as the principle of unity in the universe is found in Philo (*Plant.* 2.8-10; *De sacr.* 18.66-67) in conjunction with the Platonic notion of the *logos* as an archetype.

226. Heb. 10.20.

227. This cosmological interpretation comes from Philo, *Vit. Mos.* 2.18.88; *Quaest. Ex.* 2.85. See also Josephus, *Ant.* 3.7.183, and Origen, *In Ex. hom.* 13.3 and the references in n. 212.

228. 2 Cor. 12.4.

229. Col. 1.16. For the different classes of angels in Gregory, see the references in Balás, *op. cit.*, p. 133. Also, Daniélou, *The Angels and their Mission*, pp. 83-94, on angels and the spiritual life.

230. Cf. note 71. The heavenly tabernacle is not only the divine nature of Christ but also the celestial world. But for Gregory this celestial world is not the world of impersonal ideas but of personal angels. Philo (*Quaest. Ex.* 2.62) had identified the cherubim of the tabernacle with the divine powers.

For this transformation of Platonism, see Balthasar, *op. cit.*, pp. xvii-xix.

231. Heb. 1.14.

232. Isa. 6.2; Ezek. 5.4; 10.1f.

233. The Jews used "Face" as a designation of God.

234. Philo, *Quaest. Ex.* 2.65.

235. Apoc. 4.5 and Zech. 4.2 are the source. Gregory refers to Isa. 11.1f. which had great influence on the ancient Church's thought about the Spirit. For the usage here, cf. Clement Alexandria, *Strom.* 5.6.35 and *Paed.* 3.2.87.

236. Rom. 3.25. For the sake of consistency this rendering departs from that of the Jerusalem Bible.

237. Phil. 2.10.

238. Heb. 13.15; Apoc. 5.8.

239. Exod. 25.4,5. The following interpretation picks up the thought of II, 22 that the skins of animals symbolize death.

240. 1 Cor. 12.12; Eph. 1.23. The tabernacle as a figure of the Church appears in Origen, *In Ex. hom.* 9.3-4; Hilary, *In Ps.* 131.16; and Ambrose, *Ep.* 4. On the following sections see more briefly *In Cant.* 2, Vol. 6, p. 44, 16ff. (MG 44.788D). Gregory anticipates the two hierarchies of the Pseudo Dionysius.

241. 1 Cor. 12.28f.; Gal. 2.9, but in the following sentence Gregory changes the order of the names. See Origen, *In Ex. hom.* 9.3, and Gregory, *In Cant.* 14, Vol. 6, p. 416, 11ff. (MG 44.1077A) for this use of Gal. 2.9, and cf. "pillars of faith" in *De beat.* 6 (MG 44.1264D).

242. John 5.35.

243. Phil. 2.15.

244. Matt. 5.14.

245. 1 Cor. 15.58 (the Douay translation).

246. 1 Tim. 3.15 (the Douay translation).

247. Ps. 141.2 (departing from the Jerusalem Bible) gives its wording to the whole statement, but see also Eph. 5.2; Phil. 4.18; Exod. 29.18; Ezek. 20.41; 1 Tim. 2.8 on the "holy hands."

248. Cf. Cyril, *Cat. Lect.* 3.2 (MG 33.428B); the following chapters refer also to the baptizing activity of Jesus, Peter, and John. Elsewhere Gregory uses the members of a body to express the various ranks in the church—*In Cant.* 7, Vol. 6, pp. 216-224 (MG 44.917B-924D).

249. Mark 1.4,5.

250. Acts 2.41.

251. Acts 8.27ff. We follow Musurillo's emendation in our translation. All the manuscripts read "laver of Candace" as if that were the name of the Ethiopian treasurer. Candace was the title of the Ethiopian queen, but was taken by Gregory (as normally) as a personal name.

252. Ps. 147.14 (v. 3 in LXX). Many mss. omit this sentence.

253. 1 Cor. 9.27. Note the praise of the monastic life—see *In Cant.* 15, Vol. 6, pp. 451-52 (MG 44.1104B-D). We recall that Gregory wrote a treatise in praise of virginity. Origen already saw in the covering of the tabernacle a figure of ascesis—*In Ex. hom.* 13.5—and he too cites 1 Cor. 9.27.

254. We have used "apprehension" to translate κατανόησις and "comprehension" to translate κατάληψις. For Gregory it is sense that "comprehends" (II, 163), and God is beyond "comprehension" (II, 164, 166; cf. II, 234). "Truth," however, "is the sure apprehension (κατανόησις) of real being" (II, 23, cf. 25), and it is the mind that apprehends reality (II, 162).

255. On the language of "negative theology" (ἄληπτον, ἀπρόσιτον, ἀπόεεητον, ἄόυτογ) see Daniélou, *Platonisme* . . . , pp. 185f.

256. Jerome, *Ep.* 64, is devoted to the interpretation of the priestly garments. Gregory gives a different moral interpretation to the vestments in *De or. dom.* 3 (MG 44.1148D-1149C). Clement of Alexandria, *Strom.* 5.6.37-40, gives a cosmological interpretation, following Philo, *Vit. Mos.* 2.23.109-27.140; *De spec. leg.* 1.85-95; and somewhat differently *Quaest. Ex.* 2.107-124.

257. Or, "Urim and Thummim," Lev. 8.8.

258. Wisd. 18.24. Philo develops the imagery, *Vit. Mos.* 2.24.118; *Quaest. Ex.* 2.117. Cf. Clement Alexandria, *Strom.* 5.6.32.

259. Rom. 12.1 (modified Douay rendering).

260. 1 Thess. 4.17. The garment of flesh, the clothing of skin, which symbolizes the life according to the flesh, is opposed to the airy tunic in an eschatological sense in *De an. et res.* (MG 46.108A) and *De Mel. epis.* (MG 46.861B). Here lightness designates the virtuous life. Similar references to 1 Thess. 4.17 occur in *De beat.* 2 (MG 44.1212C) and *De or. dom.* 4 (MG 44.1165D); cf. *De beat.* 1 (MG 44.1208B). In *Ep.* 3.2, Vol. 8, 2, p. 20, 19 (MG 46.1016C) Gregory uses *Phaedrus* 246c in speaking of the resurrection as one becoming like a cloud in lightness.

261. Ps. 39.11 modified.

262. The necessity of having all the virtues is a thesis of Gregory—*De virg.* 16, Vol. 8, 1, pp. 313-316 (MG 46.385B-388B)—which comes from Basil (David Amand, *L'ascèse monastique de Saint Basile* [Maredsous, 1949], p. 171). Cf. Jaeger, *Two Rediscovered Works*, pp. 128ff., and E.G. Konstantinou, *Die Tugendlehre Gregors von Nyssa im Verhältnis zu der Antike Philosophischen und Judisch-Christlichen Tradition* (Würzburg, 1966), pp. 120-124.

263. 1 Tim. 1.19. On the symbolism of the bells see Justin, *Dial.* 42.1, who assumes there were twelve bells which therefore represent the Apostles; and Clement Alexandria, *Strom.* 5.6.37. Philo sees in them the harmony of the cosmos, *Quaest. Ex.* 2.120.

NOTES

264. The pomegranates are a favorite image with Gregory to express the idea that virtue, after contradicting our false nature, introduces us to the pleasantness of inner nourishment—*In Cant.* 7, 9, and 15, Vol. 6, pp. 230, 10ff., 282, 12ff., and 455, 14ff. (MG 44.929B, 969C, and 1108B); and cf. II, 285.

265. Heb. 12.11.

266. The LXX in a mistranslation introduces tassels (κόσυμβοι) at Exod. 28.39 (v. 35 of LXX).

267. 1 Cor. 9.13,14.

268. 1 Cor. 9.18; cf. 2 Cor. 11.7.

269. 1 Cor. 4.11.

270. 2 Cor. 6.7.

271. Cf. Philo, *Quaest. in Ex.* 2.114.

272. *Ibid.*

273. See II, 22. Cf. also *In Cant.* 11, Vol. 6, p. 329, 17ff. (MG 44.1005D).

274. A reference to the numerous conversions in the 4th century—cf. *Or. cat.* 18 (MG 45.53D-56A).

275. 1 Tim. 6.13.

276. "Idol-mad" is characteristic of Gregory, see PGL, *s.v.* εἰδωλομανέω.

277. "Usefulness" is the great principle of Origenist interpretation; every passage of the Bible has to have a useful content—Daniélou, *Origène* (Paris, 1948), pp. 180ff.

278. Exod. 32.26 (the Douay translation).

279. A similar exegesis occurs in Philo, *Ebr.* 15.67-17.71. Philo discards any literal interpretation (16.69), but Gregory was able to give an acceptable literal interpretation also.

280. See II, 51ff.

281. Gregory here synthesizes the two interpretations of "false brother" as an evil angel (210) and as the innermost thoughts *(logismoi)* of our nature (208). This ambiguity of the personal or impersonal character of temptation was in Origen.

282. Gen. 3.1ff.

283. Exod. 32.29.

284. 2 Cor. 3.3. The same theme is developed in *In Cant.* 14, Vol. 6, pp. 411, 18—415, 12 (MG 44.1073A-1076C). For Gregory's different interpretations of the finger of God writing on the stones, see the summary n. 436.

285. 1 Cor. 2.10 modified.

286. The view of natural law expressed here corresponds to Gregory's view of the true nature of man as his supernatural life. See Daniélou, *Platonisme . . .* , pp. 48ff., and works cited, n. 29.

287. Gen. 3.4.

288. Exod. 32.18f., LXX.

289. On θεοδόχος see *Or. cat.* 37 (MG 45.97B) and PGL *s.v.*

290. Luke 1.35 modified. Here is another figure of the incarnation, for which cf. Irenaeus, *Proof* 26 (ACW 16: 64). The Exodus account of the tables of stone is sufficient to suggest the idea, but is there also an allusion to Daniel 2.34, 45, which is used by Gregory—*In bapt. Christi* (MG 46.589A-B)—in reference to the virgin birth?

291. Luke 11.20 and Matt. 12.28 (cf. Exod. 8.19 and Deut. 9.10).

292. Exod. 34.29ff.

293. Matt. 25.31.

294. Arianism was regarded as a Judaizing heresy—*De fide* (MG 45.137A); *C. Eun.* 3, 7, Vol. 2, p. 217, 26 (MG 45.804C).

295. Isa. 26.10 (the Douay translation). The parallel of the glory of the visage of Moses with that of Christ is in 2 Cor. 3.7-4.6, itself an application of Exod. 34.

296. See Introduction and bibliography in note 60.

297. Daniélou, "*Akolouthia*," pp. 236ff.

298. Exod. 33.11. Cf. *In Cant.* 12, Vol. 6, p. 356, 1-16 (MG 44.1025D) for the same context commented on in a similar way to what follows.

299. Ἀπελπισμός. Gregory uses ἀγελπιστία in *In Cant.* 13, Vol. 6, p. 369, 15ff. (MG 44.1037B-C) to express the state of the soul in never attaining to God. Cf. Philo, *De post. Cain.* 4.12-5.16.

300. Exod. 33.21-23 (the Douay translation).

301. On the whole pericope, cf. Philo, *De spec. leg.* 1.41-50 and *De post. Cain.* 48.168-169: God remains invisible, but His ὀπίσθια are his traces in the world, which are his powers. Gregory Nazianzus, *Or.* 2.3 (MG 36.29B), refers to this Exodus passage in developing the impossibility of man's comprehending God in his essence, but he too takes the back of God as referring to the traces of his activity which God leaves in the world. See n. 208.

302. One of the principles of the Alexandrian exegesis was that a statement unworthy of God points to an allegorical meaning. See Introduction.

303. The same figure appears in *De beat.* 2 (MG 44.1213B-C), cf. 6 (MG 44.1272D-1273A), and *Or. cat.* 6 (MG 45.29A). There are two parts of our nature: "The intellectual part would naturally move upward and the material part downward"—*In Cant.* 12, Vol. 6, p. 345, 11-19 (MG 44.1017C). For man as μεθόειος, the meeting place of the earthly and heavenly, see Ladner, DOP XII (1958): 71; Weiswurm, *op. cit.*, pp. 48ff.; J. Daniélou, *L'être et le temps chez Gregoire de Nysse* (Leiden, 1970), pp. 116-132.

304. The theme of the flight of the soul, associated with wings, comes

from Plato, *Phaedrus* 246b, 249a, 255c, and *Theaetetus* 176a. Gregory utilizes it often—II, 244; *In Cant.* 15, Vol. 6, p. 449, 12ff. (MG 44.1101B-C); *De or. dom.* (MG 44.1145A-B); *De virg.* 11, Vol. 8, 1, p. 294, 7ff. (MG 46.365C-D)—but for him the wings are those of the dove, the Holy Spirit—*ibid.* The theme is used by Justin, *Dial.* 2.6; Clement Alexandria, *Strom.* 5.14.94, and Origen, *De princ.* 3.6.1; cf. Plotinus, *Enn.* 1.2; 1.2.3ff. See P. Courcelle, "Tradition néo-platonicienne et tradition chrétienne du vol de l'âme," *Annuaire du Collège de France* 63 (1963): 376-388 and 64 (1964): 392-404; Daniélou, *Eranos Jahrbuch* 23 (1954): 396-400; Cherniss, *op. cit.*, pp. 33-49; Ladner, DOP 12 (1958): 65.

305. The theme of the attraction by the Good comes from Hellenistic philosophy, influenced by Plato and Stoicism (*Herm.* 10.6; 16.5), but it is also biblical (John 6.44; 13.22). The basis for the flight of the soul is the attraction of like for like—Cherniss, *op. cit.*, esp. pp. 48f. Gregory in *De an. et res.* (MG 46.97A-B) has the attraction of the soul by God's love if it is not held down by material things (cf. 44.876B).

306. Phil. 3.13. We arrive at the essential passage which is the text for the book.

307. The ever-increasing participation in the Good is always the point of departure for new progress. The creature "never halts at what it has reached, but all that it has acquired becomes by participation a beginning of its ascent to something still greater"—*C. Eun.* 3.6.74, Vol. 2, p. 212, 10-12 (MG 45.797A). "The boundary of what has been attained becomes the beginning for the discovery of higher goods"—*In Cant.* 8, Vol. 6, p. 247, 11f. (MG 44.941C). This is possible because the soul has been created as a receptacle with an ever-increasing capacity to receive what is poured into it—*De an. et res.* (MG 46.105A-C). See Daniélou, *Platonisme* . . . , pp. 291-307.

308. Plotinus, *Enn.* 5.8.4, 26.

309. Gen. 28.12. The theme of the ladder is in Plato, *Symp.* 211c, and Plotinus, *Enn.* 1.6.1,20. Gregory more often employs the figure of step or stages (βαθμοί)—*De virg.* 11, Vol. 8, 1, p. 292, 10ff. (MG 46.364B-C); *In Cant.* 5, Vol. 6, p. 158, 19ff. (MG 44.876B). See Jaeger, *Two Rediscovered Works*, p. 79.

310. For the constant increase in the desire for God, cf. *In Cant.* 12, Vol. 6, p. 366, 11ff. (MG 44.1033D-1036A). Although one fills himself to capacity, because of the infinite nature of God he is able to grow greater in proportion to his growth in grace—*In Cant.* 8, Vol. 6, p. 245, 19—246, 15 (MG 44.940D-941B). Thus the spirit, unlike flesh (n. 83) never knows satiety—*In Cant.* 14, Vol. 6, p. 425, 14ff. (MG 44.1084C-D); only love for the Beautiful knows no limit—*De an. et res.* (MG 46.96A and 97A). See II, 232, 235, 239.

NOTES

311. The use of ἕεως is a reference to Plato, *Symp.* 201d. Gregory explains that by ἕεως he means an intense form of ἀγάπη—*In Cant.* 13, Vol. 6, p. 383, 9 (MG 44.1048C). See G. Horn, "L'Amour Divin: Note sur le mot 'Eros' dans S. Grégoire de Nysse," *Revue d'ascétique et de mystique* 6 (1925): 378-389; Daniélou, *Platonisme* . . . , pp. 199-208; Aubineau, SC 119: 177, 195; Weiswurm, *op. cit.*, pp. 196ff.; Jaeger, *Two Rediscovered Works*, p. 76; Leys, *op. cit.*, 53-55. For a view of ἕεως opposed to that of Daniélou, *op. cit.*, and H. v. Balthasar, *Der versiegelte Quell* (Einsiedeln, 1954²), p. 11, see Mühlenberg, *op. cit.*, p. 183, n. 3.

312. Cf. n. 208.

313. God is the Good and the Beauty—Aubineau, SC 119: 150.

314. Cf. Origen, *De princ.* 2.9.1-3. See reference on satiety in n. 310. Ivánka, *Hellenistisches und christliches im frühbyzantinischen Geistesleben* (Vienna, 1948), pp. 48ff.; Daniélou, *Eranos Jahrbuch* 23 (1954): 400-407, 417. For the contrast with Origen's spirituality, Otis, DOP 12 (1958): 108f.

315. Exod. 33.20.

316. Basil, *Ep.* 234.2 (MG 32.869C); Gregory Naz., *Or.* 45.3 (MG 36.628A). Cf. Völker, p. 41.

317. A Platonic polemic against Stoicism's καταληπτικὴ φαντασία—the phrase is also in *In Cant.* 12, Vol. 6, p. 357, 6 (MG 44.1028A). For the refinement of Gregory's opposition to Stoicism in this respect, see v. Balthasar, *Présence et Pensée*, pp. 60-67.

318. N. 191.

319. See I, 7 and note 14.

320. Same root (συνεπεκτείνω) as in Phil. 3.13 (cf. II, 225). See *In Cant.* 1, Vol. 6, p. 31, 6ff. (MG 44.777B).

321. Comparable formulations in *In Cant.* 12, Vol. 6, pp. 369, 24-370, 3 (MG 44.1037B) and *In Eccl.* 7, Vol. 5, pp. 400, 21-401, 2 (MG 44.720C). One notes the progress of this formula over that which defines the earlier vision at Sinai, "the seeing that consists in not seeing," II, 163. Gregory does not deny a real vision of God, but he asserts the deficiency of any possible vision of God in relation to what he is. Philo, *Quaest. Ex.* 2.51, "For the beginning and end of happiness is to be able to see God. But this cannot happen to him who has not made his soul . . . a sanctuary and altogether a shrine of God." On the theme, see K.E. Kirk, *The Vision of God* (London, 1932).

322. Thus is achieved the demonstration of the thesis posed in the Introduction that perfection is in progress (I, 10). Cf. Balás, *op. cit.*, p. 156.

323. Rom. 8.28, reading the text of the Alexandrian family.

324. Exod. 33.21.

325. Phil. 3.13.

326. Almost an exact parallel in *In Cant.* 5, Vol. 6, p. 159, 12ff. (MG

44.876C). Cf. Joseph Maréchal, *Études sur la psychologie des Mystiques* II (Paris, 1937), pp. 107f., who develops the idea that Christ is the rock and the place.

327. Exod. 33.21. There is a very similar discussion of "rock," commenting on Cant. 2.14, in a context of knowing God but without reference to Moses in *In Cant.* 5, Vol. 6, pp. 160, 10—163, 10 (MG 44.876D-877D). Irenaeus in commenting on the Exodus passage says it teaches two things: that it is impossible for man to see God, and that man shall see Him in the last times in a rock, namely in His coming as a man—*Adv. haer.* 4.34.9 (Harvey, II, 220).

328. By this paradox Gregory opposes physical movement which is cyclical and stationary to spiritual movement which is progressive and stable. Daniélou, in *Eranos Jahrbuch* 23 (1954): 400-408 and *Platonisme* . . . , p. 282.

329. Eph. 4.14.

330. Epicurus, *Fragment* 470 (Usener). The sand image appears in *In Eccl.* 1, Vol. 5, p. 290, 1ff. (MG 44.628C-D); *De mort.* (MG 46.500D-501D).

331. Ps. 39.3, but Gregory changes the verse so that it is man doing it instead of having it done to him. The verse is correctly cited in a similar context in *In Cant.* 11, Vol. 6, p. 331, 15 (MG 44.1008B).

332. 1 Cor. 10.4. Cf. *In Cant.* 11, Vol. 6, p. 331, 16 (MG 44.1008B). *In Cant.* 5, Vol. 6, p. 161, 15-18 (MG 44.877B) has the Gospel as the rock. Christ as the "rock" is treated in *De perf.*, Vol. 8, 1, p. 192, 20ff. (MG 46.269A). *De beat.* 6 (MG 44.1264C) has "steep and sheer rock" in connection with the inaccessible knowledge of God; cf. *In Eccl.* 7, Vol. 5, p. 413, 4ff. (MG 44.729D) for the lack of sure footing in the spiritual quest.

333. 1 Cor. 15.58.

334. See n. 304.

335. 2 Cor. 5.1.

336. 2 Tim. 4.7.

337. Christ as the ἀγωνοθέτης appears many times in Gregory—*De beat.* 8 (MG 44.1296C and 1301A); *C. Eun.* 3.1, Vol. 2, p. 3, 14 (MG 45.573A); *De S. Theod. Mart.* (MG 46.737D-740A). For other references see PGL, *s.v.*

338. In the *De perfectione* for the first time in the history of theology a theology of the divine names is unfolded (cf. Jaeger, *Two Rediscovered Works*, p. 30). Although the names of Christ here seldom stand unconnected, Gregory does not seem to have yet understood the names of Christ as steps on an endless ladder to virtue. This understanding is at the basis of his presentation of the names here. They are steps which lead to the desired object, sparks which illuminate a little of its essence (for a discussion and

references, see Völker, *Gregor von Nyssa*, pp. 39f.). On the whole subject, see Mühlenberg, *op. cit.*, esp. pp. 183-195.

339. Gen. 2.15; 3.23f. Also, *In Cant.* 1, Vol. 6, p. 24, 8 (MG 44.772C); *De beat.* 5 (MG 44. 1257D). Daniélou, "Terre et Paradis chez les Pères de l'Église," *Eranos Jahrbuch* 22 (1953): 433-472; E.F. Sutcliffe, "St. Gregory of Nyssa and Paradise," *The Ecclesiastical Review* 84 (April 1931): 337-350.

340. 2 Cor. 5.1.

341. John 14.2,23.

342. Luke 16.22f. Also, *Vita S. Mac.* Vol. 8, 1, p. 398, 2 (MG 46.984D).

343. Ps. 26.13; 114.9. Also, *De beat.* 2 (MG 44.1212A).

344. Ps. 22.2. Also *Vita S. Mac.* Vol. 8, 1, p. 398, 1 (MG 46.984D); *De beat.* 2 (MG 44.1212A); *C. Eun.* 3.8, Vol. 2, p. 241, 8 (MG 45.829D), applied to Christ.

345. Gal. 4.26. *In Christi res.* (MG 46.617B-C) identifies Paradise and the celestial Jerusalem.

346. A common term in Matthew, e.g. Matt. 13.44, etc.

347. Phil. 3.14.

348. Prov. 1.9; 4.9.

349. Prov. 4.9.

350. Isa. 62.3.

351. Ps. 60.4.

352. Isa. 65.11-14? The Lukan passage in note 354 below may supply the basis for the phrase.

353. Prov. 25.4, 8 may be behind the phrase.

354. Luke 22.30; Matt. 19.28.

355. Deut. 12.5.

356. Ps. 26.5.

357. Col. 2.3 and Eph. 1.3. Gregory had a fondness for this sort of listing. Cf. the list of names of Christ as "King" which forms the framework of his treatise *De perf.* About Christ as containing all good, cf. Origen, *Comm. Joh.* 1.9.52ff.

358. Cf. Irenaeus, *Adv. haer.* 4.34.1 (Harvey, 2, p. 213).

359. John 1.18 (n. 43); 1.3.

360. John 14.6; 2 Tim. 4.7.

361. John 14.2.

362. Deut. 13.4. Gregory now develops a new aspect of the spiritual life: not only to seek God but also to follow Him (cf. II, 52). Cf. *In Cant.* 12, Vol. 6, p. 356, 12f. (MG 44.1025D-1028A), where the vision of God is defined as a "continuous following of God." Cf. R. Leys, *"L'image de Dieu chez Saint Grégoire de Nysse,"* p. 52, on how "looking toward God" is becoming like him. The Neo-Pythagorean idea of philosophy was to follow God,

and Armand Delatte, *Études sur la littérature pythagoricienne*, p. 76, points out that "to follow God" was based on the *Phaedrus* myth of two horses obeying the driver. This idea of philosophy was adopted by Philo, *Migr.* 23.131. Cf. Clement of Alexandria, *Strom.* 2.19.100.4; *Paed.* 1.5.20.4.

363. Ps. 91:1,4 (the Douay rendering modified). Gregory is playing on the phrase "broad of the back."

364. Ps. 63.8.

365. Luke 9.23.

366. Luke 18.22.

367. See n. 301.

368. Exod. 33.23.

369. For a fuller treatment of opposites, see *C. Eun.* 3.7, Vol. 2, p. 232, 16ff. (MG 45.820B). See Bk. I, n. 12.

370. Exod. 33.20.

371. On the vestments of glory with which Adam and Eve were clothed in Paradise and with which we shall be clothed again, see *In Cant.* 11, Vol. 6, p. 330, 1ff. (MG 44.1005D); *De or. dom.* 2 (MG 44.1144D) and 5 (MG 44.1184B-C); *In bapt. Christi* (MG 600A-B). To these vestments are opposed in this passage not the tunics of skin of Gen. 3.21 (cf. II, 22) but the fig leaves of Gen. 3.7, a symbol of the shame which follows sin—cf. *De virg.* 13, Vol. 8, 1, p. 303, 14ff. (MG 46.376A), which shows that Gregory makes no distinction in significance between the "leaves of shame" and the "dead skins." See Daniélou, *The Bible and the Liturgy*, pp. 37-40, 49-53.

372. Gen. 4.24.

373. Some Hellenistic handbook discussion of envy may stand behind this sentence. Cf. Plutarch, *De invidia et odio*; Dio Chrysostom *Orations* 67 and 68; Stobaeus *Ecl. III*, 38. On the image of the nail, cf. *De an. et res.* (MG 46.97C) and *De virg.* 5, Vol. 8, 1, p. 277, 11ff. (MG 46.348C); it comes from *Phaedo* 83d. See P. Courcelle, "La colle et le clou de l'âme dans la tradition néo-platonicienne et chrétienne (Phédo 82e, 83d)," *Revue belge de philologie et d'histoire* 36 (1958): 72-95, and "Variations sur le clou de l'âme," *Mélanges offerts à Mademoiselle Christine Morhmann* (Utrecht, 1963), pp. 38-40.

374. An analogous enumeration on the theme of envy is in Clement of Rome 4.7-13 (discussed by Karlman Beyschlag, *Clemens Romanus und der Frühkatholizismus: Untersuchungen zu I Clemens* 1-7 [Tübingen, 1966]). Cf. Wisd. 2.23f. In Gregory, cf. *Or. cat.* 6 (MG 45.28D-29C) and *De beat.* 7 (MG 44.1285-1288) on envy. He uses these experiences of Moses in discussing his personal difficulties in *De castig.* (MG 46.316A-C). Cf. Basil, *Hom.* 11 on envy (MG 31.372B-385C).

375. For this feature of ancient science see Pliny, *H. N.* 11.279; Clement Alexandria, *Paed.* 2.8.66. The symbol of perfume was a favorite of the Neoplatonists, cf. Dionysius Areopag., *De ecclesiastica hierarchia* (MG

3.473C, 477C, 480BD). Elsewhere Gregory uses perfume to describe the divine nature, cf. *In Cant.* 1, Vol. 6, p. 36, 9ff. (MG 44.781Cff). See G. Horn, "L'amour divin. Note sur l'mot 'Eros' dans S. Grégoire de Nysse," *RAM* 6 (1925): 383ff.; M. Harl, "A propos d'un passage du *Contre Eunome* de Grégoire de Nysse," *Rech. Sci. Rel.* 55 (1967): 220; and Daniélou, *Platonisme* . . . , pp. 232f.

376. Moses had attained perfect ἀπάθεια where he was inaccessible to the passions—see n. 422. Moses was superior to anger and desire—*De an. et. res.* (MG 46.53C). The imagery of the archer, but in a different context, is in *In Cant.* 4, Vol. 6, p. 127, 7ff. (MG44.852A-B).

377. Rom. 13.14.

378. John 15.1 provided a point of departure for this common typology in the ancient Church—Justin, 1 *Apol.* 32; *Dial.* 54; Irenaeus, *Proof* 57 (ACW 16: 85); *Adv. Haer.* 4.20.2 (Harvey 2, pp. 173f.); Hippolytus, *De Chr. et Antichr.* 2.11 (MG 10.735-738); *Ben. Is. Jac.* 18 (PO 27, p. 83); Clement Alexandria, *Paed.* 2.2.19; Origen, *Comm. Ier.* 8.51. See Corrado Leonardi, *Ampelos*, Bibliotheca "Ephemerides Liturgicae" 21 (1947), pp. 151ff. for a discussion of the grapes of the promised land as a symbol of Christ on the cross in the Church fathers.

379. Deut. 32.14 modified. For the "blood of the grape" cf. *In Cant.* 3, Vol. 6, p. 95, 18ff. (MG 44.828C-D).

380. Gregory makes allusion not only to interior repentance but to the ecclesiastical reconciliation which he has treated in the *Ep. can.* (MG 45.221B-236D) and *De castig.* (MG 46.308A-316D). He lists confession of sins among the "customs of the church" in *C. Eun.* 3.9, Vol. 2, p. 285, 28f. (MG 45.880C-D).

381. The water which flowed from the rock is compared to the blood and water which flowed from the pierced side of Christ on the cross (John 19.34). The rabbis had said that the striking of the rock brought forth blood and water—*Midrash Rabbah, Exodus* 3.13. Among the Church fathers the symbolism is sometimes eucharistic (and this seems truer to 1 Cor. 10.4)—Theodoret, *Quaest. in Ex.* 27 (presumably); Chrysostom, *In 1 Cor. hom.* (PG 51.299); Ambrose, *De Sacram.* 5.1. Among earlier writers it is more commonly baptismal—Tertullian, *De bapt.* 9; Hippolytus (J. Crehan, *Early Christian Baptism and the Creed* [London, 1945], pp. 172f.). Cyprian, in criticizing the eucharistic interpretation, appeals to John 7.37ff.—*Ep.* 63.8. The water from the rock appears as a baptismal type (apparently) in certain representations from early Christian art—C.F. Rogers, *loc. cit.* The interpretation which sees in the second episode of the rock the "second repentance" is new with Gregory. It attests the baptismal interpretation of the water from the rock, for ecclesiastical confession was regarded as a "second baptism" (cf. Tertullian, *De poen.* 12).

382. Cf. Wisd. 16.6f. The image of the serpent erected in the wilderness as a figure of Christ on the cross comes from John 3.14. Gregory alludes to it also in *In Cant.* prol., Vol. 6, p. 8, 3ff. (MG 44.760A-B). For ancient testimonies see Barnabas 12.6; Justin, *Dial.* 94; Tertullian, *Adv. Marc.* 3.18; *Adv. Jud.* 10.10; *De idol.* 5.5; Cyril Jer., *Cat. Lect.* 13.20; and Daniélou, *From Shadows to Reality*, pp. 167-70.

383. Num. 21.8.

384. Gal. 6.14.

385. Ps. 118.120. For the spiritual life likened to death and resurrection, cf. *In Cant.* 12, and 14, Vol. 6, pp. 342, 12ff. and 404, 22ff. (MG 44.1016C-D; 1068A).

386. This is a different symbolism of the nail from II, 257.

387. Rom. 8.3 (the Douay translation).

388. Treated more fully in II, 29ff.

389. Gal. 5.16f.

390. This interpretation is influenced by Philo's comments on the episode, *Leg. alleg.* 2.19.76-21.85, but for a cure Philo offers only a serpent "opposite in kind . . . namely, self-mastery." Gregory often likens pleasure to animals—cf. *In inscrip. Ps.* 2.14, Vol. 5, p. 156, 20-27 (MG 44.588A); *In Eccl.* 2, Vol. 5, p. 311, 7 (MG 44.648A); *De or. dom.* 4 (MG 44.1172A-B); *De prof. Chris.*, Vol. 8, 1, p. 137, 17ff. (MG 46.245B). See Daniélou, *Platonisme* . . . , pp. 74ff.; Plato, *Repub.* 588b.

391. Cornutus uses τύπος with the meaning of "symbol" (p. 6, 9 Lang). Philo uses ἀλληγοεία in connection with the same passage (see preceding note).

392. John 3.14.

393. On οἰκονομία see n. 185.

394. This criticism of ecclesiastical intrigues makes allusion to events in Gregory's own life. Cf. *Ep.* 1, Vol. 8, 2, pp. 3f. (MG 46.1000C-1001A). Similar criticism of those who desire to be priests but are not worthy are in Gregory Nazianzus, *Or.* 36.2 (MG 36.268A) and Basil, *Sermo de renun. saec.* 4; 10 (MG 31.633B; 648A-B).

395. Num. 16.31-35.

396. Ordination was viewed as God's appointment and blessing— Chrysostom, *In Act. hom.* 14 (MG 60.116); *In 1 Tim. hom.* 5 (MG 62.525-27). See Ferguson, *Ordination in the Ancient Church*, pp. 350-352.

397. The same symbolism is applied to the pomegranate in II, 193. This application comes from Philo, *Vit. Mos.* 2.33.178-34.184. See also Origen, *In Num. hom.* 9.7. That Aaron's rod was harsh on the outside but sweet on the inside is also found in Ambrose, *Ep.* 41.3. *Midrash Rabbah, Exodus* 23.10 speaks of scholars who are ugly on the outside (unprepossessing) but beautiful within (full of good things).

NOTES

398. Cf. Luke 16.19; Amos 6.6.
399. Luke 6.43 paraphrased. A similar criticism of priests is in Gregory Nazianzus, Or. 42.24 (MG 36.488A).
400. Aeschylus, Supp. 997-98.
401. Num. 20.7. Philo makes the "royal road" a symbol of the reason which leads to God (Gig. 14.64).
402. Matt. 7.14; Deut. 28.14. See also Clement Alexandria, Strom. 4.2.5, for the bringing together of the Philonian "royal way" and the "hard" way of Matt. 7.14. In In Cant. 11, Vol. 6, p. 330, 15f. (MG 44.1008A) it is Christ who is the "way," following Origen, In Num. hom. 12.4. The In Cant. passage warns against turning either to the right or the left. For the journey and road motif cf. Philo, Quaest. Ex. 2.26.
403. This doctrine of virtue as the just mean is Aristotelian, Nic. Eth. 1106 27, 36. Already Philo had applied the mean between excess and deficiency to the "royal way" (Spec. leg. 4.32.168; Imm. 34.159-35.165). Cf. In Cant. 9, Vol. 6, p. 284, 5-15 (MG 44.972A); In Eccl. 6, Vol. 5, p. 375, 4ff. (MG 44.697D); De virg. 15, Vol. 8, 1, p. 313, 8-13 (MG 46.385B). Cf. Muckle, op. cit., p. 69 and E.G. Konstantinou, op. cit., pp. 112-117.
404. Matt. 10.16.
405. See n. 120.
406. 1 Tim. 4.2.
407. 1 John 5.19 (the Douay translation modified).
408. Λεωφόεος in opposition to ἀνοδία in reference to the royal way is found already in Philo, De post. Cain. 30.102, and Clement Alexandria, Strom. 7.15.91.
409. In Num. 22.22ff. it is the angel and not the ass who informs Balaam of what he is to do. The birds are mentioned in 24.1 of the LXX.
410. See Bk. I, n. 117 for the affirmation of the demonic character of magic. For this episode, see Origen, In Num. hom. 13.5.
411. Mark 5.9 (Luke 8.30).
412. Mark 1.24 (Luke 4.35) and Matt. 8.29.
413. Titus 2.8.
414. Num. 23.8.
415. The same formulation in Lucian, Apol. 9; Julian, Or. 6.185a.
416. Plato, Timaeus, 69d; Rep. 579b.
417. Origen, In Num. hom. 20.5, develops the episode in a spiritual sense whereas Gregory takes it in a moral sense.
418. Cf. Ps. Phocylides 214, λυσσάω πεὸς μειϑιν.
419. Referred to in De beat. 6 (MG 44.1276A). The lance of Phineas is a symbol of the destruction of the old man by baptism in In bapt. Christi (MG 46.597C).
420. Passion transforms man into an animal. See n. 390. See Abraham

192

NOTES

J. Malherbe, "The Beasts at Ephesus," *Journal of Biblical Literature* 87 (1968): 71-80.

421. Prov. 6.28, 27. Proverbs was sometimes cited by the name Wisdom in the fathers—*Vit. S. Mac.*, Vol. 8, 1, p. 373, 20f. (MG 46.961D); Justin, *Dial.* 129.3; Eusebius, *H. E.* 4.22.9. Wisdom is the speaker in the citations in I *Clement* 57.3 and Clement Alexandria, *Strom.* 1.19. Cf. Sophocles, *Antigone* 618, 619.

422. On ἀπάθεια see Daniélou, *Platonisme* . . . , pp. 63ff., 92-103; Aubineau, SC 119: 166f.

423. Matt. 5.28f.

424. Jaeger, *Two Rediscovered Works*, p. 78, for parallels on "sweat of brow" involved in advancement in the virtuous life.

425. Hesiod, *Op.* 289.

426. See I, 8.

427. On the imagery of the eagle, see *In Inscrip. Ps.* 1.8, Vol. 5, p. 52, 13 (MG 44.465D).

428. These "summaries" are more than just that; they serve to emphasize the theme of progress.

429. Following modern translators we give what must be the sense.

430. Gregory develops the illustration more in *In Inscrip. Ps.* 2.11, Vol. 5, pp. 115-117 (MG 44.544A-D); *In Cant.* 14, Vol. 6, p. 407, 17ff. (MG 44.1069B-C). The image is Plotinian, *Enn.* 1.6.9. On the influence of *Enneads* 1.6 on Gregory, see Daniélou, "Grégoire de Nysse et Plotin," *Association Guillaume Budé. Congrès de Tours et Poitiers* (1953) *Actes du congrès* (Paris, 1954), pp. 259-262.

431.

Philo saw in Moses' death a kind of apotheosis (*Vit. Mos.* 2.288ff.), but Palestinian Judaism saw it as expiatory for the sins of Israel (Bloch, *Moïse*, p. 131).

432. Deut. 34.5-7 modified. On the ideal of service to God already in Philo, see Völker, *op. cit.*, pp. 330ff.

433. Num. 12.7 and Heb. 3.15. "Moses the faithful servant" is a favorite expression with Justin, e.g., *Dial.* 46.3; 56.1; 79.4; 130.1.

434. Gregory plays on the double meaning of "end" and "goal."

435. For other oxymorons by Gregory see II, 163 with n. 198 and II, 281.

436. Gregory has applied the symbol of the tables inscribed by the finger of God to the original creation of the soul (then broken—II, 215) and to the incarnation (God writing on human material—II, 216); here he sees an image of the action of the word of God in the soul, even as Paul compares the Spirit writing on our hearts in 2 Cor. 3—cf. *In laud. frat. Bas.* (MG 46.812A-B) and *In Cant.* 14, Vol. 6, p. 414, 12ff. (MG 44.1076B). The

NOTES

finger and the tables are compared to the baptismal inscription in *Adv. eos qui diff. bapt.* (MG 46.417B-C).

437. The golden calf is also differently interpreted above, II, 203. Gregory never felt confined to only one interpretation.

438. A new symbolism for Balaam. The theme of the magical power of passions is in Plotinus (*Enn.* 4.3.17). It is frequent in Gregory—*In Cant.* 10, Vol. 6, pp. 313, 17ff. and 316, 4 (MG 44.993C and 996A-B). On becoming animals through the passions, cf. n. 390.

439. See another allusion to the philtre of Circe in *De beat.* 2 (MG 44.1216C) and in another context in *C. Eun.* 3.2, Vol. 2, pp. 77, 25—78, 11 (MG 45.645B-C). See Homer *Od.* 10.212ff.; Horace, *Ep.* 1.2.23-26.

440. Literally "naked of evil." This is one of the similarities with Gregory of the Ps. Chrysostom "Homily on the Pascha of 387," noted by F. Floëri and P. Nautin in their edition for SC (No. 48, Homélies Pascales 3).

441. The theme of the image of God appears here for the first time in our work, but it holds an important place in the work of Gregory—see R. Leys, *op. cit.*, H. Merki, *op. cit.* and Walter J. Burghardt, *The Image of God in Man according to Cyril of Alexandria* (Washington, 1957), p. 4, with the literature cited. For Gregory, as for Athanasius, there was no difference between εἰκών and ὁμοίωσις. It is possible that this explains why the image of God appears as the end of the spiritual life. "The aim of the life of virtue is to become like God"—*In Cant.* 8, Vol. 6, p. 271, 11f. (MG 44.960D-961A).

442. These traits are those by which Gregory characterizes the image of God. Cf. Daniélou, *Platonisme* . . . , pp. 48-51; Muckle, *op. cit.*, pp. 64-69; Leys, "La théologie spirituelle de Grégoire de Nysse." *Studia Patristica* 2 (1957): 499ff.

443. See Introduction, pp. 2f.

444. Exod. 33.17,12, LXX.

445. Exod. 33.11.

446. On Moses as intercessor see Bk. I, n. 79.

447. Philo, *Quaest. Ex.* 2.40.

448. Philo, *Quaest. Ex.* 2.21, for this Hellenistic sentiment. The threefold motives for serving God appear *In Cant.* 1, Vol. 6, pp. 15, 15—16, 10 (MG 44.765B-C). Cf. Völker, pp. 250-253.

Index to Preface, Introduction and Notes

202

Index to Texts

205

76, 80, 81, 92, 109, 110, 124,
125; rod of, 35, 36, 38, 39, 61,
62, 68, 72; and Sinai, 42, 43, 45,
46, 81, 93–98, 110, 114; teaching
of, 46, 80, 126; theophany of, 34,
35, 59, 60, 114; virtue of, 34, 64,
112, 113, 115, 121, 122, 123,
124, 133, 135, 136, 137; and war
with Amalekites, 41, 90, 91.
Mt. Sinai, 42, 44, 91–120, 134,
135.
Mysteries, 81, 84, 86, 90, 93, 99,
100, 107, 123; of cross, 86, 91,
92, 125; divine, 94, 101, 111,
135; and faith, 98, 124; as
protection, 58, 83; and
tabernacle, 98, 102, 103, 135;
understanding of, 94, 95; and
Virgin, 59, 88.

Nature, 78, 98; of Being, 60, 115;
divine, 30, 43, 61, 71, 82, 93, 93,
96, 99, 100, 112, 115, 116, 130;
and the good, 30, 31; human, 31,
32, 47, 55, 59, 61, 64, 70, 84,
93, 104, 109, 110, 111, 124, 132;
as mutable, 55, 61; sinful, 62, 70;
state beyond, 46, 47.
Nile, 33.

Obedience, 29.

Paradise, 99, 118, 120.
Pasch, 84.
The Passion, 101, 123, 124.
Passions, 61, 75; and evil, 32, 56,
84, 85, 121, 131, 132; and fall,
55, 126; freeing from, 72, 83,
102, 125, 128; of Israelites, 47,
50, 131, 132, 134; and sin, 70,
71, 124, 125.
Patriarchs, 45, 105, 106, 118.
Paul, cf. Apostle; 88, 98, 101, 104,
105, 118, 124.

Perfection, 31; counsel on, 29, 30;
growth in, 31, 33, 133, 136, 137;
limitless, 30, 31, 133;
unattainable, 30, 31.
Peter, 101, 102.
Pharaoh, and exodus, 37, 38;
hardened, 71, 72; and magic, 36,
62, 68, 69; as the tyrant, 33, 35,
36, 55, 56, 61, 65, 68, 71, 80,
109, 133.
Philip, 102.
Philosophy, 57, 60, 62, 63, 68, 81,
104, 106.
Phineas, 50, 131, 134.
Piety, 75.
Plagues, 36–37, 68–78.
Prayer, 101, 102.
Preparation, 89, 90.
Priests, 46, 85, 91, 98, 103, 131;
and Aaron, 47, 49, 91; dress of,
45, 46, 47, 103, 134; God-given,
49, 125, 126, 127, 135;
institution of, 46, 47, 110, 114,
134.
Promised land, 48, 50, 122, 123,
134.
Prophets, 59, 61, 86, 93, 94, 100,
101, 124.
Providence, 64, 65.
Prudence, 79.
Psalmist, 104, 117.
Psalms, 119.
Psalter, 94.
Punishment, 47, 73, 104; of
transgressions, 46, 108, 130, 131,
137.
Purification, of guilt, 46, 131, and
law, 44, 80, 108; rites of, 41, 42,
47, 87, 92, 93, 103, 124.

Reason, 60, 80, 85, 130; and soul,
65, 103; and virtue, 56, 59, 64,
79, 117.
Red Sea, 38, 39, 114, 134.

THE CLASSICS OF WESTERN SPIRITUALITY
A LIBRARY OF THE GREAT SPIRITUAL MASTERS

"The Paulist Press' recent 60 volume series on the Western mystics is to my mind the most hopeful sign in American publishing."

Kenneth L. Woodward
Religion Editor, *Newsweek* Magazine
in *Publishers' Weekly*

GREGORY OF NYSSA—THE LIFE OF MOSES
translation, introduction and notes by Everett Ferguson and Abraham J. Malherbe, preface by John Meyendorff.

"Such an experience seems to me to belong to the soul which loves what is beautiful. Hope always draws the soul from the beauty which is seen to what is beyond, always kindles the desire for the hidden through what is constantly perceived... And the bold request which goes up the mountains of desire asks this: to enjoy the Beauty not in mirrors and reflections, but face to face." Gregory of Nyssa, c. 332–395

This great spiritual master of the fourth century was born as the general persecution of Christians was ending. One of the Greek Cappadocian Fathers (the other two were Gregory's brother, St. Basil the Great, and their mutual friend, St. Gregory Nazianzen), Gregory has come to be regarded increasingly as the most brilliant and subtle thinker and most profound mystical teacher of the three. Whether or not one agrees with Jean Daniélou who saw Gregory as the founder of mystical theology in the Church, there can be no doubt of Gregory's major importance within the Christian tradition.

The Life of Moses has special significance because it reflects Gregory's "spiritual sense" of the Scriptures. He maintained that the ultimate purpose of the Bible was not its historical teachings but its capacity for elevating the soul to God. Gregory saw the totality of the spiritual life as an "epektasis," a continual growth or straining ahead, as in the words of St. Paul, "Forgetting the past, I strain for what is still to come."

Gregory frames an immensely significant synthesis of the earlier Hellenistic and Jewish traditions in this work. He describes the spiritual ascent as taking place in three stages, symbolized by the Lord's revelation of Himself to Moses, first in light, then in the cloud and, finally, in the dark. This translation and introduction, winner of the Christian Research Foundation Award, has been expertly rendered by Professors Abraham Malherbe of Yale University and Everett Ferguson of Abilene Christian University.

In his preface Father John Meyendorff, the eminent authority on Orthodox spirituality, says of Gregory's spiritual sense, "Communion with God is a constant ascent 'from glory to glory'....Thus in meeting God, there is never frustration, or satiety, but only the discovery of true Love. It is on this point —more clearly than on any other—that Gregory, while being Greek, transcends the Greek mind itself and indicates to his contemporaries and to future generations, including our own, the path to the Living God."

PAULIST PRESS
NEW YORK • RAMSEY • TORONTO
ISBN: 0-8091-2112-3

TRANSLATION, INTRODUCTION AND NOTES BY
EVERETT FERGUSON AND ABRAHAM J. MALHERBE
PREFACE BY
JOHN MEYENDORFF